Fresh Eggs
and
Dog Beds

Book Three

Nick Albert

Copyright © Text, Nick Albert, 2019
Copyright © Cover Illustration, Nick Albert, 201
Published by Ant Press, 2015
First Edition

The author asserts the moral right under the Copyright, Designs and Patents Act 1988 to be identified as the author of this work.

All rights reserved. No part of this publication may be reproduced, stored in a retrieval system, or transmitted, in any form or by any means without the prior written consent of the author, nor be otherwise circulated in any form of binding or cover other than that in which it is published and without a similar condition being imposed on the subsequent purchaser.

This one is for my mum.

Contents

Author's Note 6
1 – The Slumber Party 7
2 – A Dicky Ticker...21
3 – Lost and Found 31
4 – Twinkle Toes 45
5 – The New Beau...59
6 – The Approaching Storm 71
7 – Strangers on a Plane 83
8 – The First Cut is the Deepest.................................97
9 – A New Hat...109
10 – Silence and Snow 123
11 – A New Year 135
12 – The Big Push...147
13 – New Friends 159
14 – Cassie Comes Home...171
15 – The Deluge 183
16 – Tumbleweed Chicken 197
17 – The Final Roar 209
18 – That Sinking Feeling...221
19 – Crash and Burn 235
20 – Twist and Shout 245
21 – Mind Your Head 257
22 – The Question 267
23 – 300 Eggs...277
24 – Highs and Lows 291
25 – Adare 305
26 – Happy Anniversary...317
27 – Tout and About..331
28 – New Beginnings 343
Acknowledgments 352
About the author 353
Ant Press Books 354

Author's Note

I have tried to recreate events, locales, and conversations from my memories of them. In order to maintain their anonymity in some instances I have changed the names of individuals and places, I may have changed some identifying characteristics and details such as physical properties, occupations, and places of residence.

1 – The Slumber Party

"Jaysus! I hadn't realised your house was so remote," Andy said, as he climbed out of his car.

"Were you beginning to worry I was secretly some lunatic axe murderer, leading you up here so I could bury your body on the moor?" I joked.

"Well..." He grinned, sheepishly running his fingers through his thick white hair.

"There's time enough yet!" I suggested playfully.

He laughed, his soft face breaking into an easy smile.

Like me, Andrew Rich is a golf coach. He has done the same job since leaving college, whereas I have only recently returned to the profession. It was a youthful passion, long discarded in favour of a career with job security, a decent pension and an income capable of feeding a hungry mortgage. Andy and I have been friends for a couple of years. We met soon after my wife and I had given up the madness of the British rat-race in favour of a new life in rural west Ireland. Well into his thirties, Andy is 10 years my junior. He has a lovely wife, two delightfully well-behaved children, a dog, a cat, and several horses. As we are both medium in height and build, we could easily be mistaken for brothers – especially if I had more hair, or he did not have so much.

It was a beautiful early spring day. After a frosty start, the sunshine had broken through, giving a welcome break from a recent run of unseasonably wet and windy weather. Today Andy and I used a rare gap in our busy teaching schedules to play a round of golf together, something we managed only a dozen times a year – less so since the Irish economy had recently gone into overdrive. As the course we played was nearby, I invited Andy back to my house for a late lunch. Even though he was Irish, following my car along the narrow and unfamiliar backroads of County Clare was a new experience for him.

"That's some views you've got up here," Andy said, shaking his head in admiration. "All that forest on the hills, and the moor stretching off into the distance. It's beautiful."

"We like it," I replied. "It's certainly and improvement on the south east of England. Essex was nice when Lesley and I were first married. At the time it was a good place to raise a family, but it's just too overcrowded now. County Clare is wonderful, particularly if you like wide open spaces, along with some peace and quiet."

"Well, you've certainly got that here," Andy whispered, turning full circle as he scanned the horizon. "Forest, moorland and fields as far as you can see. And not another house in sight. I don't suppose you get much traffic either?"

"Not much," I nodded, smiling. "Perhaps a dozen cars will pass, 13 if it's a busy day."

"Have you much land?" The phrasing of the question was typically Irish.

"Just a few acres, not that it makes much difference up here. Our land begins on the other side of this wood and runs alongside a farm track behind the house." I pointed south. "That tree line to the side of the hill is the boundary. It follows a single track lane along to the main road, stretching from the lake on the left, to our quarry over there on the right."

"So that quarry we passed is yours?" he asked.

I nodded.

Andy frowned. "Why did you buy a quarry?"

I shrugged and grimaced. "It came with the land. Actually, it's kind of cool. There's an old lime kiln up there and the geology is really interesting, I've already found a few fossils. Of course, as it's so remote, it's home to loads of wildlife."

"You should open up a caravan site," Andy suggested, "or perhaps put in a zip line. The tourists would love it!"

"You think?"

He nodded enthusiastically. "Or you could split the land into building plots."

"But we've just got here," I pleaded. "I'm not ready to sell just yet."

"Well, you have road access on three sides, so planning approval would be easy. You'd make a fortune!"

"I'll put your suggestions on my 'To Do' list," I laughed.

"Mind I get some commission!"

"You have my word."

"If you're staying, you should cut the grass and put in a little golf course."

"Now that's a good idea," I laughed. "But I think, for now, we'll probably keep it for the wildlife. They prefer the quiet, and so do we."

"I don't blame you, Nick, it's truly a lovely spot."

I smiled and put a guiding hand on his shoulder. "Welcome to Glenmadrie! Come on indoors, Lesley is looking forward to meeting you."

We had taken just a few steps when the front door opened and my wife stepped out to greet us. She was wearing her old jeans, a red check lumberjack shirt and her long auburn hair was held back by a brown scarf. I thought she looked ravishing.

"You're early," Lesley shouted. "I didn't expect you so soon!"

She grinned and waved at us with the paintbrush she was holding, but her wide smile faltered when she was almost bowled over as our dogs pushed past her legs. They exploded through the front doorway, a tumble of fur, teeth, and legs, racing to investigate our visitor. The four unruly mutts charged along the driveway, ignoring Lesley's shouts of admonishment and causing a wide-eyed Andy to pause and take a cautionary backwards step.

Leading this melee with a staccato babble of high-pitched barks was Amber, our Pomeranian Terrier. Not much larger than a healthy rat, with fur the colour of antique pine, a long snout, black button eyes and a curly tail, she is intensely competitive and fearless to the point of stupidity. In her effort to defend her home from invaders, real or imagined, she has been known to go toe-to-toe with chickens, ducks, horny stray dogs, badgers, cars, tractors, aircraft and even the International Space Station when it made an ill-advised overflight one hot summer night. Despite her commendable bravery, little Amber lacks the weaponry to be anything other than a noisy irritation.

In joint second place, side-by-side racing to meet the visitor, were Lady and Kia. Both are rescue dogs. Saved from certain death a year earlier, the cute puppies had quickly blossomed into delightful, if somewhat rambunctious, dogs. Despite their physical differences, they were as close as sisters.

Lady is a Fox Hound, perhaps mixed with a hint of Beagle, which would account for her legs being marginally shorter than average for the breed. She has tight beige fur, with a dark brown saddle, white socks and a long face framed by floppy ears, punctuated with intelligent brown eyes. Always unable to settle on her bed until she has irritated everyone in the house, dogs and humans alike, Lady is the undisputed pack leader.

Kia is a Collie. She lives life to the full, but with the minimum of effort. Like a working dog who retired early, when Kia is not asleep she's happiest just watching the world go by. As black as coal yet as soft as silk, her medium length coat is a delight to stroke. She has droopy ears, dark brown eyes, a black nose and a white muzzle with a corresponding flash on her chest, as if she had just dribbled some vanilla ice cream. Kia is gentle and kind, yet quick to use her rotund physique to her advantage when barging her way to victory in the chase for a tennis ball. Whenever Lady goes hunting, nose down, tail up and howling like a wolf, Kia will never be far behind. These forays, always unsuccessful and usually in the wrong direction, are harmless fun for the dogs, no more than useful exercise. However, while Lady will come back spotlessly clean and grinning with excitement, Kia will return panting heavily, smeared in mud and carrying the evidence of every bush and ditch she encountered as she dutifully followed her leader.

The final dog to push past Lesley's legs was Romany. She is an aged Lhasa Apso. Reminiscent of a myopic, overweight and cantankerous miniature lamb, Romany came with us from

England. Less than knee high, with thick white fur, short legs and a dislike of anything cold or damp, she is as suited to the Irish climate as flip-flops or a bikini.

As the canine stampede approached, Andy took a second backwards step and turned his pleading eyes in my direction.

"Don't worry, they won't hurt you," I said.

"Err..." he croaked, his voice trembling.

"Stand your ground, show no fear," I commanded. In truth he was in no danger, but I couldn't resist a little devilment.

Having encircled our guest, whooping and baying like Native American warriors around a pilgrim waggon train, the dogs quickly decided he was not a threat and switched to full welcome mode. Vying for attention and jumping up, they rapidly decorated Andy's immaculate black trousers with hair, streaks of dog slob and muddy footprints. Romany moved to one side where she performed her bum balancing act, like an acrobatic sheep.

"Lovely dogs!" he laughed, staggering to maintain his balance under the onslaught.

"Hello, Andrew," Lesley said, shaking his outstretched hand. "It's nice to meet you."

"You too, he replied. "Please call me Andy."

"Sorry about the mutts, I was planning to keep them indoors for a bit, but they slipped by."

"Not to worry," he replied. "I love dogs. We have one and so does my dad."

"GET DOWN!" Lesley yelled.

Andy flinched and half ducked, before realising the command was directed at the unruly canine horde. They half-heartedly complied, continuing their competition for attention with marginally diminished enthusiasm.

"Come on indoors, I'll put the kettle on," Lesley said, leading the way. The pooches followed, always hopeful of a biscuit.

While we waited for the kettle to boil, I led Andy on a quick tour of the house and outbuildings. Lesley and I were three years, and about a third of the way, through renovating the old farmhouse. Although I had shared a few photos and discussed the refurbishment with him, this was the first time my friend had seen the property.

"It's a much bigger place than I imagined," he said as he sat down at the kitchen table. "It seems to go on forever."

"The rambling style of the house and outbuildings was one of the first things we loved about this place," I replied.

"It's certainly different," Andy observed.

"I'm not sure if it was ever designed to be like this," I said. "I expect it just evolved and developed over time."

"We were going to rename it Higgledy-piggledy House," Lesley said. "But Nick thought it might be bad luck to change the name, so we stuck with Glenmadric."

"Undoubtedly a wise choice," Andy nodded. "Is it true you bought this place on a whim?"

"More or less," Lesley replied. "Nick had just had a health scare, and there was the continuing prospect of him being made redundant."

"It was a combination of factors," I added. "In the end, we decided enough was enough. So we resolved to get away from all that hassle, living under a mountain of debt and suchlike, and look for a place in the countryside were we could begin a new life. So here we are!"

"And you'd really never visited Ireland before you came over to buy a house?"

"I know it sounds mad when you put it that way," I agreed, "but our first visit here was planned as a combined holiday and scouting trip, mixed with a little house hunting. After three days, we just fell in love with the place."

"Ireland has that effect on people." Andy smiled.

"You'll have a bite to eat?" Lesley asked. She was sounding more Irish every day, albeit with a Birmingham accent.

"Oh, yes please."

"A cheese sandwich with some homegrown tomatoes okay?"

Andy and I nodded enthusiastically.

"And some cake?" I added, wiggling my eyebrows and

grinning.

"Of course," she sighed dramatically.

My wife makes delicious cakes, and jams, and pickles, and chutney. It's a small miracle I can still fit into my trousers.

"Can I help?" I asked.

Lesley shook her head.

"I'm not holding you up from your decorating?" Andy asked.

"No. I'm done for the day. I was just touching up a few bits in the guest wing."

"You've done a grand job," Andy said. "Are you going to live out there until the renovations are finished?"

I grimaced. "That was the plan, but–"

"I've decided we should live in the main house," Lesley interjected. "That way we have an added incentive to finish the project with some haste."

"Well, I think this kitchen looks fantastic. Nick showed me some pictures from before. It's a real transformation."

Lesley nodded. "It was horribly dark and the ceiling was only this high." She waved a buttery knife somewhere above her head.

"Do you know the history of the house?"

"Pretty much," I answered, pointing towards the sitting room. "As far as we know, the centre was once a traditional Irish thatched cottage, probably built around 1850 or so. In the early 1900s it was converted to a two-storey building. And from 1970 onwards, a succession of underfunded but overenthusiastic amateur builders added bits whenever the mood took them."

"That's quite common in rural Ireland."

"Yes. They're not big on planning permission out here," I agreed. "Anyway, this two-storey extension was added in 1975. The date's carved into the stonework above where the new doorway was knocked through. The matching extension at the other end was much later, sometime around 1995."

"So you end up with a long thin house with lots of outbuildings linked to the ends," Andy said. "A sort of bastardised Dutch barn design."

"Higgledy-piggledy house!" Lesley interjected.

"Perhaps you should change the name after all," Andy laughed.

With our hunger sated, we retired to the sitting room with our mugs of tea and enjoyed the welcoming warmth of the fire.

"That's a magnificent stove you've got," Andy sighed, stretching out his legs.

"Dual purpose," I mumbled, indicating the circle of dogs on the hearth rug. "It warms the house and keeps the pooches organised."

Andy pointed at two pipes snaking across the bare wooden ceiling. "What are those for?"

"I've just added a back boiler to the stove. Those pipes are spliced into the heating system. Extra efficiency and all that."

"The blue string is quite striking," he laughed.

"Bah! It's all very temporary," I explained. "This will all be coming down soon."

"All of it?" he asked, his eyebrows raised in surprise.

"Yep." I nodded.

"If there is no upstairs floor in the middle, how will you get into the rooms at the ends of the house?"

"I guess I'll have to fix up a couple of ladders," I explained.

Andy looked up at the ceiling, casting his eyes over the creosote-dark rafters, woodworm riddled floorboards and ancient cobwebs. "And you can't save any of it?"

Lesley shook her head. "The joists are weak and rotten, so we're ripping it all out. Everything you see will soon become firewood. Nick's going to put in new floors, raise the ceiling, and upstairs he'll build an extra bedroom, a family bathroom and a corridor. That way the rooms are all separate. Not like now."

"Phew!" Andy rolled his eyes. "It sounds like a huge job. Are you really doing it all yourself?"

"Unless you want to help?" Lesley joked.

"I would, but I'm so busy doing golf lessons," Andy explained, quickly backing out of a potential trap. "Or I will be, now the weather has improved."

"Same here!" I added. "The way the economy is booming, I think we're going to be even busier than last year."

"So how are you going to find the time to do all these renovations?"

I shrugged noncommittally. "I guess I'll just have to make the time."

Lesley huffed. "Nick's been teaching from dawn till dusk since the snow cleared. Most nights he's asleep on the couch before nine. We came here for a more relaxed life, but now he's working around the clock. I'm truly worried he's overdoing it."

"I guess we're slipping back into old habits," I added.

"You should take a holiday," Andy suggested. "Go to Spain and have a rest."

"Not Spain again!" Lesley laughed. "I think we're probably banned."

"Why?" Andy asked.

My wife pointed at me. "On our last trip, *he* kept falling asleep."

"You're joking me!"

Lesley and I shared a smile at Andy's typically Irish phraseology.

"Everywhere we went, on the coach from the airport, at the beach, at the bar, and even over breakfast, Nick kept falling asleep," Lesley explained.

I grinned and scratched my cheek. "In my defence, I had a heavy cold."

"I guess that's understandable!" Andy leaned back, shut his eyes, giggled, and shook his head, basking in the warm glow from the stove.

"But that's not all," Lesley added. "The holiday ended with an incident at the strip club."

"It wasn't a strip club," I corrected. "It was one of those cabaret shows, like that place in Paris. The Mad something…"

"The Crazy Horse Club," Lesley corrected.

"That's it!" I clicked my fingers. "It was very posh. All part of the package deal. We sat right at the front."

"Anyway," she continued. "There were all these beautiful topless girls, dancing in a line. Lovely long legs flying up and down. Plenty of food and wine. It was a fantastic show."

"Very artistic," I added defensively.

"But then I noticed some of the girls pointing," my wife growled.

"There was a lot of wine," I mumbled.

"And when I looked to my left, there was Nick, head back, mouth open, drool running down his chin and snoring like a hibernating bear!" Lesley laughed at the memory.

Andy made no comment. For a moment, I thought he was shocked by our story, but as I leaned forward the reason for his silence became obvious. A good lunch and the warmth of the room had taken its toll. My friend was snoring softly, fast asleep.

***

Spring arrived in an explosion of flowers, birdsong and, for me, golf lessons. For the first time since moving to Ireland, I began turning away work, just to maintain a little free time for other duties. Most weekday mornings I gave group lessons, and after a hurried snack, the afternoons were busy coaching a seemingly never-ending succession of club members and the occasional tourists. From four o'clock until twilight every weekday evening, I taught regular groups of junior golfers. Multiple after-school lessons of music, dance, art, languages, and sports were expensive, but becoming commonplace for most children. These activities were a good barometer of the growing uncontrolled heat within the Irish economy.

Already, many wise observers were questioning if such a bright fire could continue to burn for much longer.

***

"How was your day?" Lesley asked as I staggered indoors.

"Exhausting," I replied, blinking at the bright lights in the kitchen. "Satisfying, but exhausting. It's great to see the kids getting so enthusiastic about golf – or any sport for that matter. And they're all so polite and well behaved."

"That must be nice. A real credit to the parents."

I nodded and changed the subject.

"While I remember, there was a Garda checkpoint just outside of Ennis. The road was quiet and I got chatting to the Guard. She told me they were looking out for a Polish guy called Prawo Jazdy."

"Bravo jet ski?" Lesley laughed, deliberately mis-pronouncing the name.

"Prawo Jazdy," I repeated, snorting. "Apparently he's a real menace on the road. Some sort of multiple offender."

Lesley frowned and shook her head. "I've never heard of him."

"That's what I said too, but now I know the name." I grimaced.

"Is he dangerous?"

"I don't think so, just a bad driver," I said. "He's probably no more of a hazard than that guy who ran you off the road without stopping."

Lesley tutted, unimpressed with my attempt at humour. "What does he look like?"

"Oddly enough, she wasn't sure," I replied. "The Guards suspect he's taken to wearing a disguise."

"Ooh! It sounds very exciting," Lesley gushed. "Perhaps he's a spy trying to discover the secret ingredient that makes Guinness so popular."

"That's no secret, it contains alcohol!" I joked.

My wife smiled. It made my heart skip a beat. It always does.

"Surely they'd have a record of his car registration number?"

I shrugged. "The poor girl seemed rather embarrassed about that. Apparently, they have records of him using several different cars and multiple addresses, but they haven't managed to get him to court. I guess that's why they were asking if anyone knows him."

"How odd," Lesley said.

"Anyway, how was your day?"

"Interesting," she replied, grinning wickedly. "I had a visitor. A young man came by to share my afternoon tea."

I frowned. "Do tell."

"He's called Nathen and he grew up here with his sister and their parents, in this very house. He lives in Holland now, but he's back here for a funeral, or something, and as he was nearby, he popped in to see the old place."

"It's not the first time that's happened here," I observed. "I remember the day you discovered that old fellow sitting in the kitchen smoking a pipe."

"He'd let himself in and even made a cup of tea," she recalled, patting her chest. "It scared the life out of me for a minute! He was a lovely chap though."

I smiled. "It's not something you would try in England, unless you're a celebrity with a film crew."

"That's for sure."

"So tell me about Nathen," I asked, leaning forward. "What did he say?"

"Well, he was only here for half an hour or so," she explained. "Mostly he talked about his life growing up at Glenmadrie. The kids used to play in the quarry, or on a rope swing they had on the big ash tree behind the new pumphouse. From what he was saying, I don't think they went to school very much, but they had a great life, playing outdoors and exploring all day."

"No internet, computer games or television back then," I said. "Did he tell you anything about the house?"

Lesley nodded. "He reckons the original property dates back to 1805."

"Phew!" I gasped. "That early?"

"That's what he was told, although they only lived here for around 15 years during the 1980s and early 90s. Nathen recalled sharing a bed with his sister because the winters were so cold. He said the house was snowed in most years, until the new road was built. Before then it was just a rough track, tough going, even for a horse and cart. They had lots of goats, which Nathen had to milk every day. To get by, they sold the milk, some cheese, and bottles of illegal hooch called Poitín."

"Ah, I wondered when we'd hear about the Poitín," I said. "I'd heard one of the previous residents liked a tipple."

"That would have been Nathen's dad. He was called Billy, after the goats he kept – although that wasn't his real name. Billy distilled the Poitín in the cowshed and stored it in small jugs." Lesley grinned. "Nathen and his sister tried it once. They fell over a lot and got very sick."

"I'm not at all surprised!" I laughed. "I've heard that stuff's like paint stripper, almost pure ethanol."

"Nathen recalled the house was always damp because the fireplace was too small and there was no central heating. They didn't even have proper windows, just sheets of glass cemented over the holes, so it got very hot indoors during the summers."

"How fascinating. No opening windows?" I exclaimed. "That must have been tough."

"I got the impression he had a thoroughly healthy and enjoyable childhood here, despite the obvious poverty."

"It's nice to hear something good about Glenmadrie, especially after all we've heard about the wild parties and shenanigans that went on before we bought it."

Lesley sniggered and looked away.

"What?" I asked.

"I haven't told you about the ablutions yet," Lesley replied, rolling her eyes.

"The ablutions?" I frowned.

"Nathen said they never had a bathroom. The one we have now must have been added much later. Back then the kids had to wash in the kitchen sink, or in a tin bath in front of the fire, and their toilet was performed down in the woods, or in an old milk churn out in the cow shed."

"A milk churn? Good grief!" I gasped. "How did they...?"

"Apparently, they had a ladder and a platform with a wooden seat and a hole," my wife explained. "You can imagine the rest."

"I'd rather not!" Fascinating as it was to learn the history of Glenmadrie, sometimes you can have too much information.

2 – A Dicky Ticker

"Perhaps he's right," Lesley said, wiping her hands on the tea towel.

"Perhaps who's right?" I asked, as I put the dinner plates away in the kitchen cupboard.

"Andy," she replied. "I was thinking about what he said."

"What did he say?" I asked, hoping she was going to suggest I built a private golf course.

"About us needing a holiday," Lesley said.

"You mean when *he* said *we* need a holiday, just before *he* fell asleep on *our* couch?" I quipped.

"He was tired and the room was warm." She poked me on the shoulder with her finger. "And he's younger than you!"

"Hey! There's no need to be unkind," I complained dramatically. "Anyway, we're living the dream here. Life's one long holiday."

"Ack!" Lesley waved my objection away as if it were a troublesome fly. "Just give it some thought."

"What did you have in mind?" I asked.

"I don't know," she shrugged. "Perhaps we need to get out more."

"Were going out tonight," I reminded her.

"I know, but that's not what I meant." My wife chewed on her bottom lip. "Perhaps we need to have more fun?"

"I'm always available for some fun." I wiggled my eyebrows seductively.

"Tusk! That's not what I meant either."

I pulled a sad expression. "I wanted to draw a moustache on Andy's sleeping face, but you wouldn't let me."

She shook her head and sighed. "Don't be so childish." Lesley gave me a hard glare. "I mean it, we should have more fun."

I shrugged and picked up a Pyrex dish and paused to scan our new kitchen cupboards. "Where does this go?"

"In the bottom cupboard next to the draws."

"Shouldn't we call it a press?" I asked, using the Irish slang.

"Would it help you remember where the dishes go?"

"Not really," I admitted.

"Then you'd best stick with calling it a cupboard." Lesley glanced at the clock. "What time does this thing start?"

"Nine o'clock," I replied. "Don't worry, we won't be there long. Probably no more than an hour. It was very nice of the golf society to ask me to do their presentation. It's a real honour. I'll just shake a few hands and give out the prizes. Afterwards we can quietly slip away. I expect we'll be home before 11."

Lesley gave a huge yawn. "I hope so. I'm dreadfully tired."

"You don't have to come." I put my hand on her arm. "You were really ill. You're not fully recovered yet. The doctor said it could take as much as a year, so it's okay to be tired. Why don't you stay here and have an early night?"

Lesley shook her head. "I'm fine. Once we get there, I'm sure I'll perk up."

"Are you sure?"

"I'm fine," she insisted. "Anyway, it will be nice to meet some new people. Come on, let's go."

***

It was a half hour drive. We found the village easily, but locating the correct pub was proving to be somewhat of a problem.

"Clancy's," I said, squinting into the darkness. "I'm sure Brenden said the presentation was at Clancy's pub."

"Well, I can't see it," Lesley growled. "We've passed six pubs and none of them were called Clancy's. Anyway, how can a village this size have six pubs? SIX! I counted."

"I'll ask here," I said, pulling the car over.

I was back in the car in two minutes.

"Any luck?" Lesley asked.

I shook my head. "I tried three pubs. They didn't know anything about a golf society presentation."

"Three to go then." Lesley pointed ahead.

Inevitably, the correct pub was the last one we tried. As we stepped inside, involuntarily blinking at the sudden brightness, Lesley frowned.

"It's not very busy," she whispered.

There were just four customers. Two elderly men were sitting at the bar, staring morosely into their half-finished pints. I decided they were unlikely to be golfers. However, the two smartly dressed ladies sitting at the back and waving in my direction, probably were.

"Are you here for the golf presentation?" I asked.

"Sort of!" They smiled then jiggled their near-empty glasses, suggesting these were not their first drinks of the night. The ice cubes made a tinkling sound.

We exchanged names and I offered to buy them a drink. Lesley asked for a large orange juice and lemonade, both ladies giggled and asked for a double gin and tonic. The barmaid took my order and kindly offered to bring the drinks to our table. As I sat down, Lesley surreptitiously tapped her watch and raised a quizzical eyebrow – and with good reason, it was already 20 minutes after nine.

"Shouldn't there be some people here by now?" I asked the two ladies.

"Bah! Don't worry," one of them replied. "You're in Ireland now. Sit back and relax."

"But I was told the presentation would begin at nine," I explained.

"Pff!" the other lady snorted. "You'll not see a soul before 11."

I looked at Lesley and winced. She was doing her best to stifle another yawn. A moment later, the barmaid brought our tray of drinks. There were two large G&Ts, a soda water for the designated driver, and two pint glasses – one with orange juice and the other brimming with lemonade.

"Err, I asked for a pint of orange juice and lemonade," I said.

"That's right," she replied, pointing. "A pint of orange juice and a pint of lemonade."

"I'm sorry," I explained. "I wanted a pint of *mixed* orange juice and lemonade."

The barmaid frowned and tutted. "Then you should have asked for a Fifty-Five."

"Oh." I grimaced. "I didn't know."

She waved a dismissive finger at our drinks tray. "Well, you've got these now."

I opened my mouth to continue the conversation, but gave up as I would have been talking to her receding back.

Over the next 90 minutes, a dozen more people arrived for the presentation. The females all joined our table, sitting with the ladies who had by now had several more drinks. A few minutes before 11 o'clock, the door swung open and a large crowd shuffled in. From their flushed faces and slightly wobbly walks, I surmised this was not the first pub they had visited. Last through the door was Brenden, the secretary of the golf society. He was a small guy, almost unhealthily skinny, but with a warm smile and abundant enthusiasm. I politely elbowed my way through the crowd and tapped him on the shoulder.

"Niiick!" he bellowed. "You're here."

"Yes, since nine o'clock," I replied.

"Good, good, excellent!" he gushed.

I introduced Lesley and, after a few polite banalities, asked Brenden when the presentation was going to begin.

"Oh, in a while," he shrugged non-committally and waved towards the crowd. "It won't be long. Circulate. Shake a few hands. Everyone's dying to meet you."

Like space dust coalescing into planets, the crowd had spontaneously formed into distinct groups, each circling their own sun – typically the largest and loudest man dispensing advice, opinions and spittle in equal measure. Taking Brenden's advice, we did our best to meet and chat with as many people as possible. We could only nip at the edges of each group, but the people were polite and welcoming, although completely unaware of my existence or any plans to hold a presentation.

Since arriving in Ireland, we had made good progress in tuning our ears to the County Clare accent. Only infrequently now would I need to cup my ear and feign deafness, hoping to have a sentence repeated without causing offence. But this night was a different challenge. Extravagant libations and the energetic exchange of passionate opinions had raised the volume and slurred speech to the point where, for us, the dialogue was unintelligible. Admitting defeat, Lesley and I moved to a quiet table so we could chat.

Our conversation soon returned to Andy's suggestion.

"Should we have a holiday?" Lesley asked, failing completely to stifle a yawn.

"I'm not sure how," I replied. "My diary is full again. I picked up three new clients yesterday. If it carries on like this, I'm barely going to have enough time to do the renovations."

Lesley took a sip of lemonade, then another from the glass of orange juice.

"Are we doing the wrong thing?" she asked.

"What do you mean?"

"Well, we moved here for a better quality of life and to get away from the daily grind and stress, but somehow we're back working around the clock again. You're either out teaching, or busy building stuff, and now you're doing a column for the local paper and trying to write a book as well. It's work madness all over again!"

"This isn't the same as before," I said defensively. "I'm only busy because I choose to be."

"That's not why we came here," my wife snapped. "You were pushing too hard before and it risked your health."

"I was fine, it was nothing!"

Lesley glared at me.

I shrugged. "I was made redundant by the same company eight times in six years. That sort of thing is bound to take a toll."

She continued to glare, her lips white with tension.

I sighed and scratched the top of my head. "I guess you're right."

"You know I am," she said, relaxing somewhat.

"On the other hand, we've been debt free since we got here and that was our number one priority. What's more, nobody's forcing me to work so many hours. Admittedly the income is handy, particularly with all the money we're spending on these renovations."

"And there's a lot more to do yet," Lesley added. "Even with all the extra money you're earning, we're slowly depleting our savings."

"True," I conceded. "Even so, I could always clear a day, or a month, if we wanted. The real problem stopping us from taking a holiday is the animals. Apart from the obvious loss of income, it would cost a fortune to kennel four dogs, and then who would look after the chickens?"

"I guess we'd need a house-sitter."

"Good luck finding someone to live in our dusty building site of a home," I laughed. "Perhaps we'd do better when the renovations are finished."

Lesley sighed. "Until Andy mentioned it, I hadn't really thought about taking a holiday."

"Well now you have." I put my hands behind my head and yawned.

Lesley responded in kind. Mine was stifled, hers was not.

"Where do you want to go?"

"On holiday?"

I nodded.

She glanced down and scratched her cheek thoughtfully.

"There's so much of Ireland we haven't seen, why would we want to go abroad?"

"For the sun?" I suggested. Lesley is such a sun lover that her decision to move to what can feel like a perpetually dull and dank country, remains one of life's great mysteries.

"True!" She nodded and then grimaced ironically. "Sunshine is fine, but not a prerequisite for a restful break. Anyway, as we're already on holiday for the rest of our lives, or supposed to be, I guess it would be nice if we had some days out around

Ireland."

"We could do that," I agreed. "Where do you want to go?"

Lesley sat up, immediately her demeanour seemed brighter and more energetic.

"There are quite a few walled gardens nearby we could visit," she suggested.

"Gardens?" I tried to look excited and failed.

Lesley thumped me lovingly on the arm, quite hard.

"When do you want to start?"

"Best wait until after The Visit," she said, her eyes twinkling and suggestively wide. Our daughter, Joanne, was due to visit soon and this time she was bringing Mark, her new boyfriend. It sounded serious. We were looking forward to meeting him.

"Wasn't I supposed to begin renovating the centre of the house right after they had left?" I asked.

"Perhaps you should pause for a bit?" she said. "There's no benefit in rushing into such a big project, particularly if you're going to be flat-out teaching."

"You sure?"

Lesley nodded. "Besides, there are enough little jobs to do around the house and garden to keep you occupied."

"Oh good." I rubbed my hands together. "I can make a 'To Do' list."

"You and your lists!" Lesley tutted. "For once, can't you just get on with things without writing a 12-page battle plan?"

I mimicked a sad face. "My lists help me get organised."

"Fine," she huffed. "Make your list."

"I have writing to do as well," I added. "And research for the book I want to write. I'd best add that to my list."

"That too, I guess," she said, with rather less enthusiasm than I would have liked.

"Okay, it's a deal."

We bumped fists and Lesley yawned expansively.

"I'll go and ask Brenden about this flipping presentation," I growled, checking my watch again.

At a quarter to midnight, the grand presentation of prizes to the successful competitors in the golf competition finally got underway. The completion of my official duties took just 90 seconds. There were no speeches or photographers, just one bleary-eyed and heavily inebriated winner, who accepted the egg cup-sized trophy with a nod and a belch. I shook his hand, stepped back and melted into the crowd like fog on a warm morning. I don't think anyone noticed we had left.

Lesley was waiting by the car, yawning and fuming in equal measure.

"Well," I said, smiling. "You can't say I never take you out!"

Somehow I dodged her swinging foot.

***

It was a couple of weeks later when I first met Ticker. Even though his lifestyle was the antithesis of the one I sought, we soon became friends. Like opposite poles of a magnet, it was our differences that drew us together.

Although we were both English, his accent was pure pedigree, perhaps cultured at Eton. Mine was more mongrel, Essex with a hint of London but trying to sound better. Physically, we were very different. We were certainly never going to be mistaken for brothers. Ticker was tall and good looking, I wasn't even tall. He had great hair – the luscious brown of expensive coffee with perfect blond highlights. It was gloriously thick, wavy, and squeaky clean. If I rubbed my bald spot hard enough, it squeaked. His face had all the right proportions that made people think of millionaires and presidents. My face reminded people of playdoh on a hot day. He was dapper and elegant with a curious habit of wearing bowties, whereas I always looked as if I had dressed in the dark.

On the upside, I had a talent for coaching golf and Ticker had an overwhelming desire to improve his game, whatever the cost.

We first met in the carpark of the golf club.

"Graham Morgan-Tucker," he boomed, shaking my hand

vigorously. "But you may call me Ticker."

"Ticker?" I frowned questioningly.

"G-M-T," he spelled his initials. "Like Greenwich Mean Time, so my friends call me Ticker."

"Well, Ticker. I'm very pleased to make your acquaintance," I replied. "Where are your golf clubs?"

"In my car." He swept his arm expansively towards a gleaming Mercedes C-Class coupe. "It's new. What do you think?"

For some reason, just occasionally, I forget to switch on my Inappropriate Comments filter. This was one such day.

"I suspect you must have a very small penis," I said, before wondering if I had indeed spoken the words out loud. One look at Ticker confirmed I had. I saw a mix of emotions dancing across his face. He broke into a wide grin, threw his head back and laughed.

"A very small penis! Oh that's funny." He wiped his eyes and patted me on the back. "Nick, I believe we're going to get along just fine."

I was justifiably relieved.

Ticker was a recent immigrant to County Clare from Dublin, where he had lived for the previous 18 months. He was a civil engineer, doing something clever and well-paid in regard to bridges. Our beautiful county has a lot of rivers, and with so many new roads being constructed, his talents were in high demand.

To begin our client/coach relationship, we agreed to play a few holes together, so I could accurately assess Ticker's golfing strengths and weaknesses.

"To let the dog see the rabbit," I explained.

Our tee shots were delayed by, of all things, a helicopter landing just 50 yards away, right in the centre of the first fairway.

"That's not something you see every day," I shouted, as we were pelted with dust and loose vegetation.

We watched in disbelieving silence as the door opened and a

man in a grey morning suit helped a child of eight or nine disembark. Like a miniature bride, she wore a pure white silk dress, with a matching veil and handbag. Father and daughter held hands and trotted across the damp grass towards the hotel carpark. When they were clear, the helicopter took off, once again showering us in fragments of grass and mud.

"How utterly extraordinary!" I remarked.

"Not at all," Ticker replied. "It happens all the time in Dublin."

"But what...?" I stammered, pointing to where the young girl was climbing into a vintage Rolls Royce.

"They're undoubtedly celebrating her first communion," Ticker explained. "It's a big thing over here."

"I guess it must be," I exclaimed. "But a helicopter and a vintage car seem a little over the top."

"It's all the rage in Dublin. Any excuse to show others how well off you are."

"That's just mad," I replied, shaking my head. "There were no helicopter rides at my first communion, even though we were living on an air force base."

"And there were no vintage cars at mine," he added. "Although we owned several."

"I seem to recall I fainted and then threw up. Afterwards, the priest gave me a little blue badge."

"Welcome to the new Ireland," Ticker laughed. "Communions, confirmations, birthdays and the debs' ball are all major events now. I guess this is an indication that opulence is alive and well, even in County Clare."

"Well, if that's the case," I said, grinning wickedly, "you're going to need a bigger car!"

3 – Lost and Found

"I see they haven't caught him yet," Lesley said.

"Who haven't they caught?" I asked, looking up from my book.

Silence. My wife sipped her breakfast coffee and turned a page of yesterday's newspaper.

I took a bite of toast and chewed slowly, savouring the flavour whilst trying to ignore the four sets of hungry eyes, enviously watching my every move. Although our dogs know table treats are forbidden, there is always the possibility of a sudden cardiac arrest or choking fit, causing a fumbled morsel to fall within reach. Therefore, in their watchful and loving fashion, they remain forever hopeful.

"Was it Lord Lucan?" I suggested.

"Mmm?" she grunted, her attention still focused on the newspaper she was reading.

"Who haven't they caught?" I said, a little louder.

"That Polish guy," she mumbled.

"Bravo Jet Ski?" I quipped.

Lesley smiled and flicked back a page to find the correct pronunciation. "Prawo Jazdy. It says here they raided a house, but it wasn't his. Apparently, he's been giving the Guards the run-around, false addresses and the like."

"Well, he's hardly a big league criminal," I said, licking some honey from my fingers. "But the hunt has some entertainment value, I'll give you that."

Lesley ignored my comment and took a sip of her coffee before turning the page.

"That reminds me," I said. "Your car test is at 12 today."

"I hadn't forgotten," she mumbled.

"The test centre is on the road opposite the railway station. I've left all the documents on the passenger seat. You need to book in at reception and pay a fee."

Lesley nodded. "It's not like the UK where you just pop down to the local garage then?"

"It's certainly different. I admit I was very impressed when I took my car. They were very organised," I said. "Are you sure you don't want me to take it?"

"It's fine." She shook her head. "I'll stop in town and do some shopping on the way home."

"It's up to you. Just don't be late," I advised, immediately regretting my choice of words.

My wife's lips tightened, but I was excused from any repercussions as her attention was captured by the next headline.

"It says here," she said, "the Government has been advised to make changes to the taxation system."

"Fascinating." I mimed a yawn and followed with a real one.

Lesley joined in.

"I'm trying hard not to think about finance anymore," I explained. "Anyway, they just had a budget and put taxes down."

"Well they must have done it wrong," she replied, waving her glasses at the paper. "Some think tank or other says Ireland gets too much of its tax income from car sales and house building. They need to diversify."

"Oh goodie," I huffed. "More taxes. I can hardly wait."

"Anyway, you're in the wrong business. You should be selling cars." She tapped the newspaper with her finger. "New car sales this year are predicted to top 250,000."

"Good grief!" I gasped. "That's a lot of new cars for such a small country."

"Slightly more than one in five households will be buying a new car this year," she read.

"That would explain why it has suddenly become harder to pull out into traffic. When we first got here, the roads were so quiet, you could almost pull out without looking. Now there's so many cars, it's almost like being back in England."

"Don't exaggerate," Lesley chided. "It isn't that bad."

"I guess not." I shrugged. "It just feels that way sometimes, especially at rush hour. There are definitely more cars, and not just new ones."

"Perhaps we should buy one."

"A new car?" I asked, frowning.

My wife nodded.

"I'd rather not." I grimaced and chewed on my lip.

"Why not?" she asked. "Christine's just bought a new car and only the other day you were complaining to me because a client was taking the Mickey out of your car."

"That was Ticker," I replied, smiling at the memory. "He'd take the Mickey out of any car I had, unless it was brand new and worth €120,000."

"He sounds a bit snobby," she grimaced.

"Ah, he's grand." I waved her comment away. "Ticker is rather a city boy. Whereas I think you have to work for money, he thinks money should be working for him. As well as a new car, he's just bought three houses over in Shannon."

"Three houses! Whatever for?"

"It's part of some new buy-to-let scheme he's doing through the bank," I explained. "He's going to rent them out and when the mortgages are cleared, he'll sell the houses and live on the proceeds."

Lesley smiled and shook her head. For a while we lapsed into a comfortable silence. My wife flicked through the remaining pages of the newspaper. I nibbled my toast and wondered what else I could add to my To Do list.

"We're having lunch at Christine's house," Lesley announced, as we cleared the breakfast dishes away.

"When?" I squeaked.

"Sunday, about one."

"That'll be nice," I replied, doing my best to keep a neutral tone in my voice. Lesley's friend, Christine, is a feisty, blonde, English lady, with a button nose, twinkling blue eyes, a ready smile and a husky voice. No taller than a sickly pit pony, what she lacks in stature, she more than makes up with energetic conviviality. She's a delightful lady, but I imagined Sunday lunch at her house would be as quiet and relaxing as attending a birthday party for hyperactive toddlers. To be on the safe side, I kept my thoughts to myself.

"While I walk the dogs, can you go to the Post Office?" Lesley asked. "Someone needs to post Joanne's birthday card."

"Sure. Is there a gift too?"

Lesley shook her head. "You sent her a case of wine from the internet. Don't you remember?"

"I do now!" I snorted a laugh. "Last time I was in the bank, I couldn't remember which month it was. I thought my memory was going, but then I realised I don't need to know the date, especially through the winter when I haven't got any lessons booked."

"Now you mention it," Lesley frowned. "What month is it?"

"Who cares?" I laughed. "It's a great life we have."

For a while we slipped back into a comfortable silence.

"Do you think we're doing the right thing?" Lesley asked.

"Going to Sunday lunch at Christine's?" I suggested, smiling.

Lesley pinched her lips and rolled her eyes dramatically.

"I meant, are we doing the right thing staying debt free?"

"Fast cars, posh houses, expensive clothes, and all the worry it would bring again?" I pulled my wife into a hug and planted a kiss on her forehead. "I think I prefer to sleep well."

"Me too," she replied.

***

Although the local village Post Office is just five miles away, the round trip took almost an hour. On the drive down the hill, I encountered a herd of cattle grazing the hedgerows along the single track road. Irish cows are generally amiable, even without access to the soporific effects of Guinness. However, these 20 hungry bovine lawnmowers were happily munching on the juicy spring grass on the roadside embankments and therefore unwilling to move along. My only option was to gingerly edge forwards until each cow stepped aside. With patience and caution I squeezed by in a little under 15 minutes.

At the Post Office, my transaction was completed with commendable efficiency, but it would have been rude to leave without congratulating the postmaster on the birth of his daughter and discussing the state of his golf game. In return, I updated him on the progress of our renovations and the health of both Lesley and the dogs.

Back in my car, I paused for a moment and listen to a blackbird serenading me from a nearby tree. I dropped my hand away from the ignition key and watched five of Amber's siblings chasing a little old lady along the road. Looking identical to my dog, they were playful but tenacious as they nipped at her heels and circled just far enough out of range to avoid her swinging umbrella. I knew from experience that this game was a daily event, no more than a habit, performed without malice or the risk of injury to either party. In an hour, the dance would be repeated in the opposite direction.

A little further up the road, someone was hanging out their washing. White sheets, towels, and several pairs of ladies' unmentionables flapped enthusiastically, keen to capitalise on the warm drying breeze. On the opposite side of the street, a lady in hair rollers and a red spotted headscarf was doggedly scrubbing her front doorstep. To my right, a fat mistle thrush was busy breaking snail shells against the pavement, keen to expose the tasty treats within. And wafting in on the wind was the sound of children playing sports at the local school. Watching these hidden treasures of village life as if through a camera obscura was a privilege to be savoured. I smiled and sighed, quietly rejoicing in the life we had chosen.

At the village shop, I bought the local paper and a litre of milk. I took a moment to chat with an elderly gent about the weather. Seamus was a local farmer. Long since retired from the daily toil of milking and mucking out, he was someone who would always wave and chat. As it was a warm and sunny spring morning, he wore ancient canvas trousers, so caked with dirt as to be of an indeterminate colour, held up with an equally ancient brown leather belt. Above this he wore only a string vest, proudly displaying his shoulders and chest, thick with curly grey hair.

The shop assistant and I shared a smile as we watched Seamus climbing into his car. I imagine he inherited the vehicle from his grandfather and, as it was never driven more than three miles from the family farm, it had never been taxed, insured, or subjected to the impertinent pokings of a mechanic during the mandatory annual National Car Test – locally known as the 'Fecking NCT'.

"That's some tan he's got there," I remarked.

"Around these parts it's called a farmer's tan." She grinned conspiratorially and leaned forward to mock whisper from behind her hand. "It comes from not having a proper wash for 30 years."

"Good to know," I replied, wincing involuntarily.

The herd of cows was still in the lane, munching happily at their free breakfast. An unavoidable trail of runny cowpats decorated the tarmac and then my wheels, evidence these bovine strimmers had moved barely a few paces since my previous journey. I tooted my horn and edged cautiously forward as we repeated our little dance until it was safe to pass.

Finally back home, I was surprised to see Lesley's car still in the driveway and the house empty. There was no sign of the dogs or my wife. Frowning at the clock, I experienced a sudden sinking feeling. The NCT was in 30 minutes, we had discussed it that morning. Why wasn't she home? Had something happened? My wife was still recovering from a severe, life-threatening illness. Although she was much improved and healing well, she was still prone to bouts of exhaustion. Immediately I pictured a chilling image of dear Lesley, laid crumpled and unresponsive on the forest path with the dogs waiting patiently nearby.

A quick inventory revealed two things: her car keys were missing, but her mobile phone was not. Lesley had an acrimonious relationship with her mobile phone, making it probably the least used gift in the history of technology. She frequently forgets to charge it and hates having it about her person, claiming it is an unnecessary impediment to her otherwise unencumbered lifestyle. In return, her innocent little Samsung goes all sulky, refusing to respond to Lesley's swearing, or the angry stabbing of her mud-encrusted gardener's fingers.

For five minutes I paced the kitchen and chewed at my lip, before deciding I had no other option but to begin a search. With no idea which way Lesley had gone, and several possible walking routes to try, I elected to set out on my trusty/rusty mountain bike.

I hadn't gone far along the single track road before I encountered a weather-beaten dark blue car, being gamely pursued by a gangly black and white dog. I knew immediately this was old Tom, a local farmer, and his enthusiastic pooch, Patch. Even though these days Tom only ventures out to inspect his cows, visit friends, collect his pension, and enjoy the comforts of a good meal along with a few pints of Guinness at his favourite pub, he probably covers five miles every day. Regardless of the wind or rain or snow, wherever Tom drives, his faithful dog is always running close behind. Splattered in mud and pelted by gravel, Patch ignores the risk to life and limb from diesel fumes and passing cars, determined to follow his master and become Ireland's fittest dog.

As the car pulled to a stop, edging into a passing place, Patch bounded past, tongue lolling and eyes alive with excitement. A few yards later he stopped and, crouching expectantly like a sprinter on his blocks, waited for the car to pass again. There was a tortured squeal as Tom wound the handle and his window rocked from side to side on its downward journey.

"Hello, Tom," I said, smiling. "Doesn't Patch ever ride in your car?"

"He likes to take rides on me tractor sometimes," he explained. "But cars is only for chasing."

Old Tom is aged somewhere on the thick end of 70. He has thick wavy hair, as white as wood ash, a ready smile and bright blue eyes, sparkling with mischief and kindness. The man in the passenger seat was considerably taller and younger. Aged around 40 and lean built, he had dark hair, hands the size of coal shovels, and the sort of ruddy complexion earned from half a lifetime of hard farming in all weathers.

"This is my boy, Tiernan," Tom said, tipping his head towards his son.

"Hello, I'm Nick." I nodded, pointing over my shoulder. "I live at Glenmadrie."

He smiled and waved a hand towards my bike. "You're out for a spot of exercise?" Tiernan spoke softly for such a big man, but his accent was thick with the County Clare lilt.

"Actually, I'm looking for my wife," I explained. "She took the dogs out for a walk and now she's late for an appointment."

"Why would you walk your dogs?" Tiernan asked, frowning. "Can't they walk themselves?"

"It's a English thing," Tom interjected, patting his son on the knee.

I scratched my chin and smiled. "I guess you've got a point. Sometimes we have to call them back from wherever they are, just so we can take them out again."

"Thaas a bit like the hospital waking you up, so's to give yous a sleeping tablet," Tiernan giggled.

"I don't suppose you've seen Lesley?" I asked, looking at Tom.

"Not today," he replied.

"Oh well, I guess I can always find another wife," I quipped.

"Watch out!" Tom shouted, pointing along the lane.

As I turned to see the cause of his sudden warning, my mouth opened in shock. A large black Mercedes was approaching at breakneck speed. With eyes wide in fear and dragging my bike, I quickstepped across the road and threw myself into the hedge just as the car thundered past. It missed my heels by a couple of inches.

"Phew. That was close," I growled, climbing out of the ditch.

"Aye, it was," Tom agreed, shaking his head.

Even Patch thought better of giving chase.

"Perhaps someone doesn't like blow-ins," I remarked. Although we had been warmly welcomed by everyone in Ireland, even those who used the term blow-in to describe anyone who wasn't born in the local area, I anticipated we would eventually encounter someone who was an exception.

"Not at all," he replied. "That fecking eejit is just a rich twat who thinks owning a Mercedes means he owns the road. It's nothing personal."

"Good to know," I replied, brushing the mud and leaves from my jeans.

"Can't wait till the sheriffs catch up with him," Tiernan added.

"Sheriffs?" I asked.

"Yous call them bailiffs," he explained. "That twat's got his motor on the never-never, but since he's lost his job, he'll never-never pay for it!"

They both laughed, sharing the joke.

"I'd better get on with my search," I explained, mounting my bike. "If you see Lesley, please send her home."

"Good luck!" Tom's car roared off in a cloud of diesel fumes, hotly pursued by Patch.

I cycled three different paths, without sight or sound of my wife. Inevitably, when I got home, she was just walking up the driveway with four muddy dogs in tow.

"Where have you been?" I demanded. "I've been looking for you everywhere."

Lesley frowned at my unexpected outburst.

"It was such a lovely day. I decided to head across the moor to see if I could find that glacial lake," she explained. "Why were you looking for me?"

I held my hands up to indicate my surprise at her question. "Your National Car Test. Did you forget?"

The look of horror on her face suggested she had. Nevertheless, she quickly recovered and parried like an Olympic swordfighter, attempting to tip the blame in my direction.

"There was plenty of time," she suggested, hands on hips.

"Why didn't you take it, instead of wasting the afternoon hunting for me?"

For once I had the upper hand. "Because you took the car keys with you!"

"Oh."

"And I was worried you'd had a fall."

"Oh."

"Luckily, I called the NCT centre and postponed the appointment until next week," I explained. "The lady was very nice and understanding."

For husbands worldwide these little matrimonial victories are rare and worthy of some discreet celebration. Mine was a little dance. Talking of which…

Once we had towelled the dogs dry and made a cup of tea, I told Lesley about the little surprise I had planned.

"We're going to a dance."

"Are we?" My wife raised a quizzical eyebrow. "When?"

"Tomorrow night, down in the village. I saw a poster in the Post Office, so I bought tickets. I thought you'd enjoy dancing again. It'll be a chance to meet some new people."

"What sort of dancing is it?" For 30 years, Lesley taught American Round Dancing in clubs across Europe. Despite her persistent bad back, she was an excellent dancer. Conversely, once the disco era was over, my clumsy and spasmodic jerks were no longer considered to be elegant or entertaining.

"Isn't all dancing the same?" I asked.

"For you it may be!" Lesley rolled her eyes at my deliberate naivety.

"The poster said it's a simplified céilí dance," I explained. "It's especially for beginners. I guess it'll be a bit like a barn dance with lots of instruction."

Lesley looked unconvinced. I reached over and held her hand.

"Don't worry, it'll be fun," I said, silently praying I would be right.

***

As if we hadn't already had enough excitement for one day, a parcel arrived – eventually.

Living in such a remote spot is delightful and relaxing, but it has its downsides. For one, the rural west of Ireland is hardly Oxford Street when it comes to shopping for bargains. Overall, this is a good thing. Most of our local shops, even those in the nearby towns, are small family-run establishments with dusty shelves, cut-down cardboard display boxes on glass-topped counters and handwritten price cards. These are all set against mahogany backdrops of cubby holes and tiny drawers that would make an apothecary proud. In such an exciting emporium, I could purchase the makings of a good breakfast and a newspaper alongside a roll of duct tape, three different size screws, a single tap washer, seven nails, a trailer hitch and some chainsaw oil. If I had such a need, at the same time I could order a ton of gravel, catch up on the local gossip and arrange a funeral. It's like living in a time warp, a charming example of the simpler life we longed for and the very thing which drew Lesley and me to Ireland in the first place.

However, if we need a particular book, long since out of print, or some new technology at a cost lower than what I paid for my car, the only option is to shop online. The exasperation of navigating the interweb thingy, when the download speed can be measured on an abacus, is exceeded only by the frustration of trying to direct the delivery driver to our home.

Having failed to negotiate the staircase and hurdle our recumbent canines in time to reach the phone before the last ring, I usually jog to the highest point of our land where I have some marginal hope of a mobile phone signal so I can call him back. From there, like an air traffic controller guiding a stricken aircraft safely to landing, I can direct the driver to my door.

"Is that Mr Aber?" the voice asked, sounding only slightly less clear than the first transmission from the moon.

"It's Albert," I corrected, twisting my posture in the hope of getting a better signal.

"Delivery driver. I've a parcel for you," the voice crackled. "Where are you? The label says Glen Maddy."

"It's Glenmadrie. Where are you now?" I asked, hoping he wasn't actually on the moon.

"I'm not sure."

"Not sure? I exclaimed. "How can you...never mind. Is there anything you can see. Perhaps a landmark or something, so I'll know where you are?"

"There's a small white cottage with a red door."

I closed my eyes in frustration. This was hardly helpful information. Rural Ireland is awash with such buildings.

"Can you see anything else?"

"There's an old rusty tractor in a field," the voice offered, sounding like he was rolling in autumn leaves.

I frowned and scratched my forehead. Ireland has more old rusty tractors than it has small white cottages with red doors.

"Can you see anything else?" I asked. This was fast turning into a ridiculous game of Twenty Questions.

"Well, there's a huge lake," he offered tentatively.

I took a deep calming breath. Ireland has more lakes than... I had a thought. Perhaps I could work with this information. There were two lakes I knew of, both with cottages. One was to the north and the other south east.

"Can you see lots of boats?" I asked. "Dozens of yachts?"

"No," the voice sizzled and hissed. "Just a rowing boat."

"Is there a long low pier, like a wooden letter T?"

"There is!"

"Right!" I sighed. "I know where you are. You need to keep the lake on your right and then turn left at the top of the hill. About a mile later, turn right opposite the red house where there's a rusty blue car with no wheels. After you pass Murphy's pub, we're five miles further along, just on the left. I'll be waiting in the road."

"Can't I just leave it at the village Post Office?" he pleaded. This was common practice in our area, particularly for some of the overworked delivery drivers trying to make up some time.

"Normally I'd say yes," I replied, sympathetically. "But you've got to drive past my place to get to the post office."

His reply was lost in an electrical crackle and terminated in a fizzing pop. I presume he had either hung up or been hit by lightning. It was the former. Two calls and 40 minutes later my parcel arrived.

"I'm sorry to put you out," I said, guiltily. "If only you'd followed my directions…"

"My fault. I'm not sure what possessed me to turn up that forest track." He waved away my apology, as if it were a puff of cigarette smoke. He was a tall man, aged somewhere south of 50, with dark eyes and curly blond hair. Away from the crackle of the mobile phone, his accent was cultured, with a hint of eastern European. He raised his glasses and squinted at his clipboard. "Perhaps you can point me in the correct direction for my next delivery?"

"Don't you have a map?" I asked.

He shrugged sheepishly.

"Hang on, I've got one indoors." I left the parcel on the kitchen table, searched through the sideboard for the correct map, told Lesley what I was doing, and hotfooted my way back outdoors. My progress was only marginally slowed by having to prevent four dogs from escaping the confines of the kitchen, all keen to greet and delay our visitor. As I stepped through the door I encountered the delivery driver, quite openly urinating in my driveway.

"Oh, excuse me," I mumbled, in a typically English reaction.

"S'ok," he replied, enthusiastically shaking off the drops as he finished the task and zipped up.

"You should have asked," I suggested, conscious that Lesley was looking out of the kitchen window. "There's a toilet just indoors."

"Why worry?" He waved a sweeping arm at the countryside. "There's nobody here."

"I guess it's okay," I admitted. "But may I ask one question?"

"For sure," he nodded, smiling.

"With so many trees and bushes available, why did you choose to pee on the wheel of my car?"

His eyes widened in a momentary flash of horror. Once again he shrugged sheepishly. "Sorry!"

4 – Twinkle Toes

Completely ignoring the valuable experience we gained from the golf society presentation, Lesley and I arrived for the dance at precisely the time shown on our tickets. Inevitably, the dance hall – a large marquee at the back of a pub – was almost empty. Even the band hadn't arrived. There were a dozen adults, sitting in two groups at opposite ends of the hall and eyeing each other suspiciously, like forest tribes protecting their territory. Despite the lack of music, the dance floor was already in good use as several children had organised an ad hoc Irish dance competition. This unscheduled event was disturbed by what appeared to be a game of Gaelic football, inspired by the presence of a party balloon left over from a previous event.

"Oh well," I sighed. "There's plenty of entertainment to watch while we're waiting for the main event."

Lesley grunted noncommittally, before pointing to our right. "Look, it's those ladies we met at the golf presentation."

"The ones who drank all that gin?" I asked, squinting into the darkness.

"That's them, Rose and Mary," she replied, nudging me with her elbow. "Look, they're waving us over."

She was right. Sitting in a tight group in the corner were the same two ladies. And, given they had been panic buying gin since 3 pm to get ahead of the predicted rush, they certainly were tight. Nonetheless, it was nice to have some company.

"Do you dance then?" Rose asked once we were seated.

"A little bit," I replied casually. "But my unique style of interpreting the music doesn't really comply with any known dance form. However, Lesley used to be a dance teacher."

Rose squinted in confusion at my convoluted description, so Mary leaned in to help.

"He can't dance, but she can."

"Oh," Rose nodded and turned the conversation towards my

wife. "Was it ballet you taught?"

"No," Lesley replied with an easy smile. "I taught American Round Dancing."

"What on earth is that?" Mary asked.

"It's like ballroom dancing, but with cues," Lesley replied.

"Huh?"

"Rather than remembering an entire dance, you just learn several moves and the cuer calls out a sequence of moves to make a complete dance," Lesley explained.

"It sounds complicated," Rose mumbled.

"Actually, it's really quite simple," I offered. "It's like getting directions for a journey, rather than learning the entire route."

"Oh, you mean like a satnav for dance?" Mary squealed, clapping her hands. "How quaint!"

Lesley winced at the simplification of what she considered to be high art, but let the unintended slight pass by.

"How ever did you get into that?" Rose asked, leaning her elbow on the table and missing. Her drink slopped over her hand, but she was quick to slurp up the spill.

"We used to live in Essex, in the east of England," I explained. "In the area were several US Air Force bases. The Americans came over during the Second World War, and never left. Germany was much the same. Anyway, they have a lot of people doing round dancing and squares too. I guess the craze spread and soon there were clubs all over Europe."

"What are squares?" Mary asked.

"It's called square dancing," Lesley corrected. "I guess it's a bit like a barn dance, but with instructions."

"Did you do square dancing too?"

"We both did."

"Lesley was very good," I added. "Me not so much."

"Well, if you can get by at barn dancing, you should do fine tonight," Mary said. "I believe you'll find the simplified céilí to be quite similar."

"Oh good." I grinned at Lesley. "We were worried we'd get it wrong and offend someone."

"Bah!" Rose waved dismissively. "It's just a bit of craic. Enjoy yourself!"

And we did.

Once the band arrived, followed by a large crowd of people from the pub, the merriments quickly got underway. Lesley and I were willingly dragged onto the dancefloor and guided, poked and prodded into our respective places. For 20 minutes we had some simple instruction and a gentle slow motion walk-through of the moves we were going to perform. Initially, I thought it was quite straightforward, particularly as many of the moves were rather similar to those I recalled from square dancing. But once the music began, things got a little more complex.

As best I can recall, there were lots of polkas and elbow hooks, some stepping in and out, plenty of swings and claps, several loud whoops and rather too many spins. Somehow I avoided making any calamitous errors, but I suspect each group may have contained a couple of 'ringers' – experienced dancers slipped in to keep the likes of me moving in approximately the right direction. The music was foot-tappingly excellent and, judging by the beaming smiles, everyone was having a wonderful time. Or perhaps they were just laughing at my clumsy stamping.

Even though poor Lesley was still exhausted after her recent illness, and having one of those days where her back felt like it was speared with broken glass, she quickly got into the spirit of things. For my part, what I lacked in ability and rhythm, I made up for with unbridled enthusiasm and quick reactions. Together we danced the Connemara and Virginia Reels, the Circassian Circle, two war-like stomps called the Walls of Limerick and the Siege of Ennis, and finally the Haymakers' Jig. Although we were grinning like newlyweds, Lesley was looking a little wan and, after so many enthusiastic rotations and two pints of Guinness, my head was beginning to spin. Puffing hard and sweating like a pair of Turkish wrestlers, we collapsed onto our chairs.

"You both did very well," Rose said.

"Especially you," Mary added, patting my hand.

I'm hardly twinkle toes, so I barely suppressed a smile as Lesley's mouth tightened at the prospect of my spasmodic gyrations receiving praise over her foot-perfect form. Given that my wife is the artistic free spirit in our relationship and I am the precise process-driven conformist, when it comes to dance, it has always struck me as ironic that she insists on precision, whereas I look like an orangutan being attacked by a swarm of wasps. She may have decades of dance instruction behind her, but I was the 1978 Skegness disco dance champion. Not a bad achievement for a shy youngster in six-inch stacked shoes, a white waistcoat and my red underpants showing through the split bottom of my flares. Whatever gives you pleasure.

"I don't know how he does it," Lesley complained. "It's almost impossible to tell he has no idea what he's doing."

"It's true," I conceded. "I just spot the gaps in the crowd and run towards them."

"Beginner's luck!" Rose concluded, as she and Mary headed towards the bar once again.

"Do you want another go?" I asked, pointing at the dancefloor.

"You go if you want," Lesley replied. "I'm done for now."

For a while, we watched the dancing and sipped at our drinks.

"Perhaps you should start a club," I suggested.

Lesley looked at me in surprise. My proposition had caught her off-guard. "Whatever makes you say that?"

"You used to love teaching," I replied, nodding towards the whirling confusion of dancers on the floor. "And clearly there is enthusiasm for dance in Ireland."

"But I teach American Round Dance," my wife pleaded. "Céilí is completely different."

"You could adapt." I shrugged. "Anyway, I'm sure there are plenty of people who would like to try something new. Americans are very welcome over here and their dancing probably would be too."

"Bah! We're too busy with the renovations to waste time setting up a dance club."

"There's more to life than work," I replied, shaking my head. "It would be good to have some distractions. Think of it as a chance to get out and meet some new people."

Lesley chewed her lip but didn't reply. We watched the dancers in silence. I slowly sipped my Guinness and cast the occasional glance towards my wife. She was deep in thought.

"Where would I start?" Lesley asked, frowning.

"Well, it was only a thought – rather a half-formed idea I suppose." I scratched my chin and tried to formulate a plan. "You've already got the records, the dance cards and all the equipment you need–"

"They're called cue sheets, not dance cards," she corrected.

"So we'd need to find a suitable venue. Perhaps there's a village hall or community centre somewhere we could rent, if it isn't too expensive."

"I'd need public liability insurance. That's a huge problem right now. Ireland is so litigious I'm positive the British Dance Federation's insurance won't cover me here."

"Now it sounds like you're putting up barriers," I chided.

"But it's true," she pleaded. "Look at all the problems you had getting your golf teaching cover. It cost about 30 quid in England. How much was the same cover over here?"

"€2,500," I conceded with a grimace. "But eventually I got a much better deal. Perhaps they'll cover you too."

"Even if we could find a hall and get insurance, there'd be advertising to pay for and still no guarantee of making any money!" Lesley rolled her eyes in frustration.

"Don't worry." I reached over and held her hand. "I know we're on a tight budget, but not everything we do has to make a profit. If you want to start a club and you enjoy it, that's all that matters."

Lesley watched the dancing and sipped her drink.

"It's up to you," I suggested.

The dancing continued. We watched in silence, enjoying the spectacle and music. It was only as we were climbing into our car, that my wife made her final comment on my idea.

"I'll think about it."
And that was that, at least for the time being.

***

Whilst it is lovely to be invited to Sunday lunch by a friend, there is a bit of me always hoping it will be cancelled at the last minute. I'm really not sure why. It's certainly not because I am antisocial, or unsure of what to say, quite the opposite. If anything is holding me back, it's that I feel rather shy, but my response to that affliction is to take centre stage and make jokes until everyone quietly slips away in search of a quieter life. Although I may be quite good at telling jokes, my faulty 'appropriateness filter' can cause my dear wife to blanch and turn away in wide-eyed horror. Fortunately she has a dreadful memory for jokes, so by the time we get home her admonishments are no more than vague references to comments I can easily deny making.

On the other hand, perhaps we're just getting to that age where going out seems like a lot of fuss and bother, and potentially less enjoyable than sitting at home with a nice cup of tea and a decent book. This is an internationally recognised medical condition known as 'old fart syndrome'. The only known cure is to get out and take a risk. Hence, Sunday lunch with Lesley's friend Christine.

Although we had visited Christine's house once before, that was some time ago and my recollection of the route was a little fuzzy. After a couple of false starts and a good bit of back-tracking, we eventually found the correct property, a jumble of buildings hiding at the end of a curving half-mile long gravel and mud driveway. There was a big bungalow, perched on the edge of a shallow hill, with views over farmland to a lake in the far distance. Alongside was a separate double garage and, to the left, a large wooden workshop with a corrugated iron roof. It was a tidy house, painted battleship grey with black guttering. These potentially depressing colours were nicely offset by the addition of deep red paint on the woodwork and windowsills. I thought the overall effect was very smart and said so to my wife.

On exiting the car, we were greeted by an ancient black Collie dog, almost as round as it was tall. Unsure of our intentions, he stood his ground with arthritically stiff legs and an incongruous demeanour. Whilst his face was fierce and barking loudly, the other end was wagging the tail with such fervent determination as to risk unbalancing the user. For a moment we watched cautiously, unsure of how to proceed. Fortunately, just then a tall man in dark blue overalls strode out of the workshop. He wore thick gauntlets and perched above his soot-stained face was a black welder's mask. I thought he looked a little like Darth Vader on a day off.

"Arthur, give over!" he shouted. The dog immediately went quiet, supplementing his barking with even more excitable tail wagging as he tottered hopefully towards Lesley's outstretched hand.

"Hello. Are you Peadar?" Lesley asked.

He nodded and gave us a toothy smile. "You must be Lesley. Christine said you was coming."

"I'm Nick," I said, holding out my hand.

Peadar pulled off his black welder's gauntlet, the hand underneath was almost the same colour. Nevertheless, we shared a warm handshake.

"Nice place you have." I pointed at the valley. "Lovely views."

"Thank you. We like it," Peadar replied. "It was part of the family farm."

"Do you farm now?"

"A bit," he replied. "But mostly I do groundworks. Driving diggers and the like."

"And a bit of welding," I added, nodding towards the workshop where the distinctive acrid tang of hot metal mixed with the fresh aroma of ozone.

"I'm just fixing the mountings on an old tractor," he explained.

"I don't recall meeting the dog. Is he new?" Lesley asked.

"Nah!" Peadar grinned. "He's older than God. I was working the day yous came last. I expect Arthur was hiding in my workshop like."

I reached down and patted Arthur's black furry head, it felt rather sticky. He grunted in delight and let off a small fart.

"Well, it's lovely to finally meet you," I said, surreptitiously wiping my hand on my trousers.

"I love your golf column in the newspaper," Peadar said. "I read it every week."

"Oh, thank you. Where do you play?"

"Tsk." He rolled his eyes. "I don't play golf. I just like your writing. It's very funny."

"He's hoping to turn it into a book," Lesley added.

"You should," Peadar replied, patting me on the shoulder. "I'm sure it will do just grand."

Our conversation stalled as the front door of the bungalow burst open.

"Cooeee-Lesleeey!" Christine yelled, waving excitedly.

This diminutive blonde whirlwind bounded along the garden path and enveloped my wife in a hug. As if a munchkin had assaulted her with an indifferent rugby tackle, Lesley staggered backwards with her eyes wide in surprise. Whatever she lacks in height, Christine more than makes up for with kindness, boundless energy, effervescent enthusiasm and bodyweight. She gave me a hug too, and a beery kiss, before turning abruptly and leading the way into the house.

"This way, this way," she called. There was a slur in her voice and the walk back indoors was slightly serpentine.

Christine is English born, but has been living in Ireland since she was a teenager. At school she and Peadar were inseparable sweethearts. They married on her 21st birthday and have since been blessed with a flatulent dog and two delightful teenage children. Their daughter is called Aoife (pronounced Eef-ah) and the son Thomas (pronounced Toe-mass).

The kitchen diner was a large well-lit oblong room. One end was dominated by an eight-seater pine dining table, in the centre French doors opened to the garden, and at the other end there was a matching kitchen. The marble counters were heaving with dishes piled high with food. On the cooker pots were bubbling on every hob. The air was a foggy pot-pourri of tantalisingly delicious smells. My mouth watered like Pavlov's dog.

"Goodness, I hope you haven't gone to too much trouble," Lesley said, as we sat down at the table.

"No trouble at all," she waved dismissively. "Most of this is for the kids. Aoife and Thomas have some friends over. They'll be eating in the den."

"It smells wonderful," Lesley replied.

My stomach growled in agreement.

"Ours is simple. Chicken and chips," Christine said, before taking a long pull at her beer. "I've done a veggie burger for Nick. There's salad too."

"Thank you," I replied. "You're too kind."

"Not at all. Help yourself to drinks."

I made a pot of tea. Christine finished her beer and reached for a refill. I knew from experience she had an impressive capacity for alcohol, but I was beginning to wonder if she would make it to the second course.

"How's work?" I enquired politely. Christine was a secretary in the local council planning office.

"Bah! The usual crap," she spat dismissively. "Too many managers and not enough people to do the actual work."

"I know that scenario," I replied. "Although for a good while I was one of those managers."

"You should be ashamed!" Christine joked, waving her bottle at me. Some beer slopped onto the floor. "Oops!"

"In my defence, I was reporting to three different managers at the time," I explained.

"I bet you're pleased to be out of that life," she said.

"You have no idea."

"Are Aoife and Thomas looking forward to the summer holidays?" Lesley asked.

"Ack, don't remind me!" Christine groaned. "They're off to a Gaeltacht Summer Course."

"What's that?" I asked.

"It's an Irish language course up in Galway," she explained. "They'll be away for three weeks, doing classes and outdoor activities. The idea is to immerse themselves in the Irish language, so no English is allowed."

"That sounds like it would be great fun," I said.

"Fecking waste of money, if you ask me," Peadar grunted from the doorway. He came in and threw himself into a chair. Arthur waddled in and came to my side. I reached down and scratched his ear. He grunted gratefully and farted.

"Why do you say that?" Lesley asked, wrinkling her nose at the smell wafting up from under the table.

"*Peadar* thinks learning the Irish language is detrimental to the kids' education," Christine hissed through clenched teeth.

Her frown suggested we had stumbled into a minefield of conflicting beliefs. I should have moved the topic to safer ground, but as usual, I couldn't help myself.

"Why is it a waste? I asked. "Don't people need a high standard of Irish to work in most professions here?"

"They do," Peadar conceded.

"And isn't retaining the Irish language seen as fundamental to protecting the culture?"

"Well, yes, but…" Peadar sighed. "I know it's contentious and all that…" He glanced accusingly at Christine, but her attention was firmly glued to her bottle of beer.

"But?" Lesley asked.

"But they're spending a lot of time learning a language that most people never use," he growled.

"That's not true," Christine said, mostly to her beer bottle. "About 40 per cent of people here speak Irish."

"Ah, away with you!" Peadar held up his hands in frustration. "Of course, a good number of people *admit* to knowing how to speak Irish, they have to learn it at school. My point is that less than seven per cent actually use it on a daily basis. There's more folk here speaking Polish than Irish."

"That's still quite a lot of people speaking Irish," I suggested.

"Indeed, but most of them are Irish language teachers and translators," Peadar replied. "If you factor them out, then the number of people really using the language is tiny."

"Even so," Christine broke in. "The Irish language is a critical part of our cultural heritage."

"I agree, but I don't see why our children should be punished for it," Peadar said.

"Punished?" I asked. "Whatever do you mean?"

Lesley kicked me under the table. I wasn't sure if it was because the dog had farted again or that she knew I couldn't resist stoking the flames below this simmering argument.

Peadar angrily tapped his index finger on the table. "My children are going to spend around ten per cent of their time learning a language they'll hardly ever use – unless they become translators or teachers. It puts them at a distinct educational disadvantage compared to students from other countries."

"When you put it like that, it's doubly impressive that Irish students end up so well educated," I said. " I read somewhere they are ranked in the top ten in the world."

"See!" Christine snapped, waving another beer. "There's nothing to worry about."

"Ah but..." Peadar held up a finger, his eyes gleaming with passion. "Think how much better they would do if they spent that time learning physics or Chinese!"

He had a valid point but, for once, I resisted my urge to extend the conversation any further. In any event, I was hungry and my shins were aching.

We had a lovely afternoon, eating too much and chatting amiably about the less contentious issues of Christine's new car, Aoife's new boyfriend, the obscenely healthy state of the Irish economy and our unusually warm spring weather. Nonetheless, as the visit drew to a close, I couldn't resist sharing a relevant story.

"Funny you should say about the children learning Chinese,"

I said, receiving an ankle kick for my trouble. "I read recently of a Chinese businessman who decided to visit Ireland in search of opportunities to expand his corporate empire."

"This story was on the internet," Lesley interjected. "So it must be true!"

I ignored her jibe and continued.

"Being a diligent and professional person, he took it upon himself to prepare fully for his trip, reading extensively about Ireland, its culture and customs, and even learning the local language. In this regard, the European Union website was most helpful, listing Irish as the official language of Ireland, which is technically correct – but rather misleading. Consequently, on the day our Chinese friend arrived at Dublin airport, he was horrified to discover nobody, apart from him, spoke any recognisable Irish, or indeed any of China's 56 official languages. History does not record how his trip progressed from this low starting point, but in my opinion, he deserved to do very well."

***

Irish is the historical language of this great country, and I support any reasonable efforts to keep it as a living language. However, any discussion about languages quickly runs into controversy, particularly because, although all languages evolve over time, there are always a few fanatical stalwarts, determined to lock theirs into some sort of linguistic time capsule. Language is a living and breathing thing, it naturally changes with use. One only needs to read a few pages of Shakespeare to understand just how much the English has changed in the last 500 years. Why else would the Oxford English Dictionary editors add around 1,000 new words each year?

Rather like the Americans, the Irish people have developed their own unique way of speaking English – as have the British. Almost every county in Britain has its own unique accent and vocabulary, and so has Ireland. But that's a good thing. The world would be a very boring place if everyone spoke with the same accent, although we might have fewer wars.

***

Coincidentally, a few days later, another language puzzle was solved. I was at the local garage getting a slow puncture repaired. Micha, the mechanic, was a tall Polish lad, very friendly and classically handsome, despite the engine oil and grease staining almost every inch of his exposed skin.

"Thees is blackthorn," Micha said, grinning and pointing to the cause of my slow puncture. "Where thee tractors cuts thee hedges. It fall on thee road and poof! You are here again."

"Poof indeed." I grimaced and nodded. Yearly hedge cutting was an essential exercise if the narrow rural lanes of County Clare were to remain passable, but the steel-sharp thorns deposited on the road would easily pierce a car tyre.

"Thees happen to me also sometime," he added.

Micha's Polish accent was strong, but its sing-song lilt was pleasant on the ear. Suddenly I had a thought, perhaps this was an opportunity to help the Guards track down the elusive criminal mastermind.

"Do you know someone called Bravo Jet ski?" I asked.

"Who?" he frowned.

"Bravow Jeski," I said again, adding my best Polish accent. "He's wanted by the Guards for a string of motoring offences, but he keeps changing addresses and refusing to answer court summons."

Micha's eyes screwed shut in thought, while he scratched his chin. "Bravo Jet ski, Brava jegsci?" he mumbled. Suddenly he threw his head back and laughed like a pantomime pirate. "Do you mean Prawo Jazdy?"

"Yes!" I clicked my fingers and pointed. "That's the name. Do you know him?"

Micha laughed again and shook his head. In fact he laughed so long and hard, I was beginning to worry he was about to have a seizure. Finally, like the distant rumbles of a receding thunderstorm, his laughter diminished to the point where he was able to speak.

"Prawo Jazdy is not name of person," he explained. "Prawo Jazdy is name for Polish driving licence!"

And he was right. For several months, Ireland's diligent traffic police had been stopping speeding Polish drivers and meticulously recording the Polish words for Driving Licence, thinking it was actually the name of the offending driver. Oh the joys of living in a multi-cultural society!

5 – The New Beau

A few days later I went over to Shannon airport to collect our daughter, Joanne, and her new boyfriend, for their visit to Ireland.

I arrived in plenty of time and joined the short queue of traffic waiting to pass through the Garda Síochána security checkpoint at the entrance to the airport. Given this road led only to the airport or the golf club, I expect the Gardaí on duty found the questioning to be somewhat repetitive. As I inched forward, I imagined the conversations happening ahead.

"Good morning, sir. Where are you going?"

"Airport."

"Right you are. Carry on so."

Next car.

"Good morning, sir. Where are you going?"

"Airport."

"Right you are. Carry on so."

"Good morning, sir. Where are you going?"

"Airport."

"Are you sure you wouldn't rather visit the golf club?"

"No thanks. I'm picking up my wife's cousin. She's coming from America."

"Right you are. Carry on so."

And so on.

It was a warm and sunny morning and I had the window down so I could appreciate the fresh sea breeze. At the same time I was enjoying my latest discovery. A new national radio station dedicated to playing the kind of music old farts like me can remember and name. After delighting me with some T-Rex, they rolled straight into another of my favourite tunes. Life was good. I couldn't sit still. Merrily dancing the buttock boogie whilst playing the steering wheel bongos, I inched my car ahead until it was my turn for the inquisition.

"Good morning," I said.

I waited, but there was no reply. Conscious the Guard was

standing hands on hips and watching my dancing antics with curious concern, I felt the need to enlighten him to what he was missing.

"Deacon Blue." I pointed at the radio and danced with my shoulders.

The young Guard frowned.

"Real Gone Kid," I explained. "It's my favourite."

With a deep sigh, he shook his head and waved me on my way without further comment. Clearly, dancing fools were not considered to be a terrorist threat.

I had only a short wait in the arrivals hall before I spotted Joanne and her new friend. Mark was an athletically-built, tall and handsome man in his late twenties. Fresh faced with a square jaw, brown hair in a tight crew cut, cool blue eyes and a slightly reserved demeanour, he could be mistaken for a secret agent on an undercover mission. In fact he is a quantity surveyor – or so he tells me. Regardless of his secrets, or the inaccuracies of my over-active imagination, Mark and I hit it off immediately. I was impressed to see how he took care with my daughter, carrying her bag and holding her hand as we crossed the road to the carpark.

Just as we reached the car, something in my jacket began playing a familiar melody. I dropped my keys as I fumbled in my pocket for my phone, managing to answer just before my wife could hang up. She was calling to check our progress.

"We're just getting in the car now," I reported. "We'll be home in around an hour."

"Is Mark with you?" she asked.

"Yes, he's here now," I replied, involuntarily flicking my eyes in his direction.

"What's he like," she asked, none to quietly.

"Well…"

Mark nudged me in the rib. "Tell her I'm fat and 50 and only after your money," he whispered, with an evil grin. Clearly we shared the same sense of humour.

Although Mark was, like me, a 'lists man', he had obviously

already given in to Joanne's somewhat chaotic approach to life. After an overnight stay at Glenmadrie, the two lovebirds were going to borrow my car and take a four-day trip to the Connemara area, a little way north of Galway city. They had no particular plans, other than to visit Galway and explore the area around the Connemara National Park. They hadn't even arranged accommodation, preferring to take 'pot luck' with the local B&Bs. I was sceptical, but nevertheless wished them well.

After a hearty lunch, we all took the dogs for a long walk up the hill and through the forest. As the hill steepened, Mark and I got a bit of a stride on and soon opened a gap to the girls, who were happy moving at a slower pace.

"We'll meet you at the top," I shouted, noticing they had stopped to examine some wild flowers alongside the forest path.

Lesley didn't even look up, she just waved dismissively in my direction. I didn't mind, it was a good opportunity to show off the beautiful countryside and chat with Mark.

"I'm very impressed with the progress you've made with the renovations," he said. "Joanne showed me some of the photos from before you started. You've really done very well."

"Thank you. That's high praise from someone in your line of work," I replied.

"Is it really true you've never done any renovations before?"

"Pretty much," I said. "We've done some decorating and a few running repairs, but nothing even approaching a project on this scale."

"And you've learned it all from a book?" His tone was something approaching incredulous.

"It's worked so far," I countered.

"Don't get me wrong," he replied, "I'm amazed, but also very impressed."

"Thanks. It may be rather over-engineered in comparison to the building code, but it shouldn't fall down."

"There's no harm in adding a few extra screws." He smiled. "Anyway, I expect it gets a bit windy up here."

"That's true." I waved my hand at the cloudless azure sky above. "It certainly isn't always as nice as this."

"When are you going to start ripping out the centre of the house?"

"Well, I *was* planning to start next week…" I replied.

"But?"

"But Lesley thinks we could do with a little breathing space. Perhaps take a few months to get out and about and see the countryside. By the end of this week, you'll probably have explored more of Ireland than we have."

"That sounds like a good idea then," Mark said.

"Anyway," I huffed. "Lesley has plenty of little jobs planned for me."

"Perhaps you could escape?" he suggested. "Come and visit Connemara. You could be our driver."

"I don't think Joanne would approve," I patted him on the shoulder. "I'm sure you'll have a great time without me to keep you company."

After 40 minutes of hard walking, we reached the highest point of the trail and sat on some old logs where we could wait for the girls to catch up. From our vantage point, on the edge of the hill, we had an unrestricted view to the valley floor 1,200 feet below. Far to our left was the huge expanse of Lough Derg glistening light blue in the morning sunshine, and to the right I could detect the grey smudge of the Shannon estuary and beyond the buildings of Limerick city.

"Wow," Mark exclaimed. "That's some view."

"That's Slieve Bearnagh." I pointed to the mountain range in the centre. "The highest is called Moylussa. It's about 1,700 feet tall. You flew over it on the way in."

"It looks like a volcano," he observed. "Have you climbed it?"

"Not yet. Maybe one day."

"Add it to your list."

I smiled and nodded.

"Maybe one day."

***

That evening, after dinner and helping with the dishes, Mark and I went out on the land. It was a beautiful evening with a stunning sunset lighting the westerly sky fire and gold. These were perfect conditions for what I had in mind. I wanted some dramatic pictures for the cover of the golf instructional book I was planning, and Mark had agreed to act as my photographer. So, armed with my new camera, we trekked up the hill to the edge of the quarry and, framed by the fiery sky, I swung my club and assumed various poses as he snapped away. Unlike my darling wife, who hates cameras regardless of which way they are pointing, Mark took some magnificent and professional pictures. I was grateful for his help and suggested a quiet drink at the local village pub as some compensation for his time. It was also a good bonding opportunity.

As this was Mark's first visit to Ireland and he was keen to blend in during the tour of Connemara and Galway, I thought it would be fun and vaguely useful if I provided him with a few cultural nuances and linguistic translations.

"Dogs walking on their own are not lost," I explained. "They're just out for a walk. Please do not try to 'rescue' them, otherwise they really will get lost."

"Good to know," he replied.

"If you see a child out in the cold rain wearing only a thin t-shirt and shorts, they are not underprivileged or being abused. All under-tens in Ireland dress like that, all the time, whatever the weather. It must be a law, or something."

Mark nodded. His cool eyes watched me inquisitively across the top of his glass as he sipped his beer. I wondered if he was assessing my sense of humour, or just beginning to doubt my sanity. Regardless, I pressed on.

"There are two types of traditional breakfasts in Ireland," I said. "One is called a Full Irish, which is a large cooked breakfast of bacon and sausages, black and white puddings, eggs, baked beans, and potato. This is served along with a pot of Barry's Irish tea. The second type of breakfast is called a Breakfast Roll, which has the same ingredients as the Full Irish, but somehow fitted into a 14-inch breadstick. This delicious monstrosity should be consumed whilst driving. It is usually washed down with half a pint of coffee.

"Talking of driving, regardless of road conditions, or how late they are, everyone drives either very fast or very slowly. There are no 'in-between' speeds."

"I shall do my best to join in," Mark dipped his head in compliance.

I narrowed my eyes menacingly.

"Just joking!" he smiled. "I wouldn't want to damage your car."

"Or my daughter," I added.

"Fair point."

"Also," I continued, "the wearing of seatbelts whilst driving is compulsory. Therefore hardly anyone complies. Conversely, it is forbidden to use a mobile phone to call or text whilst driving, but almost everyone does, even the police."

Mark's eyes widened.

"Go figure." I shrugged. "Most cultures are either rule takers or rule breakers. I guess the nation of Ireland likes to stand shoeless on the wet lawn, so it can irreverently wiggle its naked toes at the 'Keep off the Grass' signs."

"Not like England with all our orderly queuing." Mark smiled and sipped his beer again.

"Don't get me wrong," I said. "People here are generally very polite. For example, they are much more inclined to let you pull into traffic than elsewhere…"

"But less likely to adhere to a speed limit," Mark added.

"Now you're getting it." I pulled a pen and a sheet of paper from my pocket.

"Is this one of your famous lists?" he asked.

"Sort of. I thought we could have a little competition. Just for fun and to pass the time."

"Go on," he said cautiously.

"I have prepared a short list of dialectal challenges, to assist you on your holiday."

"And you know this stuff, how?"

"Some I guessed and some I had to ask," I admitted.

"Well that's hardly a fair competition," he observed.

"Humour me," I insisted, tapping my glass. "If you get five, I'll buy the next round."

"Okay." Mark sat back and crossed his arms. "Do your worst."

"Right. We'll begin with an easy one," I said, rubbing my hands in glee. "What does 'he's very comfortable' mean?"

Mark scratched his head and frowned. "Wealthy?"

"Close, but…" I did that so-so hand wave.

Mark shrugged. "But the police are probably looking for him?" he suggested.

"Good enough!" I smiled and recorded his first point with a dramatic sweep of my pen. "By the way, over here the police are called Guards."

"Oh. Like Guardians of the Galaxy, but on a smaller scale?" he quipped.

"Question number two," I continued. "Isn't it well for some?"

Mark squinted in thought. "Probably to do with having the 'flu?" he suggested.

"No. It means, 'how the hell can they afford that?'" I replied. "Medical terminology is different. For example, the standard response required if you hear someone has contracted a communicable disease, dysentery, yellow fever, or an infection acquired from inappropriate contact with space aliens etc. would be to say, 'Sure, look-it, that dose is going around,' whilst rolling your eyes."

Mark snorted a laugh into his beer.

"How about, 'Ah, no, I'm grand thanks,'" I asked.

"I imagine it means no, but I expect it doesn't."

"Correct." I added a second point to his tally. "In Ireland, no does not always mean no. Any beverage, kindness, or gift offered, may be refused up to three times, before this refusal becomes legally binding. Obviously, alcohol does not come under this rule, as it is hardly ever refused."

"Of course," Mark nodded. "Especially Guinness."

"Gat," I corrected.

"Huh?"

"It's slang for Guinness, the national drink of Ireland," I explained. "As in, 'I'll have a pint of Gat,' although I've never heard it used."

"Probably because you've never offered," Mark complained, jiggling his almost empty glass.

"Be patient, or you'll end up ossified." I raised my pen quizzically over the page.

"Drunk," he exclaimed. "When you've consumed too many Gats."

"Correct." I added another point. "But if you're driving, you should stick to minerals."

"Soft drinks?" he suggested.

"Well done. That's four points. Minerals are indeed what the Irish call soft drinks. 7 Up and white lemonade are two particular favourites – primarily because they go well with alcohol."

"Much the same as the UK," he added.

"Here's a tricky one," I said. "What does 'Going to head' mean?"

"That's easy. It means heading to the toilet," Mark said triumphantly.

"Wrong," I replied with equal gusto. "You're thinking of the nautical phrase 'Going to hit the head' which means restroom or toilet. This phrase may have been derived from 'Head on out' and it simply means go, or go on ahead. 'I'm going to head, before the shops shut,' for example. By the way, the jacks is the catchall name for the restrooms. Many establishments will have the Irish *Fir* for men and *Ban* for ladies written on the toilet doors."

"Ah yes," he nodded. "That almost caught me out at the airport."

"Last one," I said. "What does 'You'll be grand' mean?"

"I know this one," Mark smiled confidently. "It means you'll be okay."

"Correct." I added his fifth point. "But context is important. It's like saying, 'What could possibly go wrong?' when encouraging a drunk friend to juggle some chainsaws. Strangely, 'It was grand' means no, it wasn't."

"I guess that would be appropriate just after the drunk guy tried juggling with chainsaws," Mark joked.

"I was thinking the same thing."

"To the winner the spoils." Mark handed me his glass. "Your round I believe."

I conceded gracefully, pleased Mark and I were getting on so well. As we drank I added a few final words of advice.

"It's all well and good to have a working knowledge of Irish words in common use, but that won't help you one bit when you're deep in the countryside and encounter your first strong Irish accent whilst asking for directions. In such a situation, and not wishing to be impolite, you can feign mild deafness in the hope your directions will be repeated a little slower and with less mumbling. However, if after the fifth attempt, you still have no clue as to what was said, just smile and drive on. With any luck you'll stumble upon your destination by chance."

"Don't you have a Satnav?" he asked.

It was my turn to snort into my beer. "Satnavs don't work here. Buy a map. A proper fold-out Ordnance Survey map. It's the only reliable way to navigate in rural Ireland."

Mark nodded.

"Oh, and one final thing you should know before you set off on your romantic trip to Connemara."

Mark raised a cautious eyebrow.

"They're very religious. The B&Bs up there only rent double rooms to married couples."

His face was a picture of disappointment.

***

A few days later, Joanne and Mark returned, beaming like

children on Christmas morning and waxing lyrical about their trip.

Being a university city, Galway was a big hit with the young couple. They had spent a happy morning exploring the narrow streets and quaint shops before enjoying a delicious seafood lunch at a quayside pub. In the afternoon, they headed west in search for Muckanaghederdauhaulia. This 22 letter place name is Irish for 'the marsh of the pigs between two seas' and is pronounced: dog regurgitating a cat, that is in turn coughing up a hairball. It also happens to be the longest name for a port anywhere in the world. However, it is not the longest place name in Ireland. With some eyewatering 25 letters, that prize goes to joint winners, Bullaunancheathrairaluinn and Sruffaunoughterluggatoora. Both are located in County Galway.

The drive to Muckanaghederdauhaulia was long and arduous. The eventual destination was little more than a few rocks huddled on a low boggy peninsular, made somewhat less inviting by a steel grey sky and driving rain.

"On a sunny day, it would probably have been spectacular," Joanne observed, "but we could barely see out of the window."

On the upside, Muckanaghederdauhaulia was a good starting point for their visit to the Connemara National Park, although they had to drive almost as far again before they secured a warm bed for the night. For the next three days they toured Connemara, famous for its desolate beauty and strong support of the Irish language. Mark and Joanne found the people friendly and welcoming, and the accommodation and food first-rate. The pictures they took could not do justice to the breath-taking scenery, but it was enough to get Connemara added to my 'must see' list. In the end, they rated their trip five stars for both romance and scenery. I did not enquire as to their sleeping arrangements.

Before their flight home, we all had a day out to Birr Castle in County Offaly.

There has been a castle at Birr since 1170. Like many such historic structures, it has been built, extended, demolished, rebuilt, burned down and repaired many times. The current structure was completed around 1860 and is contained within more than 1,200 acres of beautiful parkland and gardens. The castle is the family home of the Parsons family, more formally the seventh Earl of Rosse and his son and daughter-in-law, Lord and Lady Oxmantown. Therefore the residential areas are not open to the public, but there is still plenty to see.

There are miles of walks along the riverside, over bridges and through expansive woodlands, filled with interesting and rare trees collected over a period of 150 years by the previous Earls of Rosse as they travelled throughout the world. As well as the formal garden, which has a world record 40-foot tall box hedge, there are also the castle terraces to explore, the suspension bridge built in 1820, and beautiful lakes and waterfalls.

For the less horticulturally minded, Birr Castle has a considerable amount of science on display. The Parsons family have a rich history of achievement in engineering and science, through their expertise in developing lenses, microscopy, early photography and astronomy. In 1884 Charles Parsons invented the steam turbine. His brainchild made cheap and plentiful electricity possible, revolutionised marine transport and naval warfare, and eventually led to the development of the jet engine.

Being science nerds, there were many interesting things for Mark and I to drool over. The most physically impressive structure was Leviathan, the great telescope which dominates the grounds of Birr Castle. When it was completed in 1845, it was the largest telescope on earth, and capable of capturing more light and seeing further into space than any telescope had done before, a record it held for some 70 years. Sadly, during the First World War, the telescope was dismantled and its metal parts melted down for munitions. It remained in storage until the 1990s, when a partial restoration returned it to pride of place overlooking the meadow.

We had a delightfully pleasant day, helped by the stunning location and some unusually warm sunshine and blue skies.

During a light lunch in the outdoor cafeteria, the elegantly dressed couple sitting opposite smiled and nodded politely as we gushed enthusiastically about the beautiful surroundings. I shared a few of the titbits I had gleamed about the telescope and Lesley commented on the history of walled gardens. In reply, the couple seemed remarkably well informed, which was hardly surprising given they were Lord and Lady Oxmantown, something we only discovered that evening when we spotted their pictures in the guidebook.

All too soon it was time to head to the airport. We took a slow stroll along the tree lined riverside path, before turning towards the carpark. Lesley and I hung back a little so we could give Joanne and Mark a little privacy. With their heads close, they held hands and chatted in secret whispers. After passing through a long archway of living bamboo, they paused on a bridge over the waterfall to embrace. Lesley put a gentle hand on my arm and I stopped walking. As Mark and Joanne kissed, my wife squeezed my hand.

"They seem serious," she whispered. "Perhaps he's the one."

Only time would tell.

6 – The Approaching Storm

Our warm spring had rolled into an unusually pleasant run of sunny weather, which in turn had become that rarest Irish gem – a proper summer. We enjoyed a seemingly endless succession of gloriously windless sunny days and sultry starlit nights. Imperceptibly, the temperature climbed and, bereft of rain, the ground dried and cracked. Grass fires became a common sight. Like faraway Native American encampments, the horizon was dotted with columns of smoke, and at night parts of the distant valley glowed deep red where the peat on the moor was burning. Fortunately, these potentially deadly conflagrations occurred well away from Glenmadrie.

Each day the skies around the house were filled with swallows, flying nonstop until sundown, when like tired factory workers, they changed shifts with our vibrant population of bats. Some evenings I took childish delight in standing outside with my torch pointed directly upwards. After a few moments, the beam of light would be alive with moths and other flying insects. There I would wait, enduring the occasional bite and waiting for the show to begin. It didn't take long. As silent as a snowflake, the first bat would swoop through the throng of insects and sweep up its prey. Soon there was a second bat and then another. Quickly word spread, and the humid air filled with a dozen fluttering wings. Some even brushed my face and shoulders, chasing the moths that had flown too close. I didn't mind. Such an encounter was a privilege.

Although I am unfazed by the close proximity of bats, I must admit to a slightly less than manly reaction when I first encountered a giant wasp. This terrifying insect is almost identical to the common stinging wasp, except it is around five inches long, sounds like a flapping umbrella and had repeatedly tried to fly up my nose. My initial reaction was to run up the garden in blind panic, screaming like a terrified schoolgirl. When

I reached the fence, I turned on my heel and ran in the opposite direction, flapping my arms around my head like a defective helicopter. Eventually, it trapped me against the wall of the house, where it made several determined lunges in my direction. At the time, I felt my life was saved by some quick reactions and several brave parries with my hat. However, my sense of bravado was short lived. A little internet research identified the species as a giant wood wasp, a harmless member of the wasp family. That devilishly dangerous stinger is an ovipositor, just a long probe used to lay eggs in the surrounding pine trees.

Still, I maintain it is better to be safe than sorry.

***

Because of Ireland's northerly latitude and the general lack of sunshine, low vitamin D levels are endemic. But on the odd days the sun does shine, thousands of otherwise pale-skinned redheads suddenly feel the urge to disrobe and 'get some rays' – regardless of the temperature. A few hours later, the chemists and A&E departments are packed with lobster-faced sun worshipers, walking like extras from the latest zombie apocalypse film and mumbling, "Don't touch me!" through their sun-parched lips. Of course, in the best Irish fashion, their mates can't resist giving them an eye-wateringly friendly whack on their bright pink backs and shouting, "That's some glow you've got going there, Seamus!"

***

As I had taken a week away from my busy golf teaching schedule to have a rest, Lesley tasked me with digging dozens of deep holes to plant some new fruit trees. Over the years, I'd watched a few episodes of her favourite gardening show and recollected how to do this digging stuff. Whenever the presenter plants a young apple tree, he'd create a suitably sized hole by gently pushing his spade into the soft loamy earth and tipping it to one side, before carefully easing the plant into its new home.

At Glenmadrie, digging such a hole requires a lot of hard work and the enthusiastic application of a spade, a pick axe and a crowbar – a ten-pound, five-foot long steel pin the thickness of a broomstick with a sharp point at one end. In many places, the top soil at Glenmadrie is barely a few inches deep, cunningly hiding a sublayer of shale and large rocks left over from when the ice age glaciers melted. Some of these rocks are larger than a car.

With a little experimenting, I discovered the best technique was to use the crowbar to probe the ground and identify a relatively rock-free spot. Then, using the combined weight and leverage advantages of the pick axe and crowbar, loosen the ground sufficiently so the rock and shale could be scooped out by hand. Once the hole was large enough, the tree could be planted along with some fresh soil, water and a generous helping of well-rotted manure. To create our small orchard, we had 20 fruit trees to plant. Most went in just south of the polytunnel, with the remainder dotted around the garden for cosmetic effect. In practice, each tree took around half an hour to rehome. We both put in a good day's work, on what turned out to be the hottest day of the year.

It was a glorious summer, with seemingly endless days of warm sunshine and barely a hint of rain. The lane at the back of the house, which doubles as a stream during wet weather, was so dry I was able to walk out with the dogs while still wearing my slippers. Ireland is without doubt a glorious place when the weather consents to be pleasant for a while – and it consented a lot that year. At the same time, the economy was superficially as bright and sunny as the weather, but I couldn't shake the feeling that dark financial storm clouds were brewing just over the horizon.

***

"Good grief," I exclaimed. "Come and look at this."

"Look at what?" Lesley asked, walking into our living room.

I pointed towards the television. On the screen a news presenter was standing on a town centre street and gesticulating excitedly. In the background, a long queue of predominantly elderly people shuffled their feet and glumly waited for the door ahead to open.

"Are the sales on in Dublin again?" she asked, squinting at the screen. "I thought everyone but us would be flying to New York for the best bargains. That's what they all did last year."

"That isn't Ireland," I corrected, nodding towards the TV. "It's England, and those people aren't queueing for bargains, they're waiting for money."

"Money?" My wife frowned.

"That's a bank, a British high street bank, and those people are waiting to withdraw their savings."

"Whatever for?" Lesley asked.

"Well, the details are a little sketchy, but…" I grimaced. Although I worked in finance for many years, my wife didn't share my enthusiasm for the subject. *'Oh well,'* I thought. *'In for a penny…'* I took a deep breath. "Do you remember I told you about that French bank which suspended trading on some of its investment funds?"

"Not really. When was this?"

"About a month ago," I said. "They were having problems because of American sub-prime mortgages."

Lesley shook her head. "What's America got to do with France?"

"It's complicated," I replied, searching for a simple explanation. "The banks all lend and borrow with each other. The money goes back and forth, like a global game of pass the parcel. The movement of money is what keeps the banking system floating. That's why it is called liquidity. A couple of weeks ago the European Central Bank put about €95 billion into the European banking system, just to keep things moving."

"Ah, yes. I remember you mentioning that." Lesley held up a

finger and smiled. "You said it was a good thing we didn't still have a mortgage."

"Or a car loan," I added, pointing towards the TV again.

"So what's happening?"

"Someone has turned off the money tap."

"You mean the game of pass the parcel has stopped?" Lesley said, correcting my simile. Apparently my wife did listen to me sometimes.

"Indeed." I nodded graciously acknowledging her reply. "That queue is people waiting outside Northern Rock bank to withdraw their money. Someone has cancelled the line of credit and now there is a run on the bank. People are panicking."

"Phew!" Lesley whistled. "I hope we haven't got any–"

"No, we're fine." I interrupted, raising a calming hand. "But I am worried this could have some knock-on consequences."

"I'm sure you'll keep an eye on things." My wife squinted at the clock and frowned. "In the meantime, we'd better get moving."

My brow wrinkled in confusion.

"Limerick?" Lesley said, hoping to jog my memory. "We're going out for the day."

"Oh yes. What fun. Trudging around the garden centres," I tutted dramatically. "No wonder I'd forgotten."

My wife threw the tea towel at me, which was a good choice. She had a frying pan in the other hand.

***

Perhaps because of my caustic comments about visiting garden centres, Lesley decided we should first go to Limerick market and visit every gardening stall. Being a man with a short attention span and abandonment issues, married to a woman who had yet again left her mobile phone at home, I had to endure a torturous hour of walking slowly and waiting patiently while Lesley inspected every plant on display.

Gardening is very much her preserve and I am careful to

know my place as the heavy lifter, digger, and clumsy idiot husband, happy to compliment her hard work and eat the beautiful vegetables she grows. Her knowledge of flora seems encyclopaedic. I am always impressed when I point out some random plant at the garden centre and she can immediately summon its name and history, although I sometimes suspect she has just made them up to humour me.

"Lesley, that's a pretty flower," I said, pointing at something blue with yellow stripes. "What is it called?"

"Oh that? It's a 'Syllyarsehusband' or 'Hubsbanda-pratticus' in Latin. It's rather a gentle little flower. It thrives best when kept well-shaded and fed a little manure from time to time."

"Well, it looks nice. Do you want me to buy one?"

"No need, dear, I already have one at home and that's plenty."

To be fair, whilst I'd been warm and dry working on the renovations indoors, Lesley had been doing great things with the garden, working outside in the rain, mist, wind, sun and whatever other weather this fine country chooses to throw at us. Under her expert hand, we now had a fully functioning polytunnel and a well-stocked greenhouse. Furthermore, several beautiful embankments featuring various sturdy bushes were providing pretty but practical windbreaks for the flowers.

There are two reasons why my wife is quite sensible to keep the garden as her domain. Firstly, it provides her with her own space within the marriage, a place of quiet sanctuary. Secondly, I am a clodhopping and ignorant horticulturist, best kept far away from anything green that isn't on a plate. I seem to have an almost dyslexic inability to recognise the difference between plants and weeds – unless I am standing in a flower bed. There I will unerringly trample every plant with my size ten Wellington boots but miss all the weeds. I have tried to help in the past, but there was an unfortunate incident with a strimmer and some weed killer that destroyed her beloved dahlias. I am now restricted to cutting the lawn, fetching and carrying the heavy things, and obliging with some carefully supervised digging.

When we reached our second garden centre of the day, a large affair run by a British DIY chain and situated in a small shopping centre, I saw my chance to escape.

"Why don't I leave you here for a bit, while I buy a few things?" I suggested.

"Aren't you worried I'll get lost?" she mumbled, whilst inspecting a pot plant as if she was a judge at a dog show.

"I doubt you're planning to wander off," I replied. "This is the only garden centre within walking distance."

"In that case, I'll be right here." She nodded to herself and smiled.

"How would it be if we met at that new café above the furniture store?" I pointed across the carpark. "Be there in half an hour, we'll have lunch."

"Okay." Lesley suddenly had a thought, eyeing me suspiciously. "What things are you buying?"

"Nothing much." I rolled my eyes. "A telephone to replace the one that got fried in that thunderstorm."

"That's the second one this year."

"Third," I corrected. "We also need some handles for the new doors in the wing, a couple of light switches and some of that leather balm for my office chair."

"Leather balm? Surely you won't get that here."

"I will. It's the same stuff they use on car seats. There's a car parts shop over there, I'm sure they'll have some," I explained.

I acquired the new telephone and light switches without any drama, but the hunt for the correct door handles took a while longer than I had anticipated, so I had to rush to get the leather balm and still make it to the café in time.

The Motor Factors was a huge store, brimming with every imaginable gift for the modern pampered car. There were endless aisles of spanners, light bulbs, windscreen wipers, seat covers and audio equipment as well as camping gear and cycles of every conceivable shape and type. Inevitably, the leather balm was carefully hidden, only to be revealed after I had given up searching for a sales assistant and asked the nice girl on the till. Carefully following her directions, I jogged to the rear of the store and returned hotfoot to the till, arriving at the same time as another customer. Perhaps sensing my haste, the kind gent stepped aside.

"After you." He motioned for me to pay first.

"Thank you," I puffed, checking my watch. "My wife's waiting."

He nodded knowingly. "At least you're not stood outside the jacks holding her handbag!"

"There is that," I agreed and held up my bottle of balm. "Just this please."

"Do you have a loyalty card?" the checkout assistant asked. Her badge told me her name was Milli.

"No." I shrugged. "Sorry."

"Would you like one?" Milli asked, with an endearing smile. "You'll get 10% off your next purchase."

"I'm really in rather a rush," I glanced behind me and mentally grimaced at the growing queue. "Maybe next time."

The young lady scanned my item with a deft flick of her wrist and smiled again. She really was polite and efficient.

"Cash or card?"

"Cash please." I handed over a €50 note.

"Would you like a receipt?"

"Yes please."

"What's your email address?"

"Sorry?" I asked in confusion. There were now four people in the queue.

"Your email address," Milli repeated. "So I can send you the receipt. If you had a loyalty card, we would already have it."

"Err… Look, just forget the receipt." The queue was now five. I picked up my change and purchase. "Oh blast!"

"Is something wrong?" Milli asked. Some people in the queue were watching me with ill-concealed curiosity.

"I've just realised this is a coloured balm," I explained. "I wanted the clear one."

"No problem," she smiled. "Get another and I'll change it."

I mimed my apologies as I squeezed by the queue and jogged to the rear of the store. I was back in 30 seconds, but by then things were going from bad to worse.

"This is a different brand," Milli observed. "I'll have to do a refund and ring it in again."

"Oh, I'm dreadfully sorry," I turned to the poor man behind who was likely regretting his earlier kindness. "Sorry."

"Ah, you're grand," he waved away my apology with typical Irish generosity.

But there was more. Milli was tugging at my sleeve.

"These are on offer," she whispered. "Buy two and get one free. You should get another."

"No thanks," I pleaded. "One is fine." I glanced over my shoulder. A very pretty girl with dyed red hair had just joined the queue. She was wearing motorcycle leathers and carrying a takeaway coffee in a cardboard cup. Her disturbingly attractive and direct eyes danced with humour as she sipped her drink.

"It's a special offer," Milli repeated. "It's great value."

She was right of course. I excused my way past the queue again to collect a second bottle of balm, conscious of the watching eyes that followed my every move. Things didn't improve as I returned to the till.

"You have to have three. It's buy *two* and get *one* free," Milli explained. "Otherwise I can't ring it up."

I shut my eyes and groaned. What a twit. In my haste, I had only picked up one bottle.

"Don't worry about it," I pleaded.

"It's alright," Milli said. "Get another one."

"There's no rush," the man behind me agreed, grinning at my unease. "Go on now."

For the third time I navigated my way past the line of people waiting to pay and made haste to the rear of the store. On my return, I was particularly conscious of the pretty girl with the red hair and motorcycle leathers. She was obviously enjoying my predicament. Her beautiful eyes were twinkling with laughter as she sipped her coffee and watched me approach with my third bottle of leather balm. Perhaps I was overcome with embarrassment, or just overwhelmed with frustration, but somehow those smiling eyes disabled my 'appropriateness filter'.

"Sorry to keep you waiting," I said, waving the bottle of leather balm. "It's for my bondage gear."

I swear, coffee came out of her nose.

***

"You were a long time," my wife observed.

"Big queue in the shop," I explained, sitting down. "Someone spilled their coffee."

"I was chatting to a nice couple in the garden centre," Lesley said. "The husband was a plumber. It turns out he fitted the Rayburn in our house."

"Ha. Small world. Do they live over our way?"

"No. They're from Limerick," Lesley said. "But they both knew the owner through attending several of his legendary house parties. Apparently, that's where they first met."

"Good grief." I sighed and shook my head. "Is there anyone in Ireland who hasn't attended a wild party at Glenmadrie?"

"Yes, dear." Lesley patted my hand. "There's us."

A waitress came over and took our order. She was quite attractive, probably from the Philippines and, despite the tight skirt, meticulously applied makeup and high bust, almost certainly a man.

"Wasn't that a bloke?" I whispered, leaning forward.

My wife looked around. "I think they all are, or at least they were."

I glanced at the three staff members behind the counter for the first time and realised my wife was correct.

"What of it?" she asked.

"Err…nothing really," I stuttered. "I meant no offence. It's just a little unusual for Limerick."

"It's a new world." Lesley patted my hand. "Get with it."

"The food looks good," I said, quickly changing the subject.

In fact the food was excellent, reasonably priced and the service was first rate. At the first taste of my delicious roast vegetable wrap with mild chilli sauce and a side order of fries, I already knew the prospect of lunch at this café would become an excuse to visit Limerick for many years to follow.

Once we had finished eating, there was nothing to do but sit back, drink our tea and watch the world go by. It seemed every table was full with happy smiling people. Casting my eye around, I saw some tables were occupied by family groups, all with remarkably well-behaved children. There were half a dozen business people, sitting alone and reading reports or quietly tapping away at their laptops while they sipped their coffees. Three tables were occupied by pairs of smartly dressed ladies, leaning in and chatting quietly. I guessed they were friends meeting for a weekly tête-à-tête. Three teenage girls occupied a table in the corner. Glowing orange with fake tan, they all wore the same clothes, demonstrating the latest Limerick fashion trend. Overly-tight, brightly-coloured jeans and tops, were worn so as to create a gap where naked rolls of hip and belly fat could show. According to our friend, Christine, this fashion is called a 'Muffin top', presumably because of the similarity to an overflowing muffin. I presume the girls were friends, but they were all so focused on their mobile phones and ignoring each other with such ferocity, it was hard to tell. In any event, it was nice to see this new café looking so busy and successful.

My attention was drawn to a slightly portly, middle-aged man standing at the till. He was waving to his wife who was seated with their young children on the other side of the café.

She frowned and mouthed, *"What?"*

In reply, he waved her debit card, shrugged and mouthed, *"What's your PIN?"*

His wife rolled her eyes and in an exaggerated stage whisper replied, *"Five, three, seven, one."*

For conformation, the man read the number back in an equally loud stage whisper, to which he received a thumbs up from his wife, as well as several other people in the restaurant. He then proceeded with his transaction. I was particularly amused by how he covered the keypad with his hand while he entered the PIN.

As we were preparing to leave, I noticed a middle-aged woman entering the café. She was pushing an elderly woman in a wheelchair. From the similarity of their features, I was in no doubt they were mother and daughter. At that moment, the tallest and most angular of the waitresses came by. The old lady's face was a picture of surprise and amusement. She raised her thin arm and pointed a bony finger

"Look, Mary," she all but shouted. "There's one of those transistorvestites!"

As we made our way to the exit, I recalled Lesley's earlier advice. "It's a new world. Get with it."

7 – Strangers on a Plane

"This can't continue," Ticker said, with a sigh. His heaving golf swing had moved the golf ball only slightly further than the enormous clod of grass and soil.

"I agree," I replied. "You could bury a small dog in that hole. You'd better put the divot back before someone falls in."

"That's not what I meant," he replied, tutting to cover his self-conscious smile. "I was thinking about the economy."

"Keep your mind on the golf," I suggested. "You need to get your weight more on your left foot *before* you hit the ball."

"I thought I did," he replied, shaking his head.

It was almost lunchtime. The air was a little cool with a light drizzle, conditions just unpleasant enough to discourage all but the most determined golfers. Consequently, the course was mercifully quiet, which proved to be a bonus given Ticker's torturous progress during this four-hole playing lesson.

"This is your left foot," I jokingly tapped his shoe with my golf club. "When you finished your swing, you were still standing firmly on your right foot. That's why you hit the ground again."

"I thought I *was* on my left foot," he pleaded.

I tossed another ball on the ground. "Have another go, but this time make a conscious effort to end up with all your weight on your left foot." For a little additional guidance, I tapped his left shoe again.

Ticker made his swing, grunting with effort as he fought the counterintuitive feelings experienced by almost every beginner golfer trying to get the ball airborne. Another huge clod of earth flew down the fairway. He swore and grimaced with disapproval.

"Actually, that was better," I intervened, quick to suppress his unnecessary anger. "You may not think so, but it was."

"It wasn't a very good shot," Ticker complained.

"Have mercy on yourself." I put a calming hand on his

shoulder. "Make good swings first. The good shots will soon happen."

"I hope so."

"I know so. Your weight should go to the right on the backswing and the left on the through swing. Now watch."

I demonstrated the correct technique.

"You make it look so easy," Ticker whispered in awe as my ball rocketed away into the distance, ripping at the misty air like a fighter jet.

"We'd better pick up these balls and head in," I said, checking my watch and wincing. I enjoyed Ticker's company so much, I'd lost track of time.

"Oh yes, you're flying to England this evening, aren't you?"

"That's right. I'm not off till six, but I wanted to pop into town and buy some nice chocolates for my mother."

"What a sweet boy you are!" Ticker joked.

"You mentioned you were thinking of the economy," I said as we began the long walk back towards the clubhouse. "What of it?"

"You don't see it so much here in the west, but over in Dublin people are spending like there's no tomorrow. There's new housing developments popping up on every spare bit of land, rents are going through the roof and people are shopping like money grows on trees. My neighbour just had a birthday party for his daughter. There were a hundred guests, a huge cake, a marquee and two bouncy castles for the kids."

"I must admit, that sounds pretty extravagant," I agreed.

"It was his daughter's eighth birthday!" he exclaimed.

"Good grief!"

"My daughter has a birthday next month. Now she's going to expect something similar."

"Or better," I teased.

Ticker glowered at me.

"Sorry," I grimaced. "At least she isn't getting married. One of my colleagues has just spent €50,000 on his nuptials, and that didn't include the honeymoon."

"Fifty grand!" Ticker cried. "You golf teachers barely earn enough to buy a pizza, how on earth can he justify spending that much?"

"Apparently he borrowed it from the local credit union, along with a huge mortgage for his new house."

"That's a hell of a way to start married life," he grunted. "It seems like the banks here are giving out money like candy to babies."

Although Ticker was an exuberant shopper, particularly when it came to cars, boats and golf equipment, he had a high-paying job and a modicum of common-sense. His parting comment made my heart sink.

"Mark my words. This is all going to end in tears."

***

Along with writing my weekly golf instructional column for the local paper, I was hard at work on producing two books as well. One was on golf and the other was a war story, based loosely on my father's experiences as a pilot and prisoner of war. Recently, I had begun using a sophisticated text-to-speech programme so I could listen to my work being read back to me once I had completed each section. As I planned on doing a little quiet editing during my visit to England, I decided to buy some earphones for my laptop.

After negotiating the lunchtime crowds for an hour, I finally located a box of handmade Irish chocolates of a size suitable for my mother's birthday gift, yet small enough to fit into my carry-on suitcase. With just half an hour to spare before I needed to set off to the airport, I popped into one of those shiny electrical shops to buy some earphones.

I wasn't looking for anything sophisticated, just a bit of wire with a 3.5mm headphone jack on one end, and a couple of earbuds on the other. I had an old set from a mobile phone, but they were not really up to the job, so I had decided to treat myself to something with a longer wire and the licentious luxury of foam protectors on the earbuds. After several minutes perusing the confusing array of electrical gadgets and gizmos, for which I had no need, desire, or money, I spotted a display that seemed to offer something resembling earphones.

The young and somewhat rumpled sales assistant, who had been propping up a counter with his bottom whilst diligently ignoring me, gave an exaggerated sigh and, with all the enthusiasm of someone visiting the proctologist, trudged towards me. I eyed him cautiously, thinking he looked like someone who had only ever used an iron to make a grilled cheese sandwich.

"Hi, I'm Rob," he said, "Is there something you're looking for?" His tone suggested a lack of enthusiasm born from a succession of fake customers using pseudo-shopping as a way to garner technical information, prior to buying their new toys online.

"Yes, Rob," I replied, "I want to buy some earphones for my laptop."

"Right!" he said, jerking awake as if he'd just been injected with adrenaline. "I have just the thing." As if by some sleight-of-hand, a pair of white earphones appeared on the glass counter-top. I thought that they wouldn't have looked out of place on an air traffic controller. Rob obviously didn't notice my negative body language.

"These are great! They're Bluetooth with a range of up to nine yards, there's adaptive noise cancellation, a carry case and a stand. They're perfect for the gym."

"Err, well…" I mumbled, "They're a bit big."

"You can make phone calls as well…" he offered.

"Actually, I'm just looking for some earphones, you see I'm–"

Rob held up a finger, indicating that I should be silent, and gave me a knowing smile. As he reached under the counter I found myself wondering if his elaborate hairstyle had cost a lot, or whether he had just slept poorly and got up late. Given that I have a naturally wipe-clean head, perhaps I was just jealous. His second headphone offering was no nearer the mark.

"They're pink," I said, stating the obvious.

"Ah, yes. But these are much slimmer. Great for the gym," he replied, his eyes flashing. "We have other colours. I can get them in black by Friday."

I shook my head, partly to check that I hadn't just stepped into an alternate reality.

"That won't do at all. I need something now."

Rob sighed and the corners of his mouth went south. "What colour do you want then?"

"Black would be fine, but the colour doesn't really matter. I just need a set of earphones with a longer cable–"

He held up the finger of silence again. I surreptitiously checked the time.

"These will be perfect, I guarantee it!" He proffered a set of black headphones that would have fitted Princes Leia, without interfering with her hair.

"I'm sorry Rob..." I looked at my watch pointedly. "I have to catch a plane soon. I just wanted something with a long wire, some earphones... The sort that go in your ears."

He snapped his fingers with mock delight. "Oh! You mean in-ear headphones! You said headphones."

"Actually, I said..." I closed my eyes for a moment while I regulated my breathing. "Yes, in-ear headphones. That's what I want."

"For an iPhone?"

"No," I said, rather more firmly than I had intended. "They're for a laptop."

"Really?" Rob exclaimed, gaping as if I had just admitted to using stone tools. "What on earth do you do with one of those?"

"As I was trying to explain, I'm a writer. I use an audio program to help me edit my work, so I need some ear– I mean *in-ear* phones. Please."

"Riiight! No problemo! I have just the thing. Fantastic sound quality. These are perfect for all of your auditory needs."

He unlocked the glass wall cabinet and pulled out a small

packet containing what appeared to be, a set of black in-ear headphones. Being understandably suspicious, I carefully read the specifications on the back of the packet, which seemed to cover all the bases, along with several features that I didn't need or understand. On the upside, a surreptitious glance at the price showed they were one cent under a tenner.

"That's great," I smiled. I'll take them!"

"No problemo. If you'd like to come over to the Customer Service desk, I'll complete the sale for you." He led the way and I meekly followed.

At said Customer Service desk, Rob performed a complicated series of manipulations on the type of elaborate computer system that, for most retail operations, has eradicated the quiet simplicity of a cash drawer, along with the ability of the staff to do basic mathematics. As the time for my flight crept ever closer, Rob scanned my purchase twice, before laboriously entering a long string of numbers by hand. Then he shot the packaging with some sort of handheld device, presumably to disable the security tag.

"Would you like insurance?" Rob asked, in a tone of voice suggestive of someone who had correctly anticipated my reply. I gave him my best quizzical look, one I had learned years earlier, by asking my teenage daughter questions like, "Should I wear this shirt?"

"Are you sure?" Rob asked. I had to applaud his persistence and blind obedience to company policy. I wondered if at any moment he was going to ask if I wanted to 'supersize' my purchase. With respect, and commendable restraint, I gave him a polite nod.

"How would you like to pay?" he asked.

"Cash."

"Really?" He raised his eyebrows. "Not with a credit card?"

With one eye on the time and commendable restraint, I refrained from giving this eager young man a lecture on the numerous virtues of living without the stress of consumer debt.

"No thank you, Rob," I said politely, "I'll stick to cash."

"As you wish."

With a dramatic flourish, I opened my wallet and withdrew a crisp ten euro note. It was still warm from the cash machine. Rob frowned at my offering, as if it were a sheet of slightly used lavatory paper. The scratchy sort that's like greaseproof paper. He offered a tight smile.

"That's not quite enough." His voice was polite, but devoid of any discernible emotion. Perhaps he was beginning to suspect I was party to some elaborate prank.

"Nine ninety-nine," I said, waving my note and pointing at the price tag helpfully. Rob shook his head and slowly brought the price tag a little closer to my nose.

"Nine hundred and ninety-nine euros." He said these words slowly, perhaps suspecting I was senile and a little hard of hearing.

I looked at the label again, this time lowering my 'seeing glasses' for better focus. Do you know what? He was right! I was aghast, horror-struck, and amazed, all at the same time. I almost asked for a chair and a glass of water.

"Good God! Who on earth would pay almost a thousand euro for a bit of wire with earbuds on the end?" I asked.

"Well, hopefully you... After all, I have rung it up," he added, with commendable optimism.

"Well you can jolly well un-ring it up! I have no intention of paying that much!"

"But these are the best in-ear headphones on the market. The jack is 18 carat gold, the wire is specially treated to prevent signal seepage, the earbuds are equipped with noise cancelling technology, and there are a host of other features."

"Look, Rob, I'm sorry for the confusion, but I only want some earphones for doing a bit of editing work."

"But these are brilliant! Your digital music collection is going to sound awesome." His voice now carried a hint of desperation.

I shrugged and politely explained. "Sorry, Rob, my 'record collection' is all on vinyl."

I saw the confusion in his eyes.

"Is that like iTunes?" He asked.

"No. It's a collection of real records on actual vinyl, played on a record player. No earphones required."

"Whatever!" he said, shrugging noncommittally. "You can use your credit card."

"No thanks."

"You know, I have one of these." He jiggled the headphones enticingly.

"You do?" I was more surprised than doubtful.

"I wouldn't listen to my music on anything else. It's worth every euro." Rob looked around and then leaned forwards conspiratorially. "I used my credit card, you should too."

He was very polite, quite insistent, but barking up the wrong tree. I was also polite and rather more insistent. Eventually, I wore him down to the point where he sold me a perfectly serviceable set of in-ear headphones, with an extra-long cable and a bog-standard 3.5mm jack. All for the bargain price of €14.99, paid in cash.

It would be disingenuous of me to suspect that young Rob had deliberately failed to disable the security tag, but during the ensuing bag search and pat down by the security guard, I noticed he was smiling broadly. On the upside, I still had enough money to have a nice relaxing cup of tea and a sticky bun before my flight. While I did a bit of editing, I made a point of bobbing my head a bit, so the young people would think I was listening to my digital music collection.

**

My short visit to England went well, despite the culture shock of revisiting the horrid traffic jams and bustling crowds. It was an aspect of urban life I had all but forgotten whilst living such a quiet existence in the peaceful and sleepy countryside of County Clare.

Aside from being noticeably shorter each time I saw her, my mother was looking remarkably well for someone of her age.

Bursting with energy and talking nonstop, she fussed around me as if I were still a toddler, and cooked more food than we could have eaten in a week, particularly as we had plans to visit a local pub for lunch. Although she scolded me for wasting my money on her gift, her sweet tooth soon asserted itself and she quickly made a substantial dent in her box of scrumptious handmade Irish chocolates. I had a couple myself, just to check they were alright.

Mum and I had a lovely time together, chatting about Dad and sorting through some old photographs. Despite my witty and interesting repartee, my mother nodded off in the afternoon. In the years since my father passed away, I have been her only houseguest. I suspect she was exhausted by the novelty, or perhaps age was just taking its toll. We retired early and the following morning, after many goodbye hugs and kisses, I set off to visit my daughter.

Compared to the high intensity of spending time with my mother, my visit to Joanne's house was as tranquil as Sunday after lunch. Despite her success in business, somehow she manages to make disorganisation into an art form. Five minutes after arriving, I was off to the shops to buy milk, bread, butter, toilet rolls and tea towels. On the upside, she had actually remembered I was coming and arranged to work from home for a couple of days. When she wasn't making phone calls or sending emails, we relaxed, sitting on the couch together and chatting about nothing in particular. Our only trip out was an afternoon at the excellent Colchester Zoo, which was really just an excuse to turn off her phone so we could walk and talk undisturbed.

It was delightful to spend a little quality time with my daughter, and I was quietly pleased to see how many new friendships she had forged since Lesley and I had moved away. Of course we missed each other, but any fears we had of leaving an emotional void in her life were unfounded. She was obviously coping better than we were on that front. As Lesley had predicted, Joanne's relationship with Mark seemed to be blossoming. There was even talk of them moving in together. The only potential fly in our happy life ointment was Lesley's mother.

Although ten years younger than my mum, Muriel lived a more sedentary lifestyle, spending much of her days sitting by the window and watching the world go by. Soon after our move to Ireland, we had become aware of a slow but undeniable decline in Muriel's mental and physical acuity. On the last day of my trip to England, Joanne and I visited Muriel for the afternoon. I brought flowers and a bottle of her favourite tipple. After tea and biscuits, I spent an hour sorting some of her financial documents. This was something I had always done in the past. While I checked everything was in order, Joanne helped by renewing Muriel's home insurance. Although it was a convivial afternoon, the conversation seemed stilted. I mentioned this to Joanne as we drove to the airport.

"I think she's struggling to speak," Joanne observed. "Particularly when there are lots of people in the room."

"That's probably why she doesn't go to bingo anymore," I suggested.

"Or the pub," Joanne added.

"Your mother phones her every couple of days, but the conversations are getting harder. The same thing happened with my dad. Frequently, as he got older, he would only say, 'Hi,' and then hand the phone to my mum."

"Do you think she has dementia too?"

"Probably too early to say," I sighed. "Perhaps she's just getting old."

"Maybe she should go to the doctor?" Joanne suggested.

"It's a good idea, but getting Muriel to go could be a challenge. I'll ask your mum to have a go. She's over in a couple of months. I suppose it can wait until then."

"I guess Muriel is managing for now," Joanne sighed. "We'll just have to keep an eye on her."

"If the worst comes to the worst, we can always bring her over to Ireland."

"Ha!" Joanne snorted dismissively. "Good luck with that. Muriel would never agree to leaving her home."

I chewed my lip and grimaced. "Time will tell."

***

One of my favourite pastimes at the airport is people watching. Perhaps it's the writer in me. Even on those occasions when the departure lounge is heaving with sweating humanity and the hot air writhes with the sounds of a hundred languages, overlaid with the pungent odours from the food court, I can still find some harmless entertainment within my imagination.

From within the crowd I will select a random stranger. I wouldn't want to sit and stare, as that would be creepy. So with a quick sweeping glance, I try to memorise as many details of the person as possible. Then the game begins. Can I construct a viable back-story in my head? As if I were writing a character for a thriller, it must be something believable, conceivable and interesting. Slowly strolling around the departure hall, I allow my eye to wander freely, until someone catches my attention.

The first is a small man, aged around 60, sitting in an angular fashion on the edge of his seat. He is wearing a well-worn and slightly crumpled beige suit. At his feet there is an ancient brown leather briefcase, the floppy kind, almost like a satchel but with a handle at the top and a single brass catch. His thinning black hair and round wire-framed glasses give him a bookish appearance. I imagine him to be an accountant, but not the sort who would file your tax return. This gent is an international bookkeeper for some drug cartel. He is obviously an experienced traveller, but only on business. Not for him the loose clothes and comfortable shoes of the holiday maker. Mr Accountant is travelling between meetings. This morning he was in Geneva and now he is chasing the sun towards Boston, with a briefcase full of untraceable bearer bonds.

The second character is a tall man with wavy black hair. His face is dark with stubble, not the designer kind, but the result of a long and difficult journey. He is wearing a dashiki shirt and matching pants. This traditional African clothing is stained and crumpled, but worn with an air of pride, as if it were a uniform. I notice his face is haggard and his eyes hollow with the pain of experiences that can never be forgotten. I decide he is a doctor, probably a volunteer with Doctors Without Borders. He is travelling home to his lovely wife after three months saving lives in some horrific war zone. My hero.

Scanning the crowd, another face catches my eye. But this one is different. Intriguingly so. At first it is the hair that attracts my attention. Long and brown, thick and curly, it frames her head in boisterous waves, bobbing about as she walks. Her whimsical face looks young, almost elfin, although I guess she is older than 25. Her frame is petite, clad in stonewashed denim and a leather jacket, but her stride exudes confidence. She is just 20 feet away, circling the crowd almost opposite my position, as if we were separate hands on the same clockface. When she stops walking, it is so sudden, the person behind murmured an expletive and sidesteps quickly to avoid a collision. Frozen in place, this strange woman begins watching someone, her eyebrows knitted in concentration. Those dark brown eyes are staring with laser-like intensity at a man a few yards away. He doesn't see her but the subliminal intensity of her inspection causes him to shift uncomfortably. Suddenly she relaxes. Glancing away, her face is illuminated with an almost beatific smile of satisfaction, but the message is clear to read, "*I know your secret*".

Fascinated, I follow, keeping a discrete distance and watching. My own game is long forgotten. This is too good to miss. Four more times she performs the same exercise. Openly studying someone with an almost unsettling intensity until the mystery of their deepest inner secrets are revealed. Then with a sly smile and a nod of her head, she moves on. I was just ten paces behind when, with all the grace of a ballerina, she spun on her heel. In an instant her eyes picked me out of the crowd. She held my gaze for what felt like an eternity. Then her face broke into a gentle smile as if to say, "*Oh. You understand me. Well, that's okay*". Momentarily, I glanced away in embarrassment. When I looked back, she was gone, somehow melting into the crowd like morning mist in the warm sunshine. Sometimes, living inside my head can be an interesting experience.

8 – The First Cut is the Deepest

Back at Glenmadrie, I'd barely had enough time to fuss the dogs and have a refreshing cup of tea before Lesley tried to drag me outside. Having just got comfortable after my long journey, I was less than enthusiastic.

"Come on," my wife insisted.

"Why?" I groaned.

"I've got a surprise for you," she grinned.

I mentally flinched, as I don't like surprises, which is hardly surprising.

When I was a child, my family moved to Scotland. We were renting a huge country house on Strathkinness High Road, St Andrews. Arriving late in the evening, I fell into my bed, exhausted after a monstrous day of travelling. My father tucked me in with the enticing promise of a wonderful surprise waiting to be revealed the following day. Despite my tiredness, I lay awake for hours, taking in the unfamiliar surroundings and speculating as to the nature of this great surprise. My eight-year-old imagination ran wild. By the time I finally slipped into the arms of Morpheus, I was convinced the morning would see me playing in my personal fortress, climbing high into a treehouse, or even racing around the garden on a junior motorbike.

The great surprise was finally revealed in the garage. With a flourish worthy of a magician, my dad pulled away a paint-splattered dustsheet to uncover a punchbag. Not a space ship, or a go kart, or my prayed-for motorbike, but a scrappy old punchbag. It was one of those upright jobs, with a baseplate and a heavy leather punch ball on a long spring. Masking my disappointment, I followed my father's instructions and gave the ball a mighty punch, sending it to the very limits of the retaining spring. No sooner had I turned to seek his approval for my manly deed, than the spring recoiled and slammed the ball squarely into my face. With a split lip and a bloody nose, I sat on the floor and howled. My dad found the entire incident hilarious. I disagreed.

So, it was with understandable caution, I followed my dear wife outdoors and waited for her big reveal.

"Well?" she said, standing at the side of the house and sweeping her arm like a car salesman extravagantly introducing the latest model.

"Well what?" I asked.

Lesley frowned. "Can you see what's different?"

"Err…well…" I chewed my lip, aware we were playing a dangerous game.

My wife crossed her arms, clenched her jaw and glared at me.

Acutely conscious nothing had hit me in the face, thus far, I searched desperately for whatever was different. Had she bought a new dress? Changed her hairstyle? Or was she just wearing a new gas mask? I mentally shook my head and chided myself for being silly. Lesley had clearly brought me outside to show me something that was *outside*. Just then I spotted it. The answer was obvious. Suddenly confident, I smiled and relaxed.

"That's a new bush," I said, waving somewhat vaguely towards the flowerbed.

"It's not new. That bush was here before we bought the house!" Lesley clenched her fists and growled.

"But the flowerbed is new?" I offered, my voice croaking.

"No it isn't!"

"Oh…"

My wife glared.

"Err…" I shrugged in defeat.

"I've moved the rockpile!" she snapped.

"Ooh!" I slapped my forehead. It was slightly less painful than being hit in the face with a punchbag.

In the four years since we began our home renovations, the pile of rubble at the end of our driveway had gradually come to resemble a small mountain. Some rocks were the size of a fist, but others were huge knee-high boulders. Now the former site of this SUV-sized rockpile was a neatly swept area decorated with three artistically planted flower pots. It was so obvious, I'd completely missed it.

"Oh," I repeated. "Did you get a man in then?"

"No," she snapped, indignantly. "I did it myself."

"Good grief!" I exclaimed. "How? I mean...Where did you put it all?"

"I used a wheelbarrow. Some of the bigger rocks I've laid alongside the driveway, but most of it went down the lane. All those huge potholes are now filled in."

"Wow." I was awestruck. "How many loads did it take?"

Lesley scratched her head and grimaced. "I didn't count. Probably more than 50."

"That's remarkable. But what about your bad back?"

"Bah." She waved away my concerns. "I managed. The exercise was good for me. Anyway, it was mostly downhill."

Lesley had casually understated the effort she had applied. Some of the potholes were more than 50 yards away and the ground was rough and steeply sloping. What would have been tough work for a strong young lad, was an almost super-human feat for a petite 50-year-old housewife with a bad back. I am happy to admit I was extremely impressed and very grateful for the help. It was a nice surprise.

***

Our kitchen worksurfaces were covered by dozens of wire cooling racks, each piled high with a dazzling assortment of cakes. Lesley was baking for her friend's party. There were cupcakes, fairy cakes, muffins, three lemon drizzle cakes and a large chocolate birthday cake, covered in thick icing. The final batch of fruit cakes were still in the oven. The accumulated heat in the kitchen was oppressive, but the smell was simply mouth-watering.

"Goodness," I exclaimed, fanning my face. "How many

people has Christine got coming?"

"Probably about 15 kids and as many adults. I think she's going to make up some finger food as well. There'll be baskets of chips and a few plates of chicken nuggets too."

"Well, it's a magnificent spread. Well done."

"Thanks."

"Perhaps you can slip in a few cucumbers?" I suggested, pointing at the large pile spilling out of the veg rack. "We appear to have plenty."

"We do seem to have rather a glut," Lesley admitted. "It's bizarre the way things have grown in that polytunnel. I'd be surprised if we've had a dozen tomatoes this year, yet I've already picked 50 cucumbers."

"50?" I goofed, opening my mouth in mock shock. "Whatever will we do with them all?"

"Not a lot really. There are a few recipes for soup, but I don't fancy it much, or pickled cucumber for that matter." Lesley shrugged. "So we'll have lots of salads, or just give them away."

We stepped outside to get away from the humidity in the kitchen. Standing in the doorway, we were shaded from the late summer sunshine, but exposed to a cooling breeze.

"That's better," I sighed. "Perhaps you should join that market you were talking about."

"I don't know," Lesley grimaced. "People probably wouldn't want to buy my stuff."

"Don't be like that." I put a hand on her shoulder. "Your cakes are magnificent and those knitted toys you made are bound to sell."

"You think?" She scrunched her nose and nibbled on her bottom lip.

"For sure." I nodded enthusiastically. "You should give it a try. Who knows, you may even shift our glut of cucumbers."

"But what about the dance club?"

"What about it?" I said. "We haven't found a hall yet."

"I suppose…"

"Anyway, the market is on Saturday mornings. If you ever

started a dance club you could do it on a midweek night."

We stood in companionable silence. Lesley was thinking and I was happy to enjoy the cool breeze while I waited for her verdict. Finally, she let out a great sigh.

"Do you really think people will enjoy my cakes?" she asked.

The answer stalled on my lips. At that moment, our black Collie dog, Kia, quietly pushed past our legs. Gently clasped in her mouth was a fairy cake she'd just stolen from the kitchen table.

"Someone does," I replied, pointing at our furry thief.

"That's settled then," Lesley replied, her beautiful eyes sparkling with laughter. "I'll do the market."

Remarkably, Kia did not eat the cake. She gave it to Lady, who was sunning herself on the driveway. Like an offering to the gods, Kia very gently placed the fairy cake by Lady's snout, before heading back towards the kitchen. Lesley and I shared a surprised look. As our lovable Collie approached, she casually nodded as if to say, "Excuse me. I'm just going to get some more."

Holding our sides and crying with laughter, we sprinted to the kitchen before Kia could help herself to another cake.

***

Apart from a small kidney stone, an irritable stomach and the susceptibility to stress which had encouraged us to move to Ireland in the first place, I have been fortunate enough to remain in pretty good health for most of my life. Perhaps because of the damper climate, my old karate injuries had recently started to ache, so my doctor had prescribed a short course of some magic jollop to lubricate my rickety joints. It was truly a miracle cure and helped me to feel a lot better. Like all medicines, it comes with a long list of possible side effects, the most notable being periodic bouts of violent and uncontrolled flatulence. The wags empowered with inventing names for such medical conditions must have been especially pleased when they came up with the title 'meteorism' for this particular malaise.

Many years of living in sunny climes and playing a fair bit of golf has exposed me to more than my share of UV rays. Consequently, since I turned 30, I've had several small skin lesions removed, purely as a precaution and always without incident. This usually requires a little local anaesthetic, a small cut, and a quick inspection of the offending lump under a microscope. Ten days later, I'll make a trip to the GP to have the stitches removed, unless I can reach to do it myself.

At my age I try to avoid looking in the mirror, but my memory is going so I have to relent when it comes to shaving. One morning I noticed a small lump on the side of my nose. Within a fortnight it had tripled in size and become painful to the touch. I assumed it was a small infected spot, but my doctor said it was another lesion and should be removed.

I've heard it said that Ireland has one of the best health services in the world, if only you can get past the waiting list. Despite my tendency to seek out the humour in what can otherwise be a traumatic event, on those occasions we have attended a hospital, I have always found the medical treatment in Ireland to be first class and the staff friendly, but overworked. In this case my appointment letter arrived just ten days later. So, while I can attest to the quality and professionalism of the staff, I can only assume to have been fortunate when it comes to waiting for treatment.

After a pre-op assessment with a junior doctor, I returned to the same hospital the following week. Arriving dead on time, I passed all the admin screening tests with flying colours and was directed to wait for an indeterminate period in the day surgery waiting area. It was a room only slightly larger than a broom cupboard, painted institutional magnolia, with uncomfortable green plastic seating, a lino floor and a single window high on the wall. The unfiltered air was heavy with the sour odour of fear, sweat and disinfectant. Perhaps in an effort to be interesting, the medical staff had christened our dank little cupboard 'chairs'. There were several other patients nervously waiting. Lacking any internet access or magazines, they were all sitting quietly and gazing listlessly at the public health posters, or watching the silent fuzzy picture on the small television.

Although generally unconcerned by the prospect of impending pain, bad news, or the loss of dignity when visiting a hospital, I am fearful of missing my name being called. I imagine there must be people who have spent days in large noisy hospital waiting areas, all because they popped to the toilet at the wrong time, or through a moment of inattention, didn't hear their name being mumbled and mispronounced by a nurse. Fortunately, there was no such risk in our little cupboard.

Periodically a nurse would lean around the door, smile sweetly and take a patient from *chairs* to the pre-op interrogation room. There they would be stripped of their dignity and clothing. A junior doctor would use a blue felt pen to draw a circle around their offending lump, sometimes adding a large arrow for humorous effect, or perhaps to help the myopic surgeon to find the circle. A little while later the person would sheepishly return to *chairs*, wearing a stiff smile and an equally stiff blue cotton gown that refused to close at the back, carelessly displaying their baggy underpants or pimply buttocks for all to see.

When it was my turn, the junior doctor spent some time reviewing my charts and may even have sneaked a quick look at the internet before he successfully located my nose. To be on the safe side, I helped by pointing to the spot with my finger. With his tongue out, he carefully drew a circle on my nose with his pen. As he sat back to admire his handiwork, I asked if he was going to add a blue arrow.

"I'm fairly confident the surgeon will find your nose without further assistance," he tutted.

"Everyone else has an arrow," I quipped.

"I'm sure it won't be necessary."

"It's no skin off my nose." I gave him a broad smile and wiggled my eyebrows in a forlorn attempt to lighten the mood, but my jocularity was wasted on him. Suddenly overwhelmed with self-doubt, and perhaps fearing the wrath of the terrifying senior surgeon for his abject failure to draw a simple arrow, the young doctor glanced around in panic.

"I had better ask a nurse, just to be on the safe side," he mumbled as he wandered off.

Moments later, with only a blue circle to indicate the whereabouts of my nose, I paid a quick visit to the gents to ease my nerves and returned to *chairs* to wait along with the other unfortunates. I felt slightly embarrassed because I had been allowed to keep my clothes on, but it later transpired I had left my flies undone, so perhaps the others didn't feel quite so uncomfortable after all. Certainly a couple of them pointed discreetly at my crotch and gave me a knowing nod, presumably appreciative of my inadvertent gesture of solidarity.

We were all a little apprehensive, and in an effort to alleviate the tension, I started to tell a few witty anecdotes. Soon another of the patients added some of his amusing stories and I responded with a further joke or two. Like soldiers in a foxhole, motivated by fear and the desire to raise our collective spirits, everyone in the room soon joined in the entertainment. Before long we were all laughing loudly, mopping at our tears and holding our aching sides.

The door burst open and a stern looking nurse came in.

"What's all this noise about?" she demanded.

As the de facto head of the entertainment committee, it fell to me to explain.

"I guess we're all a little nervous," I offered, smiling. "We were using some collective witticisms to keep our spirits up."

The nurse slowly turned in my direction and gave me the full force of her fiery stare. I suddenly felt rather cold.

"Jokes is it?" she asked incredulously. "Well stop it at once. I could hear you right at the other end of the corridor. I will not permit laughing in my ward." With that she spun on her heel and marched out of the room.

We sat in stunned silence for a few seconds before, like a

group of naughty schoolchildren after the teacher had left the classroom, we burst out laughing. With our spirits lifted by humour and our fear dissolved through our camaraderie, we sat back and waited in contemplative silence for whatever was to follow.

Soon a nurse came to summon the first patient to the theatre, and ten minutes later she returned for a second and then a third. Was I the only one to notice the patients went out, but never came back? Finally, it was my turn. After waving farewell to my remaining compatriots, I bravely followed the nurse towards whatever fate awaited. A few steps along the corridor I noticed a side room. My fleeting glance within revealed a wizened and ghostly pale figure laid in the bed, surrounded by several grieving relatives and overlooked by a priest clutching a Bible. Suddenly I understood why our loud laughter had been inappropriate. I swallowed hard to clear the lump in my throat.

The nurse was cheerful and efficient. She led me to another set of chairs outside the operating room, where I was given blue paper booties to cover my shoes and an elasticated hat for my balding head. There I sat alone, trying hard not to think about what was to follow, as the hospital bustled around me. It was almost a relief when I was escorted into the operating theatre. This was a strangely shaped room, which seemed to have been fitted into an unused alcove in the corridor which may once have been used for storing surplus equipment.

The surgeon had an almost unintelligible accent. I imagined it was Pakistani mixed with some French and spiced with an Irish lilt. Wearing a sterile mask, his eyes greeted me with busy indifference as he proceeded to examine my nose, which he seemed to find quite easily, even without the assistance of a junior doctor or a blue arrow. He hummed, sucked his teeth and squinted at my medical notes, while his team busied around preparing for the surgery. It was all very professional and I was beginning to feel quite optimistic, until he disparaged my lump.

"Is that it?" he asked. His tone of voice reminded me of a

conversation I once had with an old girlfriend. "I expected something bigger."

"I'm sorry," I said, indignantly. "I thought size didn't matter."

"Ha!" snorted one of the nurses, safely hidden behind her mask. "You were misinformed."

The surgeon ignored the nurse's jibe. "I meant that this lump is hardly worth removing."

"That's as maybe," I explained, "but I am here now and my doctor is quite insistent. He said it has to come off."

"Oh well, okay then," he sighed. "Hop up on the table and we will cut it out."

I resisted the urge to grab his crotch and whisper, *"Now we're not going to hurt each other, are we?"*

Once I was settled, he told a nurse to hold my hands. This was either to stop me interfering with the surgery, or to ensure I didn't attempt to steal his wallet. Without warning, somebody liberally painted my face with cold yellow water that smelled like cheap lavatory cleaner. Next, some thick gauze was placed over my mouth. It made it difficult to breathe and almost stopped me from cracking more jokes. It was time to begin.

Although members of the medical profession describe an impending injection as 'a slight scratch' or warn that it 'may sting a little', I can now attest having a local anaesthetic injection into the end of your nose is eye-wateringly painful. Particularly when one is unable to flinch or pull a face in compensation. After a few moments, the surgeon tapped the side of my nose and asked if it was numb.

"I think so," I said, "it's a bit hard to tell without touching it myself."

"Don't do that," he snapped. "You're not sterile."

He tapped again.

"What about now?" he asked.

"I think so," I replied.

"You may feel some slight tugging," he warned.

"Owwww!" I squealed and began talking in tongues as the scalpel sliced into my definitely un-numbed nose.

There was a flurry of quiet swearing, along with some fumbling for medical instruments and gauze, before a second attempt could be made to numb my rapidly swelling conk. In his haste to put things right, the surgeon managed to stick the needle completely through my nose and squirt local anaesthetic across my chin. Nevertheless, once my proboscis was correctly numbed, the remainder of the operation went swimmingly. Fifteen minutes and three stitches later, it was all over.

"We'll send you an appointment to return in ten days for a wound check," the surgeon explained.

"Isn't someone going to look at my lump under the microscope," I asked, peering over his shoulder.

"Tsk!" He rolled his eyes. "We're too busy to do that here. We'll see you in ten days."

As I left the theatre I was treated to several shy smiles and a few rolled eyes from the nurses who had stopped pretending nothing was ever amiss.

9 – A New Hat

I gave my daughter a huge joyful hug, almost lifting her off the ground. She squeaked and wriggled free so she could breathe.

"How was your flight?" I asked, smiling.

"Very smooth and efficient."

It was Friday afternoon and Joanne was visiting for the weekend.

"Thanks for coming. I'm so glad you're here." I kissed her on the forehead. "Your mum's really looking forward to seeing you too."

"I figured it was the last chance before Christmas."

"You're coming for Christmas?" I asked, surprised.

"New Year," she corrected. "We're spending Christmas with Mark's parents.

"That'll be nice." I picked up her bag and led the way towards the car. "I'll have to find out where we can go to see the New Year in."

"I'm sure we'll have a great time," Joanne replied. "Whatever we do, it's bound to be a memorable night out. It is Ireland after all. Mark is already looking forward to the festivities."

"It's a bit soon now, but I'll sort something out nearer the day," I replied.

We climbed into the car and set off north towards Glenmadrie. For a while we were silent. I concentrated on driving and Joanne sent some messages from her phone.

"I'm always surprised by how quiet the roads here are," my daughter said, dropping her phone into her handbag.

"This is the rush hour," I quipped. We were on the motorway, which was empty save for one car far in the distance.

"You're so lucky to live here," Joanne smiled. "I had to drive to Colchester yesterday. The traffic was just horrendous. It took ages."

"I hear it gets bad around Dublin," I replied.

Lost in thought, Joanne hummed quietly as she watched the countryside go by. Suddenly, she clicked her fingers.

"What about a fireworks display?"

"Huh?" I frowned.

"For New Year," she clarified. "We could all go to a fireworks display."

"We don't really have those here."

"Why ever not?" she asked.

"Well, it's illegal to sell fireworks in Ireland," I said. "With the history of terrorism, I don't think the government is very keen on things that go bang unexpectedly."

"Figures," Joanne nodded.

"So a pub it is then," I suggested.

"Don't leave it too late," she warned. "In England, you have to buy tickets to get in to the best events."

"I'm sure we'll sort something out," I replied. "But not until December."

Joanne nodded and chewed on her lip. She had something on her mind. I concentrated on driving.

"Mark's moving in," she said.

"That's nice." Unsure of the correct response, I made an effort to keep my voice neutral. "Has Rebecca moved out then?"

"Soon." She smiled. Obviously everything was good in her world.

"That's nice," I repeated, more enthusiastically. "We like Mark."

"Good." My daughter squeezed my arm. "So do I."

"How's Muriel?" I asked.

"Not too bad." Joanne sucked her teeth. "Perhaps a little worse, but she's coping. At least for now."

"Your mum and I were talking about trying to organise some home help for Muriel," I said.

"What did you have in mind?"

"Whatever we can get. She's entitled to some assistance from the local health service, Meals-on-Wheels, perhaps a cleaner and a care assistant every morning to help her get washed and dressed."

"That would be great," Joanne said. "Nan could certainly do with the help."

"The thing is," I grimaced, "Muriel's a bit resistant to the whole idea. I suppose she sees it as giving up her independence."

"That's understandable, I guess."

"It's hard to convince her on the phone and we're not over until next year," I drew a long sigh. "So I was wondering…"

"If I could talk to her?" Joanne finished my hanging thought.

"Could you? Please?"

My daughter nodded.

I patted her hand.

"I'll say it's the right thing for her," she said.

"It's an entitlement," I suggested. "This isn't charity. She's paid taxes all her working life to pay for it."

"Excellent point." She clicked her fingers. "Turning away a home help would be like refusing to take her pension."

"That's a great rebuttal." My daughter was a successful saleswoman. She knew how to sell an idea. I smiled and relaxed a little. "Muriel will like that."

"I'll see her next weekend."

"Thanks. I'm very grateful. Your mum will be too."

Joanne leaned forward and squinted at me. "What happened to your nose?"

"I had a knife fight with another golf professional," I joked. "It happens all the time."

"Daaad!"

"I had a lump removed." I waved casually. "It was nothing."

"I thought perhaps you'd hurt yourself doing the renovations."

"Fat chance," I groaned. "We've both been so busy, we've barely had enough time to do any building work. Your mum's been flat out gardening and I've had a really hectic time teaching. I'm planning to start work on the centre of the house right after New Year."

"Not before?" Joanne asked. "Mark would be happy to chip in."

"And I'd appreciate his help, but I don't think you'd appreciate spending the holidays on a building site." I gave her a sideways grin.

Joanne frowned. "I don't understand."

"It's not as if we're just doing a bit of decorating. The entire centre of the house has got to come out, from the floor all the way up to the roof."

"Including the staircase?"

"Yep," I nodded. "And the upstairs and the bedroom and the bathroom."

Joanne whistled. "Big job."

I nodded. "Once I've installed the new rafters and repaired the staircase, I can lay the floor, fit new wiring, plumbing and install the walls for the bedroom, bathroom and corridor."

"Are you adding insulation and drylining, like you did in the kitchen?"

"That's right," I said, involuntarily raising my eyebrows. "I didn't realise you'd taken such an interest."

"Mum told me." Joanne grinned sheepishly. "She said it was a lot warmer in there."

"I've just finished doing the same thing in the guest wing," I added. "It was really cold and damp out there, even in the summer, but it's better now. I've also insulated the floor and laid some laminate. It's much warmer than the stone tiles, particularly in the bathroom."

"That's good. I remember how cold it was the last time I had a shower out there. I practically froze my bare feet."

"Hopefully it will be warmer now," I said. "You're sleeping out there, so you can let me know how you get on."

"I'm sure it will be fine," she said. "Anyway, the weather forecast looks good."

***

Sometimes the most mundane activities can be unexpectedly subject to the quirks of our weather and the associated dangers. This is particularly evident in the west, where we are more exposed to the whims of the Atlantic Ocean. Sudden changes in the elements have left hill walkers stranded in snow, motorists trapped by flash floods and dozens of holidaying boaters in need of rescue when unprecedented winds turned Lough Derg into a raging maelstrom. Even cutting the grass can be a hazardous activity, as I almost found to my cost on the last day of Joanne's visit.

Our property sits high in the hills. Whereas we can sometimes find ourselves basking in glorious sunshine while the valley below is encased in fog, more often these roles are reversed as the low clouds envelop our house in a thick blanket of humid vapor. On such days, anything exposed to the air will quickly become waterlogged. Given enough time, the forest floor, every exposed rock and even our cars will acquire a multi-coloured pallet of lichens or a coating of moss. With such clean air and high humidity, many of the trees are hung with long strands of Spanish moss, as if they were pale green wigs discarded by the fairies.

The winters at Glenmadrie are not unpleasant. Because of the altitude, we will always have some snow at the house, which makes an agreeable change from the rain. As the effects of climate change have become evident in Ireland, severe wind storms are more frequent, as are the associated power outages. Once spring arrives and the average temperature rises above seven degrees Centigrade, every plant in our garden will burst into life with almost unsettling enthusiasm. After months of mud and beige foliage, suddenly everything is green. Some days the plants grow so quickly I can hear the soft crackle of nature at work, although Lesley insists it's just the sound of a million slugs chewing on her prized vegetables.

One tricky problem resulting from our peculiar weather up on the hill is getting the grass cut. In early autumn, we can have periods where the northerly winds keep the air so cool as to supress any significant growth, but as soon as the warm, moist, westerly winds return, the temperature rises and so does the grass. Almost overnight, the previously sparse and dry grass on the meadow becomes long, lush, soaked with dew, and impossible to cut. Even my modified American-built mower will struggle to get through such thick wet sward. So timing is everything.

On Sunday afternoon, when lunch was over and the dishes were done, I found I was feeling at a loose end.

"I think I'll go out and cut the grass on the south lawn," I announced.

"Isn't it a bit late in the day?" Lesley asked.

I looked out of the window. The sky was thick with glowering clouds, heavy with moisture and as dark as a bruise.

"It's probably going to rain soon. I wanted to cut the grass up there last week, but it was just too wet. It's been sunny all day, if I get on it now, it shouldn't be too bad," I said, trying to avoid the guilt of abandoning our guest.

"It's fine by me," Joanne said, with a non-committal shrug, "Mummy and I were going to sort through her box of art supplies. I wanted to do some drawing."

I looked at Lesley, my eyes pleading.

"Go on!" she huffed.

The 'South Lawn' is just the posh name we gave to the swathe of grass I had cut on the three-acre hill overlooking our house. At first we had rented this meadow to a local farmer in exchange for a few trailer loads of well-rotted manure, but overgrazing soon took a heavy toll on what had been fine quality land. Unlike goats, that will consume almost anything, cattle tend to eat only the best grass, leaving large open spaces for weeds to invade. By the third summer our lovely pasture was thick with rushes and bracken and became a sea of sticky mud in the winter. Much as our vegetables appreciated the manure, the damage to our land was untenable. We amicably ended the arrangement with our farmer friend, and I took over the management of the land. After I'd killed off the rushes and weeds, the grass gradually began to thrive again. With regular cutting it became lush and green. On the slopes too steep for any mower to negotiate, I allowed the wild flowers to flourish, bringing back the butterflies and bees.

By the time I had the mower fuelled and running, the clouds, backlit by the low sun, looked like cotton soaked in dirty oil, and the air was sticky with humidity. Conscious a downpour could start at any minute, I slipped on my ear defenders and began cutting. My trusty mower was making good progress, rattling and roaring as it tore through the thick lush grass. Above me, the clouds were looking more threatening by the minute, but the rain held off, so I kept my head down, gritted my teeth, and walked as quickly as was possible, without choking the cutting deck. The south lawn is slightly less than an acre in size and it took almost 90 minutes to finish the job. By the end, my back was stiff and I needed a cup of tea. However, the cloud had dissipated, taking with it the threat of rain. Now the sun was low on the horizon, turning the sky crimson and orange. Even though I was tired, I took a few moments to look west, enjoy a spectacular Irish sunset and give praise for our wonderful, carefree life.

Back indoors, our oak dining table was covered in enough art supplies to operate a good-sized kindergarten. My girls were so busy drawing they hardly noticed my return.

"All done!" I announced proudly.

"You were brave," Joanne mumbled.

"What?" I asked, frowning.

"You were brave," she repeated, looking up for the first time. "Carrying on cutting the grass right through that thunderstorm."

"What thunderstorm?" I asked.

"The big storm we just had," she replied in a matter-of-fact tone. "It was really scary."

"I didn't hear it," I pleaded.

"The electric went off," Lesley added, helpfully.

"It came right over the house," Joanne exclaimed. "Lots of lightning, but no rain. It was very odd."

I was shocked, or at least I could have been, probably terminally.

"With my ear defenders on and the engine running, I can't hear anything," I growled through clenched teeth. "Didn't anyone think to come and warn me?"

"We figured you'd come in on your own, particularly if it rained. But it didn't," Lesley explained.

"No, it didn't," Joanne added, helpfully. "Just lots of lightning and thunder."

The two girls lost interest in the conversation and returned to their artwork, but I felt the need to push the point. After a minute of silently clenching my fists, I spoke to the back of their heads.

"Well then," I snapped, "I suppose it was lucky I didn't get hit by lightning."

As I turned away, someone mumbled, "Very brave... Very brave."

***

The Outpatients department of the hospital was crammed into a building that resembled an old Georgian farmhouse, cunningly hidden in a forgotten corner of the grounds between the carpark and what may have been a morgue. The clinic is always chaotically packed and it is not unusual to be seen three hours after your stated appointment time, as was the case when I returned for my post operation wound check.

In due course I was ushered into a small room with three connecting doors. Against one wall there was an antique examination bed and a vanity screen, possibly left over from the Boer War. The walls were painted institutional bland and the floor was lovingly fitted with cracked and faded linoleum. A metal army surplus desk sat in the centre of the room. It was painted dark green and piled high with papers and charts. Peering through a small gap in the centre of this administrative forest was the doctor who had performed my surgery ten days earlier. He slouched comfortably into a sumptuous leather office chair, while I was expected to perch precariously on a rickety white bathroom stool.

The room seemed to be in chaos with an endless parade of nurses, cleaners and kitchen staff using the office as a shortcut to wherever they needed to be. Some marched through, but others paused momentarily to deliver or collect charts from the desk and chat with the doctor. After looking briefly at my wound, the surgeon needed three attempts to locate the correct chart before he began to review my case. In between discussions with other members of the medical staff, and several telephone calls, he delivered my histology results.

"Now I see that we…"

He paused and turned to the nurse who was waiting expectantly for his lunch order.

"A cheese sandwich with pickle and a scotch egg."

Back to me.

"…removed a lesion…"

A secretary strode forward an thrust a chart under his nose.

"Tomorrow at three," he snapped. "…ten days ago and…"

The secretary held her ground and tapped the chart with a bright red fingernail.

"No. I said I'll see him tomorrow," he growled. "At three."

The secretary snapped to attention and strode away.

The doctor glanced back at my chart. As he opened his mouth to speak, the phone rang. He snatched it to his ear and listened.

"Tell my wife not to worry," he sighed and rolled his eyes. "I'll discuss it with her tonight."

Back to me again. "…the carcinoma was fully excised…"

Another interruption. This time the mobile phone on his desk began to vibrate, rattling and dancing across the files and papers. He glanced at the caller display, smiled and answered, trapping the phone between his shoulder and ear to keep his hands free.

"Jerry? How are you fixed for golf on Sunday at two?" He covered the microphone and glanced towards my file. "…the wound is healing well..."

"It's an excellent film, but a little long..."

"...see your doctor next week to have the stitches removed..."

Another nurse came in and thrust a note under his nose.

"I'll see him in two minutes." As she walked away, the doctor raised his arm and clicked his fingers to attract her attention. "Coffee with two sugars."

"See you Sunday." He cut the connection and dropped the mobile phone into his pocket.

"...follow up in six months. Good day." He slapped my chart shut and started hunting for his next case.

I remained seated, resolutely ignoring the nurse who was hovering nearby, ready to whisk me away at the first opportunity. In response, the doctor ignored my continued presence, ostensibly enthralled by something he had just spotted in the chart he was holding. I coughed lightly, like a man unsure if his recent attack of diarrhoea had passed. The surgeon looked at me over his glasses, like a headmaster considering a disobedient student.

"Are you still here?" he asked, as if noticing me for the first time. "What do you want?"

"Err... Sorry. Can you just repeat the middle bit again?"

He huffed and rolled his eyes, in a perfect parody of a disgruntled teenager, then pulled my chart and read slowly, "The wound is healing well, go and see your doctor next week to have the stitches removed."

"Actually I think there was a bit before that."

He flipped back a page and mumbled something incomprehensible.

"Sorry can you say that again?" I asked.

"The carcinoma was fully excised." He looked up and smiled.

"Carcinoma?" I leaned forward and tried to squint at my chart. "Isn't that another word for cancer?"

"That's right," he replied brightly, closing my chart and tossing it aside.

"I have cancer?" I croaked, my throat suddenly dry. "Really?"

"Yes, but fully excised," he said proudly.

"What does this mean? What do I do now?"

"Pfft." The doctor waved his hand dismissively. "Don't fuss."

"But... Cancer?" I squeaked, none too bravely. "Should I write a bucket list and stop reading long books?"

"Ack!" He rolled his eyes in disapproval and huffed audibly. The nurse edged a little closer. I crossed my arms and sat still.

"What cancer is it?" I asked, rather firmly.

He mumbled something unintelligible.

"Pardon?"

"Squamous cell carcinoma," he repeated slowly. "Ask your doctor about it."

I was numb and barely able to contain my anger. Closing my eyes, I waved a finger at his desk.

"Write it down please."

With an audible sigh, he checked his watch before scribbling the name of my cancer on a Post-It note. In a deliberate and obvious gesture, he held up the yellow paper square so I had to stand and lean across the desk to pluck it from his fingers.

"Look it up on the internet if you want more information," the nurse said, as she took me firmly by the arm. "Or ask your doctor."

"But..." I pointed at the doctor sitting at the desk, who seemed strangely unwilling to discuss anything beyond his food order.

Before I could utter another word, she quickly guided me out through the back door and left me standing alone in the carpark. I drove home with my head spinning. Lesley had gone out to visit a friend, so I made a cup of tea and set about doing some internet research. By the time my wife came home, I was able to explain the diagnosis with a little clarity and the aid of some printed notes.

"Squamous cell carcinoma is the second most common form of skin cancer. It's usually found on areas of the body damaged by UV rays from the sun or tanning beds," I read. "Sun-exposed skin includes the head, neck, ears, lips, arms, legs, and hands. This type of skin cancer appears as a scaly or crusty spot. While not as serious as melanoma, squamous cell carcinoma can quickly spread if left untreated."

"So you're okay then?" Lesley asked.

"Well..." I chewed my lower lip. "It says here that unlike other types of skin cancer, it can spread to the tissues, bones, and nearby lymph nodes, where it may become hard to treat. But when it's caught early, it's easy to treat. So I guess I'm okay, at least for now."

"Phew." My wife gave me a hug. "That's a relief, but you should still check with our doctor."

"I'll ask him on Monday, when the stitches come out."

While the internet had provided some quick answers and marginally reduced my stress level, my GP was much more helpful and happy to give me the time I needed to understand the reality of the diagnosis. He explained there was little for me to worry about, as long as I continued to use a high factor sunscreen, wear a hat and check regularly for any new lumps. As my cancer had been detected at an early stage and removed promptly with minimal damage, it was unlikely to reoccur in the same place. In the unlikely event of it spreading, the prognosis was good, with only ten per cent of cases proving to be fatal.

In an effort to remain optimistic, I turned the event to my advantage by using it as an excuse to buy some smart trilby hats. I proudly wear these on sunny days, to make me look taller and ensure my ears and neck are protected from the damaging UV rays. In a quiet moment on the internet, I even treated myself to a brown fedora hat. However, any hope I fostered of being mistaken for Indiana Jones was scuppered when Lesley said I looked like a fat bloke in a silly hat.

For a little while, the copious sun cream and unusual hats I wore caused a few sideways looks from my clients and the need for a little explanation. It wasn't long before I encountered what I can only describe as cancer snobbery.

"Squamous cell carcinoma?" my client spat. "Pfft! That's

nothing. Last year I had a stage one melanoma. Look." He pulled up his sleeve to reveal the sort of scar one might expect from a lion bite. "And I had to have a sentinel lymph node biopsy as well."

Another client was less forgiving. "Ack! That's not a proper cancer," he sneered. "My uncle was diagnosed with pancreatic cancer. Two months later he was dead. Now that's a proper cancer!"

"Oh, I'm sorry," I replied, unsure if I was referring to his unfortunate uncle or my less than manly malaise. "I hope he didn't suffer."

"Nah!" he replied, with an evil wink. "The bus hit him and that was that!"

On a positive note, every bump and protuberance I have now has to be surgically removed. Even only slightly suspicious lumps will be cut out or fried with a laser within a month of detection. Personally, I see it as a useful part of my weight loss programme.

10 – Silence and Snow

If our move to the rural west of Ireland has taught us anything, it is how life here moves at a different pace.

In England, I had a proper job. Along with the benefits of a regular salary, a car and a generous pension scheme, came rules, responsibilities and the need to plan almost every minute of my time. My meetings were scheduled days, weeks, or sometimes months ahead, as were the associated travel plans. Holiday dates were approved at regional manager level, usually many months in advance. Sickness leave was permitted, but frowned upon. Such a structured existence made us very conscious of time and how quickly it was passing.

Although I was fortunate enough to fall into paid work almost before we arrived at Glenmadrie, I became my own boss, free to manage my time as I saw fit. Once Lesley and I were settled, our days were very much our own, unless we chose otherwise. So time passes differently for us, particularly from October to May, when the weather is less than perfect and golf lessons are a rarity. During those long winter months, we rise when the barking of our dogs becomes too persistent to be ignored, and only retire to bed when we're sleepy. Living so far west of London, but still operating on Greenwich Mean Time, in December the sun doesn't rise over Glenmadrie until 9 am. With no need to manage a diary, the passing of time is not measured by the clock or calendar, but by the progress of our DIY projects and the passing of the seasons. For me it is the winter solstice, that glorious time when the nights start getting shorter, which marks the beginning of our new year. As if we were living on an isolated island, the winter days at Glenmadrie pass almost unnoticed. More than once we have taken and early trip to Limerick for some DIY supplies, only to discover it was Sunday and most of the shops were closed.

There is a silence here. It is not so much a physical quietness as one of the mind. In the absence of traffic and chattering crowds of people, the wind and rain and bird songs are surprisingly loud. The silence I am referring to comes from a calm mind, a quiet heart and a stress-free lifestyle. Perhaps it is something one can only understand through experience. Standing alone deep in the forest, the leafmould soft under my boots, the humid air thick with the scent of pine and fungi, listening to the melodic song of a blackbird sitting high in the treetops, I feel so calm and relaxed I almost have to remind my heart to beat. Such silence has a value beyond baubles and trinkets, but it is easily misplaced.

In the first three years at Glenmadrie, our downtime had become increasingly rare, particularly with the spiralling demands for golf lessons combined with our hectic program of renovations to the house and garden. In 44 months we had mixed approximately 200 loads of cement, rewired and plumbed a third of the house, built a 500 square foot wing, a 300 square foot coverway, a huge greenhouse, and renovated the master bedroom. At the other end of the house, we had converted three floors into two to create a new kitchen and a second bedroom. Outdoors we had dug a pond, landscaped an acre of garden, built a pumphouse and installed a well, erected a 50-foot polytunnel and created a huge vegetable garden. In doing so much so quickly, we had almost lost sight of the lifestyle we originally sought.

So at the beginning of our fourth year, subliminally realising we had misplaced our silence, we decided to take some time off. Our loosely constructed plan was to get out and about, visiting some local attractions, whilst we recharged our batteries in preparedness for the major renovations we had yet to tackle. However, nature abhors a vacuum. The free time I created by delaying the renovations to the centre of the house was quickly consumed by a sudden surge in enquiries for golf lessons, and a similarly large surge in spousal demands for various minor maintenance tasks to be completed. At the same time, the glorious summer inspired Lesley to redesign and extend several areas of the garden. Consequently, our wish list of distant and exotic Irish tourist attractions was pared down to a small basket of easily accessible local day trips.

With Lesley in charge of editing, almost magically, most of the locations on our shortlist had the word garden somewhere in the description. There were private gardens, show gardens, Victorian walled gardens, plant nurseries and a variety of historic structures, all set in several acres of gardens. Even that rare treat of a meal out felt suspiciously hijacked whenever the convoluted route somehow encountered a garden centre along the way.

My grinning wife always claimed this horticultural bias was purely incidental, but I'm not entirely convinced.

Fortunately, not every outing involved a gardening theme. As the growing season passed, I occasionally got to choose the destination for a trip.

"What are you pointing at?" Lesley asked, squinting at the Ordnance Survey map I was holding.

"It's a waterfall," I replied, tapping the map with my finger. "It's not far. Just a 20-minute drive and then a short walk."

"Define short walk." My wife eyed me suspiciously. I loved long walks, she preferred knitting. "The last one turned into a ten-mile hike."

I carefully measured the distance on the map and held up a hand with my finger and thumb an inch apart. "About that far."

Lesley frowned daggers.

I grinned defensively and waved away the joke. "It's probably a 20-minute walk, half hour tops," I explained, pointing at the map. "Look, we can park here and follow this logging track until this intersection. From there it's just a short walk downhill to the waterfall."

Somehow my enthusiasm won the day.

"We'd better leave the dogs behind," she suggested. "I wouldn't want them running off after a deer."

"Especially Lady," I agreed. "We could spend the rest of the day waiting for her to come back."

I parked at the entrance to the logging track. Even though the surface was overgrown and showed no indication of any recent traffic, I was careful to leave enough room for a lorry to enter. The early frost had dissipated, but the air still had a fresh chill. After pocketing my compass and the map, I led the way up the hill at a gentle stroll.

"Phew," Lesley gasped. "Slow down!"

"I thought I was."

My wife glared.

"Sorry," I shrugged, slowing my manly stride.

"Wow, look at that!" Lesley pointed.

To one side was a small meadow enclosed by the forest backdrop. Standing forlornly alone in the field was a huge bull. It was blond, perhaps five feet tall at the shoulder, four feet wide and muscled like a bodybuilder on an excess of steroids, but without the associated genital shrinkage. As I took a couple of photographs, he obligingly swung his blocky forehead in our direction. Between the short horns, two shark-like eyes regarded us with cool indifference.

"That forehead is wider than my bottom," I whispered.

"If we were in that field, he probably use it on you."

"Nah." I shook my head.

"You couldn't outrun that bull," Lesley said.

"I know," I nodded, "but I'd easily outrun you."

"Hey!"

I laughed and danced away from her swinging boot. "Anyway," I added, when it was safe. "We'd better keep an eye out for any bulls when we cut through to this waterfall."

We held hands and walked on, comfortable in companionable silence.

"This is nice," Lesley said.

"Even though there's no garden centre?" I quipped.

"We don't *always* go to garden centres," my wife exclaimed. "What about when we went to Limerick with Joanne?"

"Oh that was great fun," I groaned, rolling my eyes. "Three hours watching you two shopping for clothes."

"Don't be so dramatic. It wasn't that bad." Lesley grinned at the memory.

"You left me sitting in the corner holding the handbags," I moaned.

"You fell asleep," she sniggered.

"It was hardly surprising. I was buried under the pile of clothes you'd both picked."

"Well it was a convenient place to put them until we were ready to pay."

"That poor manager was so embarrassed," I exclaimed. "She mistook me for a homeless guy trying to keep warm."

"Understandable, considering how you dress," Lesley joked.

"I'd have bought some new clothes, but you spent all the money," I teased. "When I told Ticker about our trip, he said I should have saved my money and bought some shares."

"Ticker?" Lesley frowned.

"He's one of my clients. Very rich. I told you about him."

"Oh yes," she nodded. "What shares?"

"He said I should buy Anglo Irish Bank shares."

"Why?"

"In January, they were rated as the best bank in the world and they've just declared record profits," I explained. "The share price is very strong just now. It's about €17."

My wife studied me through narrowed eyes. "You're not thinking of buying, are you?"

I shook my head and sighed. "That's not the world we live in now. It was just a passing thought, momentarily attractive and then gone."

"That's a relief."

"Ticker was very enthusiastic though. He's bought loads."

"Good for him," Lesley said. Her voice was noncommittally neutral.

"Not to worry." I squeezed her hand. "More money for buying plants in the spring."

"The thought never crossed my mind," she grinned.

Learned in the Boy Scouts, my old-fashioned map reading

skills proved to be timeless and we soon made our way to the waterfall, navigating the final hundred yards by following the roar of falling water. The river was at right angles to our approach, flowing from left to right. Directly ahead, the stream was around 20 feet wide, no more than a flat expanse of gravel and mossy rocks where the shallow water flowed and meandered into the distance, before disappearing around a bend. It was pretty, but unexciting. However, to our left lay the source of the noise. The target of our quest. There was an elevation change of maybe 50 feet, causing the peat-stained golden water to crash and bounce down a hundred-foot slalom of sharp drops and rock pools. The noise was terrific, pounding into my chest in physical waves of energy. Nature and gravity combining to take my breath away.

"Wow. This is magnificent," Lesley shouted.

"It should be a tourist attraction," I replied. "In America or Britain, there would be a carpark, play area and gift shop."

"Goodness, this is every bit as impressive as that waterfall I stopped at in north Wales."

I shook my head in disbelief.

"You've got to love Ireland for its understated approach to tourism."

***

Although it is fair to describe Ireland's climate as temperate, largely due to the warming influence of the Gulf Stream, our exposure to the Atlantic Ocean can cause some pretty significant meteorological events. The weather here can be bad, but it is seldom extreme. That being said, I recall joyfully watching one of those television SAS survival experts being reduced to a shivering, snivelling wreck during a night on an Irish hilltop. Admittedly, the weather was pretty grim. Cold and windy, with lashing rain – or what we in Ireland would describe as 'a fine, soft evening'.

Whereas cities like Dublin, Limerick, Galway and Cork can

mobilise resources and manpower in response to flooding, snow or storm damage, here in the rural west we are pretty much left to cope on our own. However, outside of owning a small generator, a chainsaw, a snow shovel, a box of candles and some emergency food supplies, there is little else we can do.

Towards the end of November, the frosty grass and blue skies were replaced by lead-grey clouds, lashing rain and high winds. The first winter storms had arrived. For two weeks the rain fell in unrelenting torrents, saturating the ground, turning our meadow to sludge and filling every pond, ditch and gutter to overflowing. At Glenmadrie, high on the hill, we were exposed to the full force of the elements, but at least the excess water flowed away. Down in the valley they had no such respite. Soon the fields, rivers and many of the roads were awash. A week into December the rain finally stopped and the sun came out, but this was just a false dawn. With clear skies and a brisk northerly wind flowing directly from above the Arctic Circle, the temperature plummeted. In the lee of the hill and sheltered from the warming rays of the sun, Glenmadrie froze.

For a week, daytime temperatures struggled to climb above freezing, falling at night to a bone chilling -16 degrees Celsius. After so much rain, everything froze, leaving the roads impassably slick with black ice. Our previously boggy meadow became steel-hard, with the grass frosted like brittle gossamer glass. The duck pond turned into a ten-tonne ice cube and, like a thought frozen in time, the small bubbling stream cascading past our house soon resembled a multicoloured ice-cream swirl of ice, peat, sticks and pebbles. Even with the heating on around the clock, some of our internal water pipes began to clog with ice. Despite heavy lagging, the regulator on our outdoor liquid gas bottles froze, refusing to release any cooking gas until it was liberally soaked with boiling water from an electric kettle. I had to install a heat lamp in our pump house to keep the water flowing and a second in the chicken hutch, otherwise we would surely have lost the entire flock.

Trapped indoors, we eked out our supplies and did our best

to keep warm. Although I had yet to begin the renovations to the draughty living room, we had stacks of waste wood to feed our magnificent multi-fuel stove with its new back boiler. The house stayed toasty warm and we always had lashings of hot water. Most days we sat indoors reading, or watching a little television while the dogs assumed various sleeping poses, stacked around the stove in order of seniority.

A week before Christmas, we had a visitor.

"Shhh!" I hissed. Catching Lesley's attention, I held a finger to my lips and nodded towards the French doors. Eyes wide in wonder, her mouth made a perfect O of surprise. My wife nodded towards our sleeping dogs and grimaced a grin. We were both thinking the same thing: if they could see what we could see, our slumbering mutts would go bananas.

Peering through the window, it's tiny paws up against the glass, was a large pine marten. Bigger than a domestic cat, but more closely resembling an otter with pointy ears, he had dark grey fur, a neck and chest of gold, a button nose and intelligent eyes. This cheeky fellow licked the glass and looked intently at our stove, as if to say, *"If only I could get through this door and sneak past those four dogs, I could curl up and sleep by that fire."* After a few moments, he shrugged nonchalantly and trotted over to the bird table where he made a good job of clearing up the fallen peanuts.

"It's because of pine martens that Ireland has red squirrels," Lesley said, as we watched our visitor through the window.

"You mean rather than greys?" I asked.

"That's right," she nodded. "Pine martens are protected in Ireland. Over in England, grey squirrels have all but replaced the much smaller reds, but here they haven't. The theory is the pine martens can hunt and easily catch a grey squirrel, but the lighter red is more nimble and better able to survive."

"Interesting," I replied. "Did you know pine marten scat smells like Jeyes Fluid?"

"I did not."

"Or perhaps the Jeyes people wanted their signature fluid to smell like pine marten scat."

My wife rolled her eyes and groaned.

I pointed at our empty log box. "I need to get some more wood in, before it gets dark."

"You'll have to wait." She pointed her chin towards our guest. "You'll scare him away."

For a while we sat in silence. I let my eyes wander around the room as I visualised how I was going to undertake the renovations. I had an idea.

"Why don't we burn the ceiling?" I pointed up at the odd-looking cedar slats someone had used to cover over the bare rafters. We suspected they had been repurposed from planked boxes used to import tobacco. "There must be two hundred planks here. I'm going to pull it all down in a couple of weeks anyway."

"You want to pull it all down now?" Lesley asked.

"No. Just what we need for the fire as we go."

My wife chewed her lip, shrugged, and with a wave of her hand graciously gave her royal assent. I rubbed my hands in glee and grabbed the most accessible plank. Most were just two feet long and four inches wide. They were bone dry and lightly tacked in place with a few panel pins. I gave the first plank a gentle tug and was pleased to find it detached with very little effort. Ignoring the little shower of woodworm dust and cobwebs, I collected six more and popped them into the stove. Even before I latched the cast iron door shut, the wood was on fire. Seconds later, the flames were audibly roaring, burning an intense white. Soon the stove was ticking in protest as the metal expanded from the intense heat. Even the dogs moved away.

"Good grief!" I exclaimed, stepping back to save my eyebrows. "This stuff is burning like rocket fuel."

"Next time you should only add two planks," she suggested.

"Building a house with something so flammable is really dangerous." I shook my head in dismay.

"It is rather." Lesley looked up at the cedar ceiling and grimaced. "Suddenly, I don't feel so safe. This place is a fire trap."

"The quicker this lot comes down, the better," I remarked.

My wife nodded stoically. "You can start as soon as Mark and Joanne have left."

"And not a minute later," I added.

***

Our Christmas decorations were up. Up in the loft, and there they would stay. As was fast becoming a family tradition, Lesley and I decided it would be pointless to hang tinsel and baubles on the sagging rafters, or to erect a tree. Especially as we were the only people who would see them and we weren't exchanging gifts. Anyway, the spiders seemed satisfied with their webs and I needed unrestricted access to the sitting room roof, so I could continue to feed the fire. Bah humbug? Not really. When we lived in England, every Christmas Eve, along with some friends, we would visit the very old and lonely in our street. I would dress as Santa and dispense good tidings, whilst Lesley distributed gifts of homemade mince pies and mulled wine. Since moving to Ireland, the money we save through avoiding the retail excess of the season, we gift to a homeless charity. I figure they need socks and gloves more than me.

Christmas Day arrived, as stealthily as the fat man in a red suit, delivering overnight a deep blanket of fluffy snow. It hung heavy on the trees, creating a landscape of extravagant beauty as the brightness of the morning sun softened through the mist and swirling flakes.

When we took the dogs for their morning walk, there was a ghostly stillness to the air. The deep snow on the ground and the swirl of the impossibly large flakes muffled all sound, except for the eager panting of Amber, who was determined to attack every snowflake like an overexcited kitten. Both Lady and Kia were in full hunting mode, hastily running from side to side, shoving their noses into the white carpet. They always seem to be more excited when hunting on such days. The new scent trails must be more distinct when the usual background smells are masked by the snow. I'm always enthralled by the number of fresh animal tracks I can spot on the virgin surface. It goes to prove just how prolific the wildlife is here.

Poor Romany, our little white Lhasa Apso, was getting old and finding it difficult to get around. Although she still liked to go for walks in the woods, she was getting noticeably slower, particularly on snowy days. I imagined her to be muttering quiet complaints to herself as she plodded along, like a diminutive fur-coated plough. Being so low to the ground, she periodically halted, waiting patiently as we gently removed the large clumps of ice adhering to her feet and belly.

Back home, the dogs collapsed by the stove, steaming gently in slumber until it was time for a biscuit. Lesley and I ate our French toast, washed the dishes and spent a few hours making phone calls to friends and family. In the afternoon we had a delicious dinner, with lashings of homegrown winter vegetables, then read books and watched old movies until the day was done. That daily routine repeated until Joanne and Mark arrived to celebrate the New Year.

11 – A New Year

In the many years since I aced my driving test on my 17th birthday, I've driven almost 300,000 miles, much of it in bad weather, including snow and black ice. During that time I've never had a crash nor even been stuck. So on the morning I was supposed to collect Joanne and Mark from Shannon Airport, I was embarrassed to discover I couldn't even get the car out of the driveway.

During the previous week, only a few tractors had braved the road at the front of the house. Their fat tyres had firmly compressed the thick snow. On the afternoon of December 29th there was a slight thaw, which refroze overnight into an inch of solid ice. It was almost too slick to stand on. Despite the treacherous conditions, I was still confident I could make the round trip to Shannon. With the careful use of my gears and cadence braking to overcome the lack of ABS on our old car, a safe journey was possible, but only if I could get the damn thing onto the road. Unfortunately, our long driveway went downhill to where it met the road at an 85-degree angle. There I had to turn left and climb steeply uphill for about one hundred yards, before the road levelled for the next two miles. After that it was downhill all the way to Shannon. However, the car simply refused to make the combined left turn and change of elevation. I wasted two freezing hours fruitlessly trying to coax it to climb the slope, but with its plump tyres and wallowing soft suspension, it was an impossible task. In defeat, I retreated indoors to warm my toes and call Joanne.

Mark answered. They were already in the arrivals hall waiting for their luggage. I apologised for the delay and explained the problem. Mark was understanding and helpful.

"Have you tried sprinkling sand on the road?" he asked.

"Yep," I replied, "and wood ash from the fire. It didn't help."

"What about backing out?" Mark suggested. "Having the

drive wheels at the back might help."

"Good thinking. Unfortunately that was the second thing I tried. It didn't work either."

"I saw somewhere that letting some air out of the tyres could help."

"That's more for driving on snow rather than sheet ice," I said. "Anyway, I've tried that too. No joy."

"Oh dear," he groaned. "I'm fresh out of ideas. Sorry."

"So was I," I replied, trying to cover my embarrassment. "Anyway, I have one other thing to try. My little Toyota Starlet has much thinner tyres and a firmer suspension. That combination may be better at providing grip."

"You could be right," Mark said.

"The thing is..." I sighed. "I've got to dig it out first and then defrost it before I can even get the doors open. At best I'll be another two hours."

"Ack! Don't worry. It's not your fault," he laughed dismissively. "We'll get some breakfast here in the airport. You drive safely."

"Okay." I sighed in relief, delighted not to have upset my daughter's new boyfriend. "Lesley will phone you as soon as I'm under way."

Although 20 years old, the brave little Toyota was in its element. It shot up the hill without a hint of slipping and made short work of the remaining miles of ice and slush on the journey. When I arrived at Shannon, just four hours late, Joanne and Mark were patiently waiting. The carpark was bathed in warm sunshine. As we set off towards Glenmadrie, there wasn't a flake of snow in sight.

"It must be the Gulf Stream." I pointed towards the Shannon estuary. "The warmth from the water has kept the snow away."

"We believe you," Joanne joked, "thousands wouldn't."

"You'll see," I replied. "Just wait until we get nearer to the house. You may need to get out and push."

"Bah!" Joanne waved away my suggestion. "I'll drive. You two can push."

"Anyway," I said, "I'm sorry to keep you waiting. I hope you got some breakfast?"

"Blech!" They both grimaced and groaned.

"Something wrong?" I asked.

"It was awful," Mark said.

"Spectacularly awful," Joanne corrected.

"Almost offal," Mark said.

"Oh dear." I winced in embarrassment. "That bad?"

"Unbelievable," Joanne groaned.

"I guess they were having a bad day because of the weather," I suggested. "It's normally really good here."

"Not today," Joanne grimaced.

"It was like a three-day-old breakfast. Glazed over and congealed to the plate, then slightly reheated," Mark added.

"But we were so hungry..." Joanne continued.

They finished the punchline together.

"We ate it anyway!"

I barked a laugh. "Well, I hope you won't be ill."

"Especially with the forthcoming New Year's Eve celebrations," Joanne replied. "Did you arrange something exciting?"

"Ah..." I pursed my lips.

"Don't tell me you forgot!"

"No." I grimaced and scratched my scalp. "The thing is..."

"What?" Joanne pleaded.

"Well, they don't really do New Year over here," I explained.

"What do you mean, 'Don't really do New Year'? It's Ireland. Surely they never miss an opportunity to have a bit of, what's it called? Krick?"

"Craic," I corrected. "Anyway, I thought the same as you, but when I phoned around, most of the pubs seemed rather surprised we wanted to do something special to see in the New Year. I thought they'd be mad for it. Like Scotland."

"Don't mention Scotland," Mark groaned.

I glanced at him over my shoulder. "Bad experience?"

"I'll say. I went to Edinburgh last year for the Hogmanay

street party," he said, his mouth set in a hard line. "Only it got cancelled at the last moment because of a storm."

I laughed. "I heard about that."

"So where are we going?" Joanne asked.

"We're going to a local pub," I explained. "I heard there was going to be a party, so I phoned them a few days ago to find out if there were any spaces left for the night of the 31st and to ask if we needed to buy tickets. Initially the young lady seemed a little confused by my enquiry, but after checking with the manager she assured me there were plenty of places left. She even suggested they would make an extra effort on our behalf. It sounds like we're in for a night to remember."

And indeed we were.

***

On New Year's Eve we arrived at the pub a little after ten o'clock to find the place almost deserted, except for a couple of local farmers and a buxom middle-aged lady with peroxide blonde hair and rather too much makeup. In the corner, three schoolgirls armed with a flute, a fiddle and a guitar were playing Irish music and being roundly ignored by everyone.

"Are you sure this is the right place?" Lesley asked, frowning.

"Oh yes," I replied, with mock bravado.

"You'd better check," she hissed, pushing my elbow.

Leaving Joanne, Mark and Lesley standing in a self-conscious huddle by the door, I approached the bar. It was unmanned. After a couple of minutes, and several dagger-like glares from my dear wife, I experimented with a couple of *Hello* shouts, but to no avail. By standing on the brass foot bar and accidentally placing my elbow in a puddle of beer, I was able to lean over the bar and see through the open door. Nobody was in sight. As a last resort, I gave a hearty whistle. I was just mopping the dampness from my jacket with a handkerchief when the barmaid appeared from behind me.

"Sorry, love. I was out in the kitchen." Stepping behind the bar, she held up a beer glass. "What can I get you?"

"Err, I was just wondering..." I looked around at the empty tables. "Is this where the New Year celebration is being held?"

She frowned momentarily, before raising her eyebrows in comprehension.

"You're the man who telephoned," she said, pointing at me.

"I guess so," I admitted.

"I thought you were." She smiled proudly.

"So this is the correct pub then?"

"Oh yes." She nodded enthusiastically.

"It seems rather quiet." I'm never one to miss the opportunity to state the obvious.

She gave me a slightly embarrassed shrug.

"Folks around here don't really do New Year's Eve, but as you'd phoned we thought we'd make a special effort on your behalf."

"Oh. I hope you haven't gone to too much trouble," I mumbled, unsure of what she meant by special effort.

"Tusk!" She waved away my concerns.

"Are you expecting many more people?"

"Don't you worry." She smiled brightly and pointed knowingly at the baskets on each table. They appeared to contain some dusty party poppers, streamers and a packet of paper hats, which may have been left over from the Millennium celebrations. "Things will soon kick off, just you wait and see. Now bring your friends. I've a special table for you around the corner."

"Oh, good," I said, cautiously.

Once we were settled, I went to the bar to order a round of drinks and some nibbles. Returning to our table, I reluctantly disclosed my growing suspicion that the night's festivities would probably only exceed our expectations if we lowered them considerably – and it would still be a close run thing.

"Look, I apologise for our lack of experience in locating the local swinging hot spots, but we're usually at home and asleep by this time on New Year's Eve."

"Don't worry," Joanne said. "I'm sure it will be fine."

"It'll be grand," Lesley added.

Mark silently sipped his pint of Murphy's Irish Stout and looked glum.

With nothing else to do, we sat in our quiet corner, listened to the lovely music, downed a few pints and had a pleasant enough evening chatting and telling tall tales. At one point the landlord came to our table. Harry was a lovely chap, chatting amiably and taking time to learn our names, relationships and occupations. By 11.30 another three people had flooded into the pub. The tiny room seem almost crowded, until the three schoolgirls decamped, presumably heading home for an early night. Perhaps sensing they were losing the moment, someone put on a CD of festive music cover versions. The lady with the platinum blonde hair pushed some tables aside to create an ad hoc dance floor and, taking centre stage, she began gyrating enthusiastically. Lesley and I smiled and nodded in time to the beat.

"This won't do at all!" Joanne slapped her hand on the table, making everyone jump. "Come on. Let's dance."

Enthused with alcohol, or in my case orange juice, we joined in with the singing and dancing. As the clock ticked down towards the New Year, we wiggled, bopped and boogied with commendable gusto. Washed along with the faux music and barely recognisable tunes, my shoes thumped the floor as if I were a barefooted man on an ant nest. Occasionally I added the decorative flourish of one of my three signature dance moves.

My wife, the former dance instructor, placed her feet precisely in time with the beat, rocking gently in place and turning discretely to avoid any suggestion she was dancing with me.

Joanne skipped around the floor grinning with joyful delight, waving her arms in the air and jiggling her hips.

Considerably less ambulatory than his girlfriend, Mark remained nearer to the wall and made a complicated series of robotic arm movements that may have been an appeal for rescue in semaphore. Fortunately this nautical distress call worked. The peroxide blonde lady swept him into her arms, crushed his unwilling face into her moist cleavage and dragged the poor lad around the floor like a farmhand moving a bale of hay. We felt sorry for Mark and demonstrated our solidarity by clapping and laughing at his predicament. He was mercifully relieved from his mammary ear defenders when the music suddenly stopped a few minutes before midnight.

I was anticipating a countdown to midnight as Harry came out from behind the bar, but he had something else in mind. Clapping his hands for silence, the jovial innkeeper asked the regular customers to line up along the wall. Lesley frowned at me, confused.

I shrugged my response. "Perhaps they're going to do a village dance," I whispered.

With a reassuring smile and a gentle wave, Harry beckoned us forward.

We shuffled ahead, until we formed a tight group opposite the first person in the line. The man stepped forward and, with great formality, shook hands with Joanne, Mark, Lesley and me. Harry respectfully explained who each of us were, where we lived and what we did with our time to make a living. Like visiting dignitaries, we tipped our heads, smiled and exchanged some uncomfortable pleasantries until the conversation petered out. With a smile of approval from Harry, the next person was waved forwards and the entire process began over again. Even though we were all standing in a room not much larger than a car parking space and everyone had heard the previous conversation, Harry proceeded to introduce us all over again. As this bizarre ritual played out, I discretely watched as the clock ticked on past midnight, completely ignored by our fellow patrons. By the time the last of the introductions were over, we were fully 15 minutes into the New Year.

"Right!" Harry shouted and clapped his meaty hands. "It's time to welcome the New Year." He led us through a mocking countdown.

At zero we all gave a desultory cheer, set off a few party poppers and exchanged the usual hugs and kisses. The night concluded with a round of 'Auld Lang Syne' followed by a rigorous, and somewhat violent, version of 'The Hokey Cokey', where everyone had the pleasure of being repeatedly squished up against the wildly enthusiastic peroxide blonde.

"Well, that was unusual," Joanne observed as we drove home.

"I guess they do some things a little differently here," I offered.

"What was with all the bizarre introductions?" my daughter asked. "It was like we were royalty or something."

"I thought it was rather touching," Lesley said.

"I thought so too," I added. "It was nice to feel connected and welcome."

"I guess so," Joanne conceded.

"I'm sorry it wasn't much of a party."

"It's alright, Dad," she said. "It was fun, in a quirky Irish way."

"You're very quiet, Mark," I said. "Was it a memorable night for you?"

"I was just remembering last year, when I travelled all the way to Edinburgh, only to discover the street party was cancelled at the last minute." He patted me on the shoulder. "I thought that would be the worst New Year ever."

"I'm sure it was."

Mark winked at me in the rear-view mirror.

"It took a lot to top the disappointment of that night," he added with heavy irony, "but you did it!"

***

By the time we arrived back to Glenmadrie, let the dogs have a comfort break on the lawn, taken some pictures of Romany wearing a party hat and settled everyone into bed, it was almost 2 am. Even so, by 10 am the next morning, I had walked the dogs, fed the chickens, had my breakfast and phoned my mother to wish her well on what would have been my Dad's 90th birthday. New Year's Day began late for Joanne and Mark. The fresh air, festivities and a comfy bed had taken a toll, so it was almost midday before they emerged, tousle-haired, bleary-eyed and wincing at the daylight. They were due to fly home the next morning, so after a plate piled high with eggs, bacon, sausages and baked beans, our guests were keen to go for a long walk in the snow.

Recently returned from their morning jaunt, the dogs were happily toasting by the fire and somewhat less enthusiastic to be dragged outside again. Nonetheless, with a little coaxing and the offer of a ball to chase, we soon got going.

Lesley stayed behind preparing the trappings for a roast dinner.

Overnight the temperature had plummeted, leaving the snow-packed road treacherously slippery. Whilst the dogs woofed and ran and played excitedly, the humans walked the first 500 yards as if on egg shells.

"Crikey," Mark commented. "I don't fancy the early morning drive tomorrow. Particularly if it's going to be like this."

"I'll warm the car tonight and again first thing in the morning," I replied. "I'm afraid we'll have to set off an hour early, but once we get going it should be okay."

"If we *can* get going," Joanne said.

"We'll be grand," I replied, sounding more confident than I felt.

"Better pack a shovel," Mark suggested.

"Good idea."

Once we reached the forest path, the walking improved considerably. The snow was several inches deep and oddly crunchy, like granulated sugar. The dogs were happy enough, bouncing about excitedly and chasing the ball. Romany was even happier. Once we were all booted and suited, she had stubbornly refused to budge and was now toasting in joyful contentment in front of the fire. Clever dog.

As we climbed higher through the forest path, chatting

amiably, the snow underfoot became deeper. It was strangely satisfying, crunching our way through so much undisturbed snow. We stopped along the way a few times to take some group pictures and action shots of the pooches playing.

It was a perfect Irish winter's day. The sky was a cloudless expanse of azure, the air was still and the sun glinted off the snow as if the ground was scattered with diamonds. The views were spectacular. It was Ireland at its romantic best.

At around this time I realised I was rather superfluous to this romantic encounter and, claiming fatigue, headed home so the youngsters could enjoy their time together unsupervised. When they reached the highest point of the hill, Mark took a photograph of Joanne sitting on a snow-covered log pile with Moylussa mountain in the distant background. Her face was glowing with love and joy. That picture has pride of place on my office wall.

Later that evening we had a slap-up roast chicken dinner, with a vegetarian alternative, and all the trimmings. The table was heaving under the weight of food. There was curly kale, a mash of swede and carrot, peas, roast potatoes and savoy cabbage. It was all home grown, as was the cranberry jelly. Afterwards we played cards and had a game of darts, which Mark and Joanne won, despite the alcohol they had consumed.

I was up at 3 am, scraping the frost from my trusty Toyota and bringing the engine up to temperature. It took several buckets of warm water to clear the ice satisfactorily, but eventually I could open all the doors and see through the windows. We set off at 4 am. Lesley came down briefly to bid farewell, before returning to the warmth of her bed. It was pitch dark and bitingly cold. Above us, the moonless sky was a stunning vista of stars. The planets were easily identifiable, as was the glowing streak of the Milky Way. Every tree and bush was crusted in frost and the road surface sparkled as if scattered with broken glass. But the dull areas of tarmac were the most dangerous, slick with black ice too slippery to even stand on. Driving with extreme caution, cadence braking at walking pace all the way down the steep hill and achieving no more than 25 miles per hour on the flat, the 40-mile journey took one hundred minutes.

"Sorry it took so long," I said as we arrived at the airport.

"At least we got here safely," Joanne replied. "Which is more than I can say for some drivers. I've never seen so many wrecked cars."

We hugged goodbye.

"Take it easy on the way back," Mark said.

"It's uphill all the way. Easy peasy." I winked.

"Send me a text so I know you're home safe," my daughter whispered as we shared a final embrace.

"Likewise."

I waited until they passed through the doors into the departures hall, before setting off home. I heard later they had enough time for breakfast. Apparently it was mouth-wateringly delicious.

Back at Glenmadrie, it was still dark and everyone was sound asleep. I quietly drank a mug of tea and ate some toast while I waited for sunrise. It was a New Year and I was ready to begin the next phase of the renovations.

12 – The Big Push

During our year of relaxation, despite being so busy at work and completing dozens of small-scale DIY projects, Lesley and I had still delivered on our pledge to get out and about – even if it was only to visit a succession of garden centres. As the New Year began and we commenced the next stage of renovations, time began to pass much more quickly. Or so it felt. Our year had been so relaxed and carefree, the clock seemed almost reluctant to acknowledge the passing of another hour, but now the days began to rush by with startling rapidity and enthusiasm. The change really was that dramatic.

With every waking hour filled with paid work, or the need to progress the renovations, our time was no longer our own. It was as if we were riding a rollercoaster. During the slow and relaxing climb to the highest point, we had sat back and enjoyed the view, holding hands and grinning like newlyweds. But once our train passed the zenith, we could only grit our teeth and hang on for dear life as our carriage plunged ahead at a terrifying rate. The way forward was beyond our control and there was no option to stop or get off. Suddenly events were flashing by in a blur. My wife and I could only clench our buttocks and pray we would somehow navigate the twists and turns ahead. Little did we realise this crazy ride would last for another four years.

Even before we moved to Ireland, Lesley and I had drawn up plans for how we wanted Glenmadrie to look when the renovations were complete. In particular, we needed the house to be warm, dry and structurally sound. Due to the amount of rot and woodworm in the old house, this simple requirement would necessitate the removal and replacement of almost all the existing woodwork.

Our second wish was to convert the internal structure of the house from an illogical and convoluted array of unusable spaces on several floor levels, to a more traditional layout, with the upper rooms occupying a common level all connected by a single corridor.

If the renovation of Glenmadrie were likened to performing cosmetic surgery on an aging movie star, thus far we had only nibbled around the edges of a mammoth task. Jobs like reshaping the land, creating gardens, erecting a polytunnel, building a pumphouse, adding a well, constructing a guest wing and painting the exterior walls were akin to giving this once beautiful lady a nose job, straightening some teeth and adding a little makeup. Even the huge task of ripping out a spiral staircase and converting the confusingly illogical, three-floored space into a delightful and airy kitchen, was just a minor makeover compared to the job ahead. The feet, hands, face and hair were looking fine, but now it was time to start on the body.

Now you're probably thinking, *"Why didn't he begin by renovating the middle of the house and work outwards?"* That's a very logical question. There is method to my madness. The centre was the least worse part of the house, which is why it was left for so long. We could get by living in a dusty, dirty, draughty and achingly cold living space. Our priorities were having somewhere to cook and wash, clean water, a dry workspace and the ability to grow our own food. With those items ticked off my list, the next task was to attack the heart of the house.

When we bought Glenmadrie, Lesley and I seriously considered changing the name to Higgledy-piggledy house, largely because of the rambling nature of the layout. This quaint feature, the product of the many enthusiastic but misguided part-time builders who previously owned the property, would make the renovations all the more difficult.

Our home is best described as four houses connected together by four-foot thick stone walls. Three are two-storey Irish cottages built end-to-end in a long row, rather like a Dutch barn, with the fourth tacked on at right-angles, forming a long letter L. The centre cottage is the oldest and largest of the houses. It is the part I was about to renovate. The building on the left houses the kitchen with a bedroom above, and the one on the right holds the master bedroom which is atop an old music studio. Given our lack of music skills, our early decision to use this space as a storage area was shrewd thinking. The fourth cottage is attached at right-angles to the back wall of the kitchen block. It is a large squarish single-storey building. We call this self-contained apartment the wing.

All these buildings are linked by a long conservatory and several coverways that wrap around the courtyard at the rear. As Glenmadrie was built on a slight hill, the internal floor levels change from room to room. Consequently, my structural drawings (including the plumbing and wiring overlay) were more complicated than a ball of knitting wool recently recovered from a playful kitten.

"I can't make head nor tail of that!" My wife tutted and scrunched her nose.

"It's easy." I leaned across the kitchen table and pointed with my pen. "This is the existing layout. The electrical wiring is drawn in red and the plumbing is blue."

"Why do we need a plan of what is already here?" she asked.

"Because we're changing the floor levels and moving the electrical fuse box upstairs, I needed to show where everything is before we start." I pointed to the second plan, knocking over Lesley's coffee cup in the process. It was almost empty, but still managed to stain some of my papers. I noticed my wife hiding a smirk while she helped me mop up the spill.

"Can't we just get started?" she pleaded.

"In a minute." I smiled gently, as if she were an excitable child waiting to board an amusement park ride. "Just let me explain, so we're both singing from the same song sheet."

"Okaaay!" she sighed, dismissively waving her hand at my papers.

"This is the new layout. The electrical wiring is in green and the plumbing is drawn in blue."

"Why is this plumbing the same colour as the other plan?"

she frowned. "Won't that be confusing?"

"I couldn't find another coloured pen." I flashed an embarrassed smile. "Anyway, it'll be fine."

"You should have asked me," Lesley teased, obviously enjoying my discomfort. "I probably have some coloured pens somewhere."

"Good to know," I replied through gritted teeth. "Anyway, as you can see, all the plumbing and electrical wiring passes through the areas we're demolishing. Obviously we can't just disconnect it or we'll have no light or heat in the other parts of the house. It'll be several months until I'm ready to install the new fuse box upstairs and redo the plumbing, so we'll have to leave it all hanging in space until then."

"What do you mean by hanging?" Lesley asked, squinting suspiciously.

"When I did the kitchen, there was enough room to leave most of the old structure in place until the new floor was installed." I sighed and tapped the new plans with my pen. "That's not the case here. This time we've got to take everything out. From the living room floor, all the way up to the roof, every wall, floor, door, bath, radiator and light fitting has to come out. In a few weeks, it will be a huge empty space, except for a lot of old pipes, and wires suspended on ropes, and a couple of ladders so we can still get into the bedrooms."

"Whew," Lesley whistled. "It'll take ages to strip the nails from the old wood and cut it for firewood."

"It will," I conceded. "But it would be almost criminal to waste it. Besides, it's going to be expensive enough to dispose of the tonnes of old plasterboard and insulation we're going to create."

"Can't we reuse the insulation?"

"Some, perhaps. But most likely it will be so caked in soot and dust as to be unusable. That's what happened when we ripped out this room. Much as I'd like to save a little money, buying new insulation is an investment we'll appreciate if it makes this place a little warmer and cheaper to heat."

"That would be nice." Lesley nodded towards the window. Outside it was snowing hard. "I wouldn't complain if it was warmer in here."

"It'll get worse before it gets better," I warned. "Especially once we rip out all the old insulation and I disconnect the radiators."

"It'll be fine. We've plenty of wood to burn." My wife nodded and began to rise. "Can we start *now?*"

"In a minute." I pointed to another sheet of paper. "I've made a list."

I saw Lesley flinch. "Of course you have."

She sat back down and crossed her arms.

"We want to save the solid wood floor in the living room and, as it's so old, I hope to rescue the staircase. Everything else will go."

"Okay."

"But first we need to move all the furniture." I pointed to my list. "Most of the big stuff, like the dining set and the sideboard, can go out in the wing. With a little jiggling, we can fit one of the couches and the television here in the kitchen. At least then we'll have somewhere to relax, if we ever have the time."

"What about the bath?" Lesley asked. "I'd like to keep it."

"Why?"

"It's cast iron. Far better than those modern plastic things."

"Okay," I conceded. "But it'll be too heavy to move very far, so it'll have to live in one of the bedrooms until I'm ready to refit it. We'll need a new sink and toilet though."

"Of course. Those old ones are disgusting."

I rubbed my hands together and grinned at my wife.

"What?" she asked.

"Shall we begin?" I joked.

She grinned back and nodded enthusiastically.

***

It took a full day to clear the furniture and stack it away safely in the wing. After disconnecting and moving the bath, I spent another two days carefully stripping out anything we could conceivably save for future use. It was painstaking work, but well worth the effort as I was able to set aside five doors and several hundred Euros worth of skirting board and architrave. With everything clear, we armed ourselves with hammers and pry bars, and began the strangely cathartic task of demolition.

We began upstairs laboriously knocking holes in the purple-painted plasterboard walls, and pulling the sheets away from the wooden framework behind. The dust and dirt was unbelievable. Every piece of plasterboard we removed was accompanied by a cascade of grit and cement powder mixed with woodworm frass. At the slightest touch, the old insulation puffed out huge clouds of microscopic glass fibres and ancient oily soot. Lesley and I both wore overalls, gloves, masks and goggles, but our masks soon clogged up and the goggles were constantly fogged with perspiration. By the end of each day we were soaked in sweat, itchy from contact with the fibreglass and as black-faced as coalminers. It was exhausting work. After a refreshing shower and a hot meal, it was all we could do to drag ourselves to bed. Despite the masks and goggles, in the morning we were puffy-faced, red-eyed and coughing up alarming amounts of black mucus. Although the demolition was a truly unpleasant task, working together with a combined sense of purpose was a great bonding experience.

"This is much better than dragging around a garden centre," I suggested, somewhat bravely.

"It has its moments," Lesley conceded. "Although it feels slightly odd to be destroying something we've paid for."

"That's true."

As I pulled another piece of plasterboard away, there was a shower of dust. It billowed away on a gust of wind blowing through from the newly exposed stonework. I pointed at a rat-sized orifice in the masonry.

"I'm sure you'll feel much happier once these holes are plugged and we have some decent insulation behind the new walls."

"It'll certainly be nice not having woodworm dust raining down on the couch," Lesley laughed, stuffing a binbag with insulation.

"I'm looking forward to building the new rooms," I said. "With any luck I can start working on the rafters while you're in England."

My wife tied off the bag and groaned as she straightened her aching back.

"About the rafters," she said, her eyes twinkling mischievously behind her goggles. "I've been thinking."

"Oh no!" I groaned. "*Please* don't do the thinking thing. That never works out well for me."

"Ack, don't be such an old stick-in-the-mud." She waved away my concerns with a deft flick of her wrist. "I've had a good idea."

I pulled off my goggles and mask, so my lovely wife could have the full benefit of my patient and quizzical expression.

"What were you thinking?" I asked.

"I was thinking…" she pulled off her goggles and mask so I could see her disarming smile and steely determination, "that we should raise the ceiling."

"In the living room?" I exclaimed.

"Yes," she nodded enthusiastically. "By about six inches."

"But, but…" I pulled a baby face and wobbled my bottom lip. "You said you wanted the new ceiling to be the same height as the old one," I moaned. "If I raise it then it won't match the floor above the kitchen."

"So put in a step," she said, dismissively. "There's going to be one at the other end anyway."

My wife had a point. I grimaced and scratched my head as I visualised how adding six inches of height would change the layout. It was tricky, but achievable.

"Pfft," I sighed dramatically and nodded. "I guess I can make it work, although I may have to add a platform with a new step to make the old staircase fit."

"That's fine." She grinned at the victory. "I'm confident you'll figure it out."

"Anyway, you'll only gain four inches," I warned. "The new rafters are two inches deeper. It's a big span and we need the extra strength."

"Four inches will do just fine." Lesley clapped her hands, sending out a billow of dust. "Goodie! I'll have more room for the curtain rails."

I tutted dramatically. "Well, as long as you're happy…"

My dear wife beamed a sooty smile. "Let's get this lot cleared away and knock off a little early. I think we both deserve a break."

**

Lesley was away in England for a couple of weeks at the beginning of February. By the time she left, everything in the centre of the house had been removed, save for the upstairs floorboards and rafters. That task I was going to tackle alone.

We had decided it would be too expensive to hire skips, particularly as the renovations would take several years to complete. I began the week by making multiple trips to the local tip with our trusty Skoda estate packed to the gills with old plasterboard and black binbags stuffed with useless insulation and other debris. I was obviously becoming a familiar face there. The staff always gave a friendly wave and were quick to help me unload any heavy or unwieldy items.

With the rubbish cleared, all the walls removed and the electrical wiring safely tied back, I could begin ripping out the upstairs floorboards. They were in a dreadful state. Many were so rotten they snapped at the slightest tug. The boards and rafters were particularly decrepit underneath the heavy cast iron bathtub. I suspect when Lesley took a long bath, the only things stopping her going through the floor were the woodworm desperately holding hands and hoping she hadn't chosen a long book.

After a couple of very lengthy days, I'd removed around 200 floorboards. They were de-nailed and securely stacked under our coverway, ready to be converted into firewood at our convenience. Even though the floorboards were shockingly rotten, they had helped to spread the load across the upper floor. With the boards removed, the rafters became disturbingly unstable. Walking across them was an unnerving experience, requiring courage, a good head for heights and feline powers of balance.

The rafters were installed around a hundred years ago when the house was converted from a single-storey Irish cottage. These woodworm-infested, creosote-blackened beams were cemented into holes in the stonework. As they were longer than the width of the house, the only way to remove them was to cut a section from the centre of each beam, thereby creating enough space for the ends to be pulled or pried from the walls. The remaining holes could then be made good with mortar. There were 24 old rafters to be removed, leaving 48 holes to be repaired, along with several dozen areas where the old lime mortar had degraded and been picked away by rodents. It took a lot of time, but the repair would help to strengthen the walls and keep out the draughts.

Lesley was staying with her mother so she could clean and decorate her house. I telephoned every morning while I ate breakfast. Our mutual exchange of war stories helped to raise each other's spirits.

"How's Muriel?" I asked. Recently Lesley's mother had been diagnosed with early stage vascular dementia.

"Not good," Lesley replied. Her voice was a husky whisper. I suspected her mother was just out of earshot.

"How so?"

"Mum's getting very forgetful and unsteady. She's really struggling to cope." Lesley let out a long sigh. "Nick, the house was filthy. I had to wash all the walls before I could consider applying a lick of paint. They were caked in tar from when she used to smoke."

"I guess it hasn't been decorated for a good while. Have you started painting yet?"

"I've nearly finished," she exclaimed.

"Oh, well done," I said. "You've been working hard."

"No choice. I've had to order new carpets. The old ones were sticky with dropped food and spilled tea. They're being fitted on Monday, so I had to finish the painting before then."

"How's she getting on with the carers?" I asked.

"She doesn't like having a home help at all, but they're doing a good job making sure she's washed and dressed. It's only an hour morning and evening, but it helps. Mum likes the Meals on Wheels though. Apparently the food is very tasty."

"That's good."

"She's fine for now, but this isn't really a long-term solution."

"You're thinking she'll need residential care?" I asked.

"Probably."

"Or we could bring her to live with us," I suggested. "We have the space, or will have, once I've finished the renovations."

"Then you'd better hurry up," Lesley joked. "How are you getting on?"

"All the floorboards and rafters are out. I've made good the walls and dismantled the staircase."

"You've been busy too," she exclaimed.

"I've certainly put in some long days," I admitted. "You should see this place. Without the floor, it's a huge space, almost like a cathedral. Today I'll begin installing the bolts for the wall plates."

"I can't wait to see it. Mind you don't fall off the ladder."

"I'll do my best."

"Are the chickens and dogs okay?" she asked.

"The chickens are grand. Still layin' eggs, even though we don't need them," I quipped. "Romany is more curmudgeonly than ever, if that's even possible. Apart from refusing to step over even the smallest piece of waste wood, and woofing at the wrong door when she's outside, with all these renovations, she's lost her spot by the fire."

"Oh, that would upset her," Lesley agreed.

"I've moved her bed into the kitchen and she's laying on it, but every time I go past I can feel her accusing glare."

"The poor thing!" she giggled. "Is Lady still running off?"

"She is," I replied with a sigh, "and it's worse than ever. Yesterday I took them all for a really long walk, but just after we got home, Lady hopped over the wall. She was gone for a good half hour."

"That is a long time."

"I guess she sees herself as the leader of the pack or something," I said. "She was in the forest behind the house, hunting for deer and hares and completely ignoring me. Despite my shouting, every few minutes I could hear her yelping as she got on the scent of some imagined prey. I don't suppose she's going to do any harm up here. I mean, it's not like she ever catches anything, but I do worry she'll get hit by a car or something."

"Perhaps she'll settle down in the spring," Lesley suggested.

"Let's hope so. Have you been following the news?" I asked.

"Been too busy," she said. "What's happening?"

"I was listening to the lunchtime finance news on the radio. Some analysts were talking about how the international credit market is drying up because of this American sub-prime mortgage crisis. Apparently the USA has just had the largest single-year drop in home sales in a quarter of a century. That must be a bad sign. You know what they say—"

"America sneezes and the world gets a cold?" Lesley suggested.

"That's right," I replied. "Talking of which, I saw Northern Rock is on the verge of going under again. Now their line of credit has dried up, their business model won't work. It looks like they'll need a bailout from the UK government or they'll go bust."

"Surely the government won't allow a major bank to fail?"

"We'll see." I chewed my lip. "You know, I dealt with Northern Rock a lot when I was working in finance. They seemed to be a professional and stable business. Seeing them sinking is ringing some warning bells in my head."

"Perhaps it's a good thing we didn't buy those shares Ticker recommended," Lesley joked. "How's the weather there?"

"Baltic!" I exclaimed. "I hear loads of people have been flooded because of burst water pipes. Fortunately, we've plenty of wood to burn here. Even so, it's still pretty cold."

"It'll be much warmer once the renovations are finished," she said, "so you'd better crack on."

"You too."

"Will do," she replied.

"Love you," I said, but my wife had already gone.

13 – New Friends

"How was your flight?" I asked Lesley as we drove home from the airport.

"A little bumpy as we came in to land, but otherwise fine. I was chatting to a nice Irish lady called Maeve. She's very much a city girl and I was telling her about country living."

"How ironic." I laughed and shook my head. "An English woman teaching an Irish lady about country living. You'd expect it to be the other way around."

"I guess Ireland has its share of city dwellers. I'm sure there's plenty of people here who have never seen a live chicken." Lesley huffed disparagingly. "Apparently, city life is the way forward."

"That's fine with me. All the more space for us country folk," I said. "Did you sell Maeve on the wonders of County Clare then?"

"I was telling her about how we still wave at each other when we're driving."

"Ah. So you explained 'giving the finger' then?" I asked.

"More or less," Lesley grinned. "I told her how a small flick of the index finger is acceptable, but a wave is bound to confuse. I think she understood the general principle."

"Ah good. Another convert," I joked. "Speaking of which. I was driving to town the other day and just before the blue farm–"

"Which is the blue farm?"

"It's the one with the black collie that always chases cars."

"That hardly narrows it down," Lesley snorted.

"There's a derelict Land Rover in the garden," I added. "It's just before the dirty farm."

"Oh yes. What of it?"

"Well, I was driving along and I'd already given the *friendly finger* to two cars and a walker, when I came past this farm.

Anyway, there was this horse leaning over the gate and, without thinking, I gave it a finger wave."

"Silly you!" Lesley laughed.

"I guess I'm just conditioned. It's like a Pavlovian response or something. But here's the best bit..." I raised my index finger. "The horse nodded it's head in acknowledgement."

"No!" my wife giggled.

"It's true," I pleaded. "I laughed all the way to town."

Lesley looked out of the window and shook her head. After a couple of minutes, she broke the easy silence.

"Why are you driving so slowly?"

"Black ice," I replied.

"Really? It didn't seem that cold at the airport."

"It probably wasn't, but it was already freezing cold when I left the house and then it started raining. This road is sheet ice. There were several cars that had slid off into ditches along the way."

Lesley peered forwards. "It doesn't look icy."

"It is. Watch." I flicked the steering wheel hard left and right, but the car continued in a straight line as the tyres lost what little traction they had. "Black ice."

"*Please* don't do that again," my wife said, through clenched teeth.

"Yes, dear."

"What else is new?"

"Andrew Rich called the other day. We had a long chat."

"That's nice." Lesley liked my fellow golf professional almost as much as I did. "How's he doing?"

I grimaced and scratched my nose.

"Not great. Him and his wife are still at loggerheads. I don't really know what's going on, but the lack of golf lessons isn't helping. He's hoping things will pick up when the weather improves but she thinks he should get a proper job."

"It might not be a bad idea," Lesley said. "It's looking grim on that front, judging by how your lessons have fallen away so suddenly."

"I guess he could look, but golf coaching is all he has ever done." I sighed in sadness for my friend's plight. "Besides, unemployment here is rising drastically. It's not a good time to begin a new career."

"You think the economy is getting worse?"

"I do. And not just here," I replied. "I heard the UK government has just nationalised Northern Rock. That's a very significant failure. A lot of people are losing money. I think Ireland is very exposed, despite what the government is saying."

"Should we move our savings?" Lesley asked.

"No point, dear." I grinned. "You're spending it quicker that I'm earning it."

My wife gave me a loving punch on the thigh.

"Did you get the wall plates fitted?" she asked, rubbing her knuckles.

"I was gloriously triumphant," I said, with mock hubris. "It took ages, but I finally got there."

"Well done," Lesley laughed. "Why did it take so long?"

"Both wall plates have to be at precisely the correct height and exactly the same as each other along the length of the room, otherwise the upstairs floors won't be level. I couldn't measure them from the floor below because the living room floor slopes."

"Much like everything else in our house," she tutted.

"It's a feature not a fault," I held up a mocking finger. "Also, the plates are bolted to the walls by means of threaded bars. These are glued into holes drilled into the walls. Anyway, if I were attaching the wall plates to a nice new brick wall, It'd be quite straightforward to drill a neat line of holes at exactly the correct height..."

"But not at Glenmadrie," Lesley added.

"Correct. Because our walls are constructed from loose granite stone, I could only fit the threaded bars in the centre of the biggest, strongest and most stable stones. So my line of bars was anything but straight. Consequently, I had a heck of a job cutting matching holes in the wall plates so they fitted correctly."

"Phew!" Lesley whistled. "Are they level then?"

"Spot on." I grinned proudly. "Probably more by luck than judgement, but they are perfectly level and at exactly the same height. To be honest, it probably helped that you changed the floor level so I didn't have to match the kitchen ceiling."

"Unlike you, I'm quietly proud of my contribution," my wife joked. "Now, perhaps you can stop messing about and get on with the job!"

"Yes, boss," I mumbled.

***

Back home, the dogs greeted Lesley's return with such exuberant enthusiasm it was all she could do to remain upright.

"Calm down, calm down!" Lesley yelled, somewhat pointlessly.

"I read somewhere, when someone goes away for a while, dogs quickly assume you've died," I said. "This lot mourned for a day and then moved on."

"So they think I'm resurrected do they?" She knelt down to give our happy hounds a good hug.

"Either that, or they're hoping you've brought them some dog treats."

"That's more likely."

Lesley had indeed brought some treats and some new toys. One for each dog. Unaware of the equitable allocation of toys, or perhaps because if it, Lady stealthily stole all the toys and brought them into a pile by her bed.

"Is she still running off?" Lesley asked.

"When it suits her and usually at the most inconvenient times," I replied. "I was almost late setting off to pick you up because of her."

"Bad doggy," she tutted.

Lady responded by wagging her tail and nailing Lesley with the full force of her beautiful chocolate brown eyes.

"I'm at a loss, apart from positive affirmation training."

My wife frowned quizzically.

"Catch her doing something right," I clarified. "I give her a big fuss and a treat if she comes back when I call her."

"Is it working?"

"Not so you'd notice," I admitted. "We can't chain her up or lock her in. It would be different if we still lived in a town, but out here..."

"Especially as 95 per cent of the dogs hereabouts are free to roam as they please," Lesley added. "And it's not like more fences would help, or be affordable."

"It's a good job we have our dogs spayed," I said. "Anyway, I don't suppose she's getting up to any mischief, other than chasing the local wildlife, but I do worry she'll end her days under the wheels of a tractor or something."

It was around a week later when Lady decided to head off on another jaunt, just as we were returning from our morning walk. I wasted a futile half hour shouting myself hoarse and demanding her return, before admitting defeat. Fortunately, her absence didn't stop me from getting on with the renovations. Inevitably, when she returned and began barking at the door, it was at the most inconvenient moment. Oh the joys of owning a dog.

Once the wall plates were bolted in place I had hung the new rafters at two foot intervals and added short connecting bridging timbers, called noggins, to help spread the load and prevent movement. Finally, I'd used top quality interlocking chipboard sheets to provide a new floor. For the time being the entire upper floor of our house was one enormous room. Lesley had been suitably impressed with the progress I'd made, but less so when I joked that the new space would be perfect for an indoor golf simulator or home cinema.

With my new electrical fuse box installed upstairs, I began the laborious process of transferring the existing circuits from the old distribution board, which was out of date, below spec and inconveniently located on the living room wall. The new board, chockfull of exciting trip switches and circuit breakers, would be hidden away in our spare bedroom – once I'd built it. I was well into the process of installing some temporary electrical sockets in the living room, when Lady returned from another hunting trip, announcing her presence at the front door with her trademark double bark. Twice I shouted for Lesley, who was out in the wing. Receiving no reply, I downed tools and trudged through to let the vexatious hound indoors myself. Inevitably, I arrived at the door two steps behind my wife.

"I shouted for you," I growled.

"I said I'd let her in," she complained, opening the door.

"Well, I *obviously* didn't hear you," I snapped.

Like a prima donna, Lady trotted between us, apparently satisfied to have caused such inconvenience.

***

The rebuilding process was slow and expensive work. As the weather improved, I began to do more golf lessons, but nothing on the scale of previous years. Although our savings were diminishing at an alarming rate, we were still on track to finish the project on budget. On the positive side, it was clear that whatever I built and however badly, it was always going to be much better than what we started with – and a good deal warmer.

Living in and around such a building site would be beyond many people, but Lesley seemed to take it all in her stride, happily doing her bit to keep the house clean and maintain some illusion of normality, although she must sometimes have questioned if the work would ever be finished. One of these days I must buy her a World's Most Patient Wife mug and tee-shirt. When we were at the height of the renovations, every part of the house was being used either for storage or as working space. There was a bath in one bedroom, the kit for our new bannisters in another and a workbench and circular saw in the sitting room. All the wires and water pipes were held up with string. For several weeks, our only bathroom was out in the wing and access to the bedrooms was by ladders – securely tied to ring bolts in the walls. Being of a certain age, I frequently had to make the nocturnal journey, climbing bare-footed down the ladder and out to the toilet, passing through the kitchen, the conservatory and the wing – stepping over several slumbering dogs along the way. In retrospect, perhaps making this journey several times each night was good incentive to get the work completed with alacrity.

The dogs seemed to take the structural chaos in their stride, except for poor Romany, who was really showing signs of her age, getting progressively more frail and confused. Her failing eyesight meant she found it very difficult to cope with simple obstructions like a length of wood lying in her path and would either set off in search of another route, or just sit and woof until rescued.

Late one night after the upper floor was laid, but before I had installed the new bannisters, she took it into her head to explore the new upstairs layout. I was awoken by the sound of a loud thump and a pathetic squeal. In slippers and not much else, I rushed downstairs to find the poor pooch laying on the floor, dazed and with a bloody nose. Unable to see in the dark, Romany had probably stepped off the edge and dropped almost ten feet onto the sitting room floor below, possibly bouncing off the staircase on the way down. We rushed her to the vet first thing. The poor old dog was obviously shaken and very confused, but apart from a few bruises, she was relatively unscathed. Although Romany was unlikely to make the same mistake again, I blocked off the ledge with boxes until the new banister was installed.

***

As we are not really pub people, don't have kids in school and are unlikely to visit a church unless I'm carrying a coffin or inside one, it can be difficult to meet new people. On the other hand,

Ireland is a very friendly country and anyone encountered in such a remote location as Glenmadrie is likely to be affable or lost. Sally was both.

I was out with the dogs early one morning when I encountered a lady and two spaniels walking in the opposite direction along the forest path. To be more accurate, the dogs had picked up the scent of someone new and run on ahead, as they rounded the bend I heard a disturbing sound. There was a sudden burst of wild barking accompanied by the frantic high-pitched shouting of a female voice. With leads in hand, swearing under my breath and fearing the worst, I sprinted around the bend.

Ahead, my four dogs were politely circling a tall, blonde, middle-aged lady and enquiring as to why her two dogs were reacting so rudely to a friendly offer of a bum sniff.

"Sorry, sorry!" I shouted as I jogged into the melee.

It took a couple of minutes to harness my pack and bring them to heel. They were all being unusually well-behaved, except for Amber, who was making as much noise as she could in direct response to the two much larger newcomers. Once order was restored, I introduced myself and the dogs. The lady reciprocated. Sally was English, a recently retired physics professor who had just moved to Ireland with her Australian husband, somewhat ironically named Bruce. My pooches were calmly laid on the path waiting for me to walk on, but Sally's two spaniels were having none of it and were still barking in excitement.

"I'm sorry," Sally said. "They're not good with other dogs. Perhaps I should leave."

"How would it be if we walked with you for a while?" I suggested. "It's probably the confrontation that's causing their stress. If we walk alongside, perhaps they'll feel we're all in the same pack and calm down a bit."

Despite this offer coming from a complete stranger on a lonely mountain path, Sally accepted. My plan worked and the dogs soon settled down. After a short while we were able to let them off their leads so they could romp along like life-long friends. Sally and I walked and chatted for around 15 minutes, but as I had already been out for an hour before we met, I had to call time and head home. Before leaving, I told Sally about Lesley and invited her to visit the house. As this was potentially a much riskier venture for a woman alone, I did not expect her to follow up on her cautious acceptance of my offer, but an hour later there was a knock on the kitchen window. After some introductions, I left the girls to chat over coffee like long-lost sisters, while I got on with the renovations.

It says a lot about the lifestyle and comparative safety of rural Ireland that lifelong friendships can be made in such a fashion.

***

St. Patrick's Day has become a worldwide celebration of Ireland and Irish culture. For one day a year, buildings and rivers turn green, and millions of people participate in the parades. Liberated by the shared joy, they become intoxicated by music, dark stout and a love for a country they may never visit. Perhaps because of birthright, red hair, a family connection, the tugging of some random strand of DNA, or just because they love the craic, they feel compelled to dress in silly hats, sup strange beer and generally have a great day. It is a wonderful testament to the magnetic attraction this small but magical green island holds for so many people around the globe. Some of the best events can be found far away from the large-scale parades, in the towns and villages of rural Ireland. In these smaller venues, the floats may be deficient in corporate glitz, but what they lack in money, they more than make up for with enthusiasm, great music and a passionate pride for their local event.

Up at Glenmadrie, our plans to visit the local parade were forestalled by persistent snow showers and the risk of turning our shared colds into something more serious. Excused outdoor duties, we sat by the fire, coughing and wheezing while we watched the Dublin parade on television. Although it wasn't snowing in the capital city, the unexpected cold snap caught many people unawares. In particular, several children riding the floats, or marching alongside, were dressed in little more than fancy beachwear and soon succumbed to hypothermia.

"Oh, those poor kids," Lesley cried. "They've probably practised all year for this. What a shame."

Elsewhere, things were heating up. A few days earlier, the US investment bank, Bear Stearns, was close to collapse. The Federal Reserve agreed to provide the ailing company with a capitalisation loan of $29 billion. This offer was quickly rescinded and on March the 16[th,] Bear Stearns signed a merger agreement with JPMorgan Chase in a stock swap worth less than seven per cent of Bear Stearns' earlier market value. The following day, as we wiped our noses and empathised with the blue-skinned, shivering children, the full force of the financial crisis hit Ireland. In what was later called The St Patrick's Day Massacre, shares on European and US stock markets plunged. The Irish stock market closed at its lowest level in three years with Irish bank and construction shares being worst hit. Anglo Irish Bank, my friend, Ticker's, top tip for investments, saw its stock fall more than 15 per cent in a single day.

***

A few days later we observed the early indications of the developing recession. I heard a car pull up opposite the front gates, a door slammed shut and the car swiftly drove away. This caught my attention as it was unusual activity in such a remote area. Suspecting someone had just dumped a rubbish bag, I walked down to the gates, but I could see nothing obvious when I looked around. However, the dogs clearly sensed something was up, so, in response to their persistent and unusual barking, I went out to look again. After a short search, I discovered a brown Collie-cross puppy, pathetically huddled in the ditch opposite the house. The poor thing was obviously terrified and confused, alternating between seeking our reassurance and trying to hide from the excited yapping of four unfamiliar dogs. I locked our pooches indoors and, with a little coaxing in a soft voice, managed to encourage the painfully skinny and shivering puppy to approach the house.

Over the next few days we checked with the dog pound several times to see if anyone had reported her missing, but the lack of any enquiries supported our suspicion she had been dumped. We had no intention of taking her to the pound and the prospect of an untimely death, and she showed no inclination to leave, so we named her Cassie and welcomed her into our lives.

14 – Cassie Comes Home

She was an achingly-pretty brown and white Collie-type puppy. Probably less than six months old, but already the same size as Lady and Kia, Cassie wore a soft, light brown coat with a bright centre stripe on her nose and white booties on her enormous paws.

"I'm guessing she's a Christmas puppy that's become uninteresting or unaffordable," Lesley surmised, as we stood outside watching Cassie cautiously inspecting us from behind my car.

"I'd say that's a safe bet," I replied. "The poor little thing. She's so underfed."

Initially Cassie was very shy and unsure of herself, choosing to sleep in the outhouse and only eating her food once our backs were turned. Gradually she came to understand our offer of friendship was true. On the second day, she ate her food with the casual manner of a dog confident this meal was hers alone and more would follow. By the third day, she would accept a gentle stroke and even licked my outstretched hand, albeit rather cautiously.

I have found the best way to start bonding dogs into a balanced pack is to take them for walks together. Once they are all facing in the same direction and doing the same thing, they soon seem to accept a shared purpose. This approach is considerably more effective than introducing the new dog into the group when they are all barking excitedly, nose-to-nose, or facing in opposite directions. Of course it's not a new idea, the same principle applies to people. In business and politics, it's far easier to negotiate with someone while you walk side-by-side, than it is when facing each other confrontationally across a desk. Many US presidents have been photographed walking and talking along the pathways of Camp David. Such an approach has delivered more peace than war.

Although we were unable to get the puppy to accept a collar and lead at first, with a little verbal encouragement she agreed to join our walks. Cassie's early participation was guarded. She would hang back, peering inquisitively from behind bushes, wondering where we were going and what we were doing. Clearly the concept of group exercise and bonding was alien to her upbringing, but the prospect of fun quickly overcame her timidity. By the fourth day, she was happily bounding across the moor with the other dogs and chasing a ball. On the fifth, she tolerated a collar and loosely held lead, and two days later Cassie ventured warily into the house.

"The assimilation is complete," Lesley said as we watched the puppy cautiously making her bed alongside Lady.

"She looks very happy," I replied. "I guess she's ours now."

"Or we're hers."

"That's probably nearer the truth," I laughed.

"I suppose I'd better take her to the vet for a check-up," Lesley said.

"Good idea," I nodded. "She probably needs worming anyway."

"Just look at the size of those paws. Cassie is going to be a big dog."

"That's fine." I pointed towards Lady. "As long as Cassie remembers who the top dog is."

Lady grunted her agreement, stretched and farted.

"Charming!" Lesley tutted.

***

At first, everything seemed to go very smoothly with our new addition. Cassie got a clean bill of health from the vet, along with precautionary inoculations and a dose of worming tablets. She was easily house-trained, got on well with the other dogs and proved to be a loving, if somewhat nervous addition to our bustling household. For a couple of weeks, all seemed well, until the day Lady went off on one of her jaunts.

It was Sunday morning and I was walking on the moor with the dogs. We were following a new route I had recently found. It departed from the official path at the highest point and looped south for around a mile, before linking up with a single-track road leading back to Glenmadrie. This walk was very much off-piste, taking a meandering course through the heather along the cliff tops, then down through a secluded valley, where it tracks a small stream uphill again to its source. From there we would head for some ancient and derelict cowsheds, where a rutted farm track plunged steeply downhill, guiding us through a small wood and back to the road. About halfway through the walk, I paused for a moment to admire the beautiful views and take in the peaceful solitude. In the distance I could hear a cuckoo. Above me the melodic song of the skylark suggested summer was nigh. Feeling wonderfully relaxed and privileged, I closed my eyes and let the warm breeze wash over my face. At that moment and entirely without warning, Lady disturbed a hare and launched into her full foxhound hunting mode.

To the unknowing observer, the ear-splitting noise of Lady's frantic yelping when she is on the scent of some imagined prey is easily mistaken for the high-pitched squealing of an injured animal. Such a sudden and unexpected delivery of noise would unsettle the best trained police horse, so it easily shattered my moment of silent contemplation. Indeed, it is a testament to the cardiac benefits of my many years of martial arts training that I didn't drop dead on the spot. Nonetheless, I inadvertently jumped several inches into the air and clutched at my chest in shock as my heart pounded wildly and attempted to burst through my ribcage. Gasping for breath, I made a perfunctory effort to call the boisterous Foxhound to heel, but to no avail. Nose down and tail up, she bounded away yelping in excitement and headed in entirely the wrong direction.

"There she goes again," I tutted, rolling my eyes at Cassie. But the puppy seemed unsympathetic to my plight and after a moment of hesitation, she bounded away in chase of the older dog.

This was a new twist. I knew Lady would eventually return, but Cassie's homing instincts were yet to be confirmed. My shouts, ranging from friendly, through angry and to increasingly desperate, were completely ignored. All I could do was finish the walk and then watch from the high spot at the top of our quarry as the two recalcitrant pooches chased their imaginary target across the moor. After another hour, they tired of this game and reluctantly returned, covered in mud and panting like cross-country runners. In spite of my admonishments and warnings of dire consequences should such disobedience reoccur, as I turned away they grinned and shared a conspiratorial wink.

Two days later, I arrived home from work to find Lesley stomping around the house and slamming doors. Using my finely developed perception I ascertained there may be something afoot and casually enquired as to what was vexing my dear wife.

"What's wrong?" she bellowed, almost turning blue-faced in the process. "I'll tell you what's wrong. Those dogs have run off again and I've wasted two hours searching for them. That's what's wrong."

"Oh dear," I replied. It was all I dared say.

Lesley frowned at me accusingly.

"I'll go and look for them," I added quickly. In any event, it was a sensible excuse to keep me out of harm's way.

Hot-footing my way outside, I threw some seed and a few greens into the chicken cage and proceeded to climb up the hill. From the top of our land I had an almost unobstructed panoramic view of the countryside. Facing the four corners of the compass in turn, I cupped my hands and bellowed for Lady and Cassie. After the third rotation I silently scanned the hills and woods for the two dogs but saw nothing. Wondering when it would be safe to return indoors, I was about to call again when I spotted movement on the moor. No more than indistinct dots against a multicoloured background, the two dogs were climbing down a distant hill and heading towards home. Although they were almost a mile away, they beat me back to the house where my wife welcomed them like long-lost sisters. Despite our energetic finger wagging and threats, these daily pseudo-hunting expeditions continued unabated. It was a harmless irritation, until an unusual problem showed up.

Lady, our Foxhound, had always been the front-runner amongst the dogs, being the fittest and fastest, continually leading the others in a chase against some imagined fox or hare. But now there was a new kid on the block. At first, Lady seemed delighted to have the company of a young apprentice, so full of energy and eager to learn, but she soon realised Cassie had a seemingly inexhaustible reserve of stamina. Each day, Lady would return from her run looking suitably hot and breathless, but Cassie would still be full of energy and ready to play. By the end of the first week, Lady looked as fit and lean as a champion Greyhound, whereas Cassie had actually gained a little weight. A week later and the hikes had become marathons. Soon Lady was carrying less body fat than an anorexic racing snake, but the younger dog looked fit and muscular. After each hunting trip, our Foxhound arrived home, eyes bulging and chest heaving as she slumped gratefully onto the cool tiles of the kitchen floor. Meanwhile, her apprentice calmly strolled in and chatted about what an invigorating jog they had enjoyed.

We were genuinely concerned by Lady's dramatic weight loss, especially as she was eating like a carnivorous horse. Katy, the local vet, was equally surprised when we took the troublesome duo for a check-up.

"Good grief," she exclaimed, after examining Lady. "This dog looks like an underweight walking stick. What are you feeding her?"

"Triple portions of Greyhound food," Lesley replied. "Just like you suggested."

"Triple portions?" Katy's eyebrows disappeared upwards under her fringe.

"Sometimes more, "I added.

"This could be the fittest dog I've ever seen," Katy said, shaking her head. "Perhaps you should consider entering her in a race."

"I considered that," I joked, "but she'll only run if Cassie is chasing her."

"And you've tried calling them back?"

"Of course," Lesley replied.

"More training?" Katy suggested, shrugging vaguely.

"Training doesn't work. Especially for these two," I replied, patting them on the head. "It seems sometimes our dogs are selectively deaf to the words we say. Whereas commands like *get down*, *sit*, and *stop it*, are roundly ignored, others are not. Words like *walk*, *chew*, *dinner* and *biscuit* elicit an instant Pavlovian response, regardless of how softly they are spoken."

Katy laughed.

"Our dogs even have an uncanny ability to tell the time, presenting themselves without fail at exactly the correct moment for breakfast, midday snacks and their evening meal," I added. "They even adjust automatically when the clocks change for Summer Time. If I were a more cynical fellow, I would suspect our dogs understand every word that we say, but selfishly and deliberately choose to ignore certain words."

"Well, we've ascertained you can't stop them from running off and they both seem remarkably healthy..." Katy nibbled her lip. "Perhaps things will settle down once Cassie has been spayed."

I grimaced. "But that's weeks away!"

"Don't worry, Nick." She patted my arm. "They'll soon tire of this game. You'll see."

Of course, Katy was right. A few days later, despite Cassie's beckoning's, Lady remained dutifully at my side until their walk was over. Perhaps she had finally developed some sense of obedience, although I consider such a development to be highly unlikely. Either way, the marathon training was over, and the two dogs returned to a slightly more sedentary lifestyle and a diet of regular dog food.

***

Even though I had just returned from a visit to England, for a bit of a treat and a day away from the drudgery of renovations, Lesley and I took a drive to a local outdoor market. For some reason I decided to take a somewhat indirect route to our destination.

"You're lost!" Lesley exclaimed after almost an hour.

"Pfft. Don't fuss so," I tutted. "The village is in the valley. As long as we head downhill, we'll get there eventually."

"The market shuts at two. If you don't get a move on, we'll miss it."

"It's only 11 o'clock," I replied. "Anyway, it's not far from here."

"Are you sure?"

I nodded and pointed ahead. Far below, the valley floor opened out to the vast expanse of Lough Derg.

"We'll turn right at the end of this road," I said. "Then ten more minutes and we'll be there."

"Good job too," she grumbled. "I still can't understand why you came this way. It's much longer."

I thought of my short trip to England. Four hectic days of travel, meeting with friends and family, meals at odd times and sleeping in strange beds. The endless traffic queues, dreary redbrick houses, rubbish-strewn streets and the stressed and overworked people, all too busy to stop and chat. For a change, England had been cool and overcast, blighted with fog and a depressingly persistent drizzle, whilst Ireland was bathed in sunshine. As the flight home passed over Dublin, the blanket of cloud ended as if cut away with some huge celestial knife. With my face pressed to the window I hummed in pleasure, drank in the beauty below and imagined I could smell the fresh Atlantic air. From wingtip to horizon, the landscape was painted in a dazzling palette of greens and browns, interspaced with irregular streaks of blue. Like moss growing on rock, a hundred thousand tiny fields spread across the land, each wrapped in intricate dry-stone walls. Shaped around the tops of almost every hill was the darker green of the pine forests and twisting through the valleys, the lakes and rivers shone iridescent blue reflecting the setting sun. Suddenly, I understood the attraction of Ireland. I too could feel the DNA tug, even though I am unaware of any such ancestral links. This enigmatically beautiful land is somehow familiar, like an inherited consciousness, it calls to me, pulling at the very fibres of my soul. Home at last.

With a sigh, I broke the comfortable silence and explained my ad hoc detour. "I just wanted to look at the countryside," I said.

***

The market was a pleasant distraction, despite its small size. There were no more than a dozen stalls dotted along the street and crammed into one end of the carpark. For an hour, we walked along hand-in-hand, pausing occasionally to make a purchase or chat with the stall holders. It was an agreeable way to flitter away a day and would not normally have merited a mention in my diary, had events not opened Lesley's eyes to future possibilities.

As it was such a warm and sunny day, I had decided to wear my new hat for the first time. And with good reason. Since I'd had a brush with skin cancer, albeit the least aggressive kind, I was under strict instructions to cover up, apply a good sun cream and wear a hat. This new model was of the wide-brimmed variety. It was a brown Fedora with a silk band and a tuft of feathers on one side. Warn at an angle, I thought it gave me a rakishly mysterious demeanour. Lesley disagreed.

"You look like a twat," my wife said, refusing to hold my hand unless I removed my headgear.

"You have no sense of style." I put the hat straight and trudged after her.

She had paused to examine some stuffed toys on a craft stall. I picked up a toy lion and inadvertently hissed when I read the price tag.

"The toy dog you made for Christine's friend was much better than this," I whispered.

"Shh!" Lesley hissed, but her expression suggested we agreed.

"I'm hungry," I said.

"You're always hungry," my wife complained. She pointed behind me at a food stall. "Get something over there."

"Okay. Those pizzas look nice. Do you want one?"

"I'm not hungry. I'll have some of yours."

"What is it with women?" I laughed and rolled my eyes dramatically. "It's the same with chips. You never want any, but somehow you eat most of mine."

"Get a big slice," Lesley suggested. "Then you won't feel so disadvantaged."

I complied, returning with a large slice of four cheese pizza. It was piping hot and smelled delicious. Despite her reticence, Lesley watched with eager eyes as I broke the pizza in half. But as the two parts separated in a web of stretched cheese, something alien appeared.

"What the..." I leaned closer.

Hanging in the gap and entwined within the cheese was a ball of hair the size of my fist. It looked like a huge dust bunny. Part dog and part human. Ginger with a hint of Alsatian.

"Oh yuck!" Lesley exclaimed. "Throw it away."

"I should take it back," I suggested. "I'm sure it was an accident. They'll probably give me a replacement."

"I've lost my appetite," she groaned.

"Me too." I dropped the pizza into the bin.

"Let's go home," Lesley said.

Back at Glenmadrie, once I'd let the dogs out and rounded them up again, we had a nice cup of Barry's tea and a thick slice of Lesley's delicious homemade fruit cake.

"This cake is excellent," I remarked. "Even though it is bereft of dust bunnies."

"Thank you." She nodded demurely.

"I was thinking..." I tapped my finger on my plate. "Your baking and crafts are as good as any we've seen today. Probably better."

"There's not as much stray hair in my food," Lesley sniggered.

"I guess it's an acquired taste," I joked. "Anyway, I was thinking. Why don't you join that market we talked about?"

My wife opened her mouth to protest.

"Before you say anything, just listen," I said. "You could easily do a little baking. Your cakes, jams and chutneys are delicious. People would love them. And as for the crafts... Well, you could knit baby clothes and make toys and all sorts of clever things. It would be an opportunity to make some friends. Why won't you give it a go?"

"I already am." Lesley grinned at my confusion.

"What?" I asked.

"While you were walking the dogs up the field just now, I phoned the market co-ordinator and told her I wanted to join. I start next Saturday."

"Oh," I gasped. "That's great."

"And next year I'm starting a dance club too," she added, her eyes sparkling with excitement.

***

And just like that, our quiet life seemed to have ended

The problem is, Lesley doesn't do small projects. She likes to create monsters. Why have a nice manageable vegetable plot, when you can farm a couple of acres? Who wants to paint one bedroom, when you can decorate an entire house all at once? For some unaccountable reason, my lovely wife sees bigger projects as always being better projects, even when she is exhausted and crippled with back pain. I blame myself for not being firm on the subject. *"Put your foot down,"* I thought. But when I asked for permission to be all manly and decisive, Lesley said no. The market idea is a good example of one of Lesley's projects getting somewhat out of hand.

It began with her knocking up a few scones on a Saturday morning, but by the end of the month she was baking all day

Thursday and Friday too. By Saturday morning, every worksurface in the kitchen would be covered in produce. There were chocolate cakes, sponge cakes, fruit cakes, lemon drizzle cakes, lemon meringue tarts, scones and muffins as well as dozens of jars of jams and chutneys. In the evenings Lesley knitted children's clothes and made stuffed toys. It felt like my wife was running a cottage industry. The parts of our house that weren't still a building site became like a factory, as if we didn't already have enough mess.

Lesley and I are very disparate people. Where I like to plot and plan my path carefully forward, she has a flamboyant, devil-may-care approach to projects. This difference is particularly noticeable in the kitchen. When cooking, I like to have my recipe at hand, my timer nearby and the listed ingredients chopped, weighed and ready in separate bowls. Because I wash up as I work, when the meal is ready to serve, the kitchen is clean and tidy. Lesley doesn't subscribe to such restrictive practices. On Saturday morning, she will load the car with her wares and roar off towards the market, leaving me to clean up the mess. Somehow my dear wife will have used every pot and pan we own, leaving them stacked in the sink ready for my attention. The work surfaces will be strewn with flour and pastry, and sticky with jam. I've even found chocolate icing on the ceiling. And what is my reward for cleaning up and being supportive? My wife loves me, and I get to eat all the leftover cakes. It's a fair trade I think!

***

The week Lesley took a well-earned break from the market to visit England coincided with the date of Cassie's operation. Although we had taken the precaution of having all our dogs spayed, she was an obvious omission. Our vet was of the opinion Cassie was now old enough to get pregnant if she encountered an unneutered dog, a likely prospect in rural Ireland. With Lesley away, it fell to me to take the pup down to the vet.

Missing breakfast and her usual morning walk, she was suspicious and tentative when we arrived at the surgery. However, this was not her first visit to the vet and Cassie demonstrated just how much she had developed in confidence in the few months since she had been dumped on our doorstep. The puppy was on her best behaviour. She licked every proffered hand, enjoying each stroke of her soft, brown coat and generally endeared herself to all the staff.

"I can't believe what a lovely dog she's become," Katy said. "When I first saw her, she was a quivering wreck. Now look at her."

There was a new assistant on duty. Kirsten was a trainee vet from Germany. She had wild golden hair, soft blue eyes and the muscular build of a farm girl happy to herd sheep or strongarm an unruly cow into submission. Kirsten also had a much softer side. Leaning down, she carefully scooped the puppy into her strong arms. Cassie responded by wagging her tail furiously and licking Kirsten's chin.

"Ziz leetle one is a poppet," she hummed. "I theenk I keep her afterwards."

"Sure," I joked, waving dismissively. "She's all yours."

"What you say Kaasi?" Kirsten tickled her tummy. "Are youse mine now?"

Cassie squirmed in delight.

"I guess I'd better keep her for now," I interjected. "Be a good girl for Katy and Kirsten."

After giving the little pup one final stroke, I set off home.

Back at Glenmadrie, I gave the other dogs their delayed breakfast and took them for a long walk up through the forest following a path that looped back to the house. I was just about to prepare a sandwich for lunch when my mobile rang. I guessed it was the vet, probably calling to update when I could collect Cassie. I was almost right.

"Nick, it's Katy," a distant voice said. "I'm so sorry…"

"What is it?" I asked.

"Cassie is dead."

15 – The Deluge

I don't remember the drive down, but I recall sitting in the car outside the veterinary surgery trying to compose myself. Cassie was such a sweet little puppy. It seemed so unfair she had been dumped and then had her life snatched away just as her outlook was improving. With damp eyes and a tight chest, I climbed out of the car and crossed the street. Kirsten was outside, loading supplies into the back of a large SUV. She spotted me and ran over.

"Hi, Kirsten," I whispered sadly. "I've come for–"

With an anguished wail, she threw her arms around my shoulders and began weeping into my chest. Rocked backwards under the unexpected weight, and unable to decipher what she was saying between the heaving sobs, all I could do was stroke her hair and wait for the crying to pass. After a minute she looked up.

"I sorry," she croaked, blinking her tear-pink eyes and wiping at her nose with her sleeve.

"It's okay." I patted her shoulder. "I understand."

"She vas zuch a preety girl. I so sad also."

Kirsten led the way into the surgery. Katy was behind the counter looking grim.

"Oh, Nick," she said, reaching for my hand. "I'm so sorry. There was nothing we could do."

I nodded and returned a tight smile.

"What happened?"

"We had her prepped for surgery," Katy explained. "She was fine, very relaxed, happily laid there wagging her tail whilst Kirsten stroked her head. But as soon as we began to administer the anaesthetic, Cassie went into cardiac arrest."

"A heart attack?" I said.

"Her heart just stopped." Katy shook her head. "I tried everything I could, but it wouldn't start again. I'm so sorry."

"I also," Kirsten added, between sniffles.

Katy took me through to the back. Cassie was lying on the operating table, eyes closed and tongue protruding slightly. Apart from a small shaved area on her front leg, there was no indication of any medical procedure having taken place. The little pup had died so suddenly, Katy hadn't even begun shaving her side in preparation for the surgery. Blinking back the tears, I gently stroked Cassie's head and flank, running my fingers through her silky-soft fur. She was still warm. With a groan I dropped my head and allowed the tears to flow. When Kirsten enveloped me in a bear-like hug and Katy patted my back, I lost it and cried like a child. Great heaving sobs wracked my body as I mourned the passing of the little dog I barely knew.

I brought Cassie's body back to the house and laid her in the conservatory, so the other dogs could come to terms with her passing. Kia, Amber and Romany sniffed enquiringly before moving away, but Lady had a different reaction. She sat with Cassie for an hour, watching carefully and giving her flank the occasional nudge with her muzzle, as if expecting her young apprentice to wake up and join her on another hunt. Finally, with her head and tail hung low, she gave a huff and simply walked away.

Later, standing alone, I made no effort to hide my tears as I dug a grave, wrapped Cassie in a blanket and gently placed her in the ground.

That night I telephoned Lesley. I had considered hiding the news until she was home, but I knew she would ask how Cassie's surgery had gone and I didn't want to lie to my wife, however well intentioned. Although she was upset and shocked, she took the news far better than I had. Perhaps she had an inkling something was wrong from the tone of my voice. In any event, I'm sure she had a good cry in the privacy of her room later.

As we finished the call, Lesley matched Katy's earlier words, "Well at least we gave her a few additional months of happiness." It was true, but of little comfort to either of us.

Despite her initial reaction, Lady seemed remarkably

unaffected by the loss of such a close companion, quickly returning to her life, exactly as it was before Cassie arrived. Or perhaps she just hid her sadness better than the rest of us.

***

For some reason, the few weeks at the end of spring and the beginning of autumn can often find Ireland basking in glorious sunshine and delightful warmth. This sandwich of meteorological anticipation often comes with a disappointing filling of cool and wet summers. Such was the case this year.

The unseasonably warm and dry spring came to an end with a succession of moorland wildfires across the country. These conflagrations were usually caused by natural combustion in the peat, or by a broken bottle or a carelessly discarded cigarette. Sometimes my morning view of the valley below was like an image of a distant battlefield, the sky striped with columns of smoke where fires were still burning, and the fields smudged black where large blazes had expired. Although there are strict regulations regarding the burning of moorland, occasionally a fire will spontaneously begin – conveniently upwind of an area which had become too overgrown to graze cattle. In October one such fire consumed several hundred acres of the moorland just opposite Glenmadrie.

I was up on our land cutting the grass and occasionally casting my eye westward across the moor to see if I could spot one of our local hen harriers. A puff of smoke caught my attention. I spied a small fire around a kilometre away. As if fuelled by petrol, it quickly developed into a one hundred metre line, with flames jumping to a height of 20 metres as the gorse and heather ferociously burned.

Turning off the mower, I sat at the top of our quarry and watched the spectacle. Crackling and popping, the fire progressed from left to right, burning gradually along the valley floor below. The breeze was from the south, pushing the blaze along at a leisurely pace. After fifteen minutes or so, I felt the wind change direction, blowing directly into my face and pushing the fire towards our house.

As a precaution, I ran indoors and called the fire brigade, taking a few minutes to ensure they knew exactly where we were before going back outside.

"What's going on?" Lesley asked as I rushed through the kitchen.

"There's a big fire on the moor," I panted, "and it's heading this way. Help me with the dogs. I'll get Lady and Kia, you grab the other two."

Frowning with concern, my wife quickly dried her hands, hooked Amber and Romany onto their leads, and followed me outside.

Within those few minutes, the fire had closed in. The smoke and embers were starting to blow over the top of the house, darkening the sky. Crackling flames were only a hundred metres away.

"Oh, my goodness," Lesley exclaimed. Her face was pale with shock.

"This has got a lot worse. It's a good job the dogs are with us."

"Surely it won't reach the house," she said.

"It will probably stop when it reaches the road," I replied, trying my best to sound more confident than I felt.

"Perhaps you should get the hosepipe connected," my wife suggested, without much conviction.

I didn't reply. We could both see the danger. On the opposite side of the road to the flaming moor was a line of tall pine trees lining the north end of our property. Once alight, the sap and pine needles would burn fiercely and carry the blaze to the house. If the fire crossed the road a hosepipe would be useless. We were helpless against such a force of nature. Hand-in-hand and with the dogs in tow, we moved to the safety of our meadow and waited.

"I think it's slowing," Lesley said.

"That field is always a bit boggy," I pointed. "Perhaps it's too damp to sustain a fire."

"It's definitely slowing," her voice carried more conviction.

"It is," I agreed, "and I can hear a siren."

"Do you think it's safe to go back indoors?" Lesley asked.

"Perhaps you should wait," I suggested.

"I left the cooker on."

"Perhaps you should go," I tutted.

"I'll take the dogs with me," she grinned. "So they don't get in the way."

Suppressed by the damp ground, the flames naturally started to die back. By the time the fire engine and a van full of council beaters arrived, the blaze was much less intimidating. I kept out of the way and watched the professionals at work. Armed only with shovels, the men quickly formed a line and expertly beat at the edges of the fire to stop it spreading further. Effectively contained, the blaze burned itself out naturally. In 20 minutes, the crisis was over.

Once it was safe and I was sure I wouldn't be in the way, I crossed the road and approached one of the firemen. He was leaning on his shovel and smoking a cigarette.

"Good work," I said. "I'm very impressed."

"Ack, this was only a small one." He waved his hand dismissively.

"Nonetheless, I just wanted to thank you all," I replied. "If it had caught these trees, it would have easily reached our house."

"Aye, that it would." He grimaced and scratched his crotch. "And it wouldn't be the first neither."

"You've attended a lot of these moor fires?" I asked.

"Loads," he replied, pointing west. "There was a big forest fire up there last week."

"I know," I groaned. "Thursday night, it lit up the sky like a sunset."

"That blaze took a good while to put out."

"I'm sure it did," I replied. "It's scary how quickly these fires spread."

"That's for sure," he grunted. "Problem is, some folks is just careless."

I would have agreed, had he not just casually flicked his cigarette into a bush.

***

It was sad to see the beautiful moor reduced to a blackened wasteland, but the fire naturally cleared the old inedible brush and gorse, making way for new growth. Within a matter of days, fresh green shoots were starting to break through and soon there was almost no sign of the damage. Given how far away we live from civilisation, I must admit to having felt some considerable trepidation and a dreadful sensation of helplessness, as I watched the flames marching unimpeded towards our house. I had some appreciation for the plight of the poor people in California and parts of Australia who lost their homes, and sometimes much more, in the annual wildfires. We are adequately insured, but no amount of money can replace the real value of a house you have committed your heart and soul to turning into a home.

***

The glorious spring turned into a dreadful summer as a loop in the jet stream created a climatic conveyor belt, sending a chain of Atlantic depressions crashing into the west coast. The weather was unrelentingly dismal, with a succession of storms bringing rain, gales and flooding so bad even the best-drained golf courses were often closed. Depending on the wind direction, the temperature fluctuated wildly. In mid-July it was just 7 degrees Celsius and we had to light the fire, but in two days the temperature rose to 18 degrees. The air was so unstable we were frequently assailed by violent thunderstorms.

Being the highest house for many miles and the last property on the electricity and telephone lines, we were particularly vulnerable to damage caused by nearby lightning strikes. Most commonly, these random static bursts destroyed the sensitive electrical components a couple of seconds before we heard the distant rumble of thunder. Although I had equipped the house with several surge protectors and we routinely disconnected the electricity whenever a storm was nearby, we were still vulnerable. Since moving to Glenmadrie, lightning had fried four expensive water pump switches and turned three telephones, six satellite boxes and a computer into quirky doorstops.

***

"What?" I shouted, turning off my drill.

Lesley leaned through the door into the living room, where I was working on the renovations.

"I said, did you hear thunder?"

"I couldn't hear," I replied, shaking my head.

"Couldn't hear what?" Lesley asked.

"Anything." I tapped my ear defenders with my index finger. "These are very good."

"I thought I heard thunder," she said. "Should we disconnect the electricity?"

"The sky has certainly gone very dark," I said, nodding towards the window. "I'll do it."

Although I'd finished installing the new fuse board upstairs, the mains switch was still located alongside the meter in our conservatory. I'd taken just four steps in that direction when the sky outside lit up with a bright flash. At the same instant, the power went out and there was a crackling pop from the electrical socket behind our television. My shoulders slumped.

"I'm guessing it's a bit late now," I sighed.

Once the power returned, I did a quick survey.

"The good news is my new wiring and sockets are undamaged," I said.

"And the bad news?" Lesley asked, quizzically tipping her head.

"The water pump wouldn't work," I replied. "I've called the

engineer, but he won't be here for a couple of days."

"There's water in the tank and we can always use the old well, so I guess we'll manage until then. Anything else?"

"Unfortunately," I grimaced and began counting on my fingers. "The kettle, the telephone, the satellite box and... the television."

"Oh." Lesley sighed and shook her head.

"It could have been worse," I added. "My computer was unplugged and somehow the fridge and both chest freezers survived."

"Those surge protectors did their job then."

"Except for the one on the TV and satellite box," I remarked. "That's fried."

"Should we call the insurance company?"

I shook my head. "It's not worth losing our no-claims discount. It would be a different matter if the house was hit–"

"Don't even go there," Lesley warned, her eyes wide with the distressing image.

I nodded then checked my watch.

"It's still early and there's bound to be more thunder today. I suggest we turn off the power, give the dogs a biscuit and go shopping in Limerick."

Four hours later, and several hundred Euro poorer, we set off for home. Our Skoda estate car was riding low, loaded with replacement electronics and enough food to last two humans and four hungry dogs for a month. I decided to head east along the Dublin road, before turning north to cross the Shannon at O'Briensbridge. This diversion from our usual cross-city route was a little longer, but had the benefit of passing near to the spectacular Slieve Bearnagh mountains. Although we were driving on dry roads, bathed in glorious sunshine, I could see dark skies ahead. A huge thundercloud hung menacingly over the hills, billowing upwards like a malevolent anvil as it dumped a torrent of water onto the land below.

"Someone's getting wet," I remarked, pointing ahead.

"Flipping weather," Lesley complained, leaning forward to

turn up the car heater. "I've never seen a summer like it. The garden is a quagmire, the flower beds are destroyed, and my potatoes are thick with blight."

"The golf course is closed again," I added.

"This damn weather has ruined your business," my wife growled. "You've had hardly any lessons this year."

"True. Although it's hard to tell if it's because of the weather or this economic crash."

"Or both."

I nodded in silent agreement while I sought a positive response. Rounding a sharp bend in the narrow road, the tarmac beneath our wheels was suddenly awash with standing water. I slowed down and tapped my hand on the steering wheel.

"On the upside… with all this free time, I've made great progress with the renovations." I looked at my wife and delivered my best toothy grin. "Next week, I can start work on building an arc."

"You might need it today." Lesley pointed ahead.

"Oh, wow," I exclaimed.

We were near the hamlet of Formoyle Beg, where the road runs along a steep hillside. To our left the postage-stamp sized fields, hedged with yellow-flecked gorse and prickly blackthorn, sloped upwards at an almost impossible angle, rising some five hundred feet to disappear into the grey cloud base. On the opposite side of the narrow road, the terrain plunged abruptly down to the river Glenomra 50 feet below. The only thing protecting a hapless motorist from an ugly fall was a dry-stone wall and a few bushes.

Although the storm had passed, the earlier deluge had obviously dumped a colossal amount of water. A small stream running down the hill had been transformed into a raging torrent of muddy water, violently flooding across the road as the fluid gave in to gravity, plunging downwards in a desperate attempt to reach the river below. The vehicles ahead were showing little respect for the stream, despite the rocks and sticks it obviously contained. Taking turns, they slowed marginally, before ploughing ahead and spraying the roadside like an exuberant speedboat ride. As my turn approached, I slowed and then stopped.

"What's the matter," Lesley asked.

"I'm not sure I can get through."

"The others did. Why can't we?"

"They were all driving 4x4s with loads of ground clearance" I explained. "That water will be halfway up the doors on this car."

As I spoke, the stream swept the stone wall away, casting the rocks into the river below.

"I think you'd better turn around," my wife suggested, her eyes wide with concern.

"I can't," I grimaced. "There isn't enough room."

There was a chorus of car horns from the growing line of vehicles behind. Feeling like a terrified child teetering on the edge of a high diving board, whilst a queue of people tutted from behind, I gritted my teeth.

"Oh well, here goes."

As I drove cautiously forward, it was obvious I was right to be concerned. The muddy water pounded into the side of the vehicle spraying up the windows, across the bonnet and pushing the car worryingly towards the edge of the road. Wide-eyed and trying not to look down into the abyss, I steered towards safety and slipped the clutch to prevent the engine from stalling. The passage through this unexpected muddy ford took just a few seconds, but it felt like an hour.

"Phew!" I relaxed, letting out the breath I didn't realise I had been holding.

"Nothing to worry about," Lesley joked.

Around the corner there was another flood, and after that, another. As going back was not an option, we pushed on, repeatedly drowning our overloaded and aging Skoda with its dodgy wiring and temperamental ignition. The god of internal combustion was with us that day. Somehow the engine continued running and we got through.

In retrospect, it was dangerous folly to attempt to ford any of these raging torrents and risk certain death had our car been washed from the road into the river, but others had passed ahead, and I felt obliged to follow. Although we got through unscathed, afterwards I felt like a buffoon.

***

By the end of August, most of the structural renovations to the middle section of the house were complete. Over the previous nine months, with Lesley's help, I had added new beams to raise the floor level, stripped and rebuilt the staircase and fully dry-lined and insulated the walls. I had built a new bathroom, bedroom and corridor on the first floor and completed all the necessary plumbing and electrical upgrades. There was still a lot of dust around, with bare floors and walls and we had yet to do plastering, decorating or any of the other twiddly bits, but we felt we were making progress.

I was fettling away upstairs, cutting skirting for the bathroom and whistling tunelessly to myself, when a movement caught my eye and I looked out of the window. To my amazement, walking up the driveway with absurdly exaggerated *let's sneak up on them* steps, were Joanne and Mark, both dressed in party hats and carrying presents. Mother and daughter had arranged a lovely surprise for my 50th birthday. Not wanting to ruin their fun, I pretended I hadn't noticed anything, but within seconds the dogs erupted in a cacophony of excited barking. The game was up.

I was delighted to see Joanne and Mark again and happy for the excuse to take a few days off – if only to celebrate surviving my first half century. That night we played charades, drank a little wine and shared my birthday cake. I couldn't have wished for a better gift.

The highlight of their visit was a magnificent meal at the Old Ground Hotel in Ennis. We ate in a section of the hotel restaurant called Poet's Corner. It can be a little crowded, not dissimilar to trying to eat your lunch on the London Underground at rush hour, but the food is excellent.

In the afternoon we took a long walk through the town and along the riverfront. It was a warm and sunny day. The river was deep, but flowing slowly, disturbed only when a gleaming white swan swooped in to land in a glistening shower of water. Along O'Connell street, the multi-coloured shopfronts could have been mistaken for the spines of books on a shelf. Each shop seemed to be selling something different, yet all were apparently doing well, despite the looming recession. With typical Irish approachability, people were nodding and smiling as we passed. It felt like a good day to be 50.

Joanne and Mark spent a lot of the day walking ahead, holding hands and giggling like a couple of teenagers on a first date. It was lovely to see two people so much in love – particularly as one of them was our daughter. Lesley and I watched them from a distance, delighted to see our Joanne so very happy. Not for the first time we pondered if their relationship could be moving towards matrimony.

Late on the Monday we gave them a tearful send-off at Shannon Airport. Mark and Joanne went back to working in London and a seemingly endless round of corporate events, hen-nights, stag-dos, weddings and christenings, whilst we quietly returned to our house, our dogs and our very pedestrian lives. We were happy, contented and, like almost everyone in Ireland, unaware of the gathering storm.

***

To forestall the recession and balance the books in the face of plummeting tax revenues, at the beginning of September the Irish Minister of Finance took the almost unprecedented step of holding an emergency budget. A few days later, heavily exposed to the sub-prime mortgage market, the American bank Lehman Brothers filed for bankruptcy, prompting worldwide financial panic. On September 17th, the UK's largest mortgage lender,

HBOS, was rescued by Lloyds TSB after a huge drop in its share price. On the same day, Anglo Irish Bank executives met with Central Bank officials to request an astonishing €7 billion emergency loan. Rumours were circulating that the Irish banking system was about to collapse. By September 29th, the situation was so dire the Irish Government took an overnight decision to guarantee the entire banking system, putting the tiny population of Ireland on the hook for potentially €440 billion.

At Glenmadrie, Lesley and I worked on the renovations and listened, helpless and open-mouthed in horrified shock, as one of the strongest economies in the world unravelled before our eyes.

***

Despite Ireland's financial problems glowering over our daily lives, the year finished with a special treat. We went to see *Get Back*, which is probably the best Beatles tribute show ever. Lesley and I have always been fans of the Fab Four. Not the screaming and crying type, just the sort that has a couple of their CDs in the car and appreciates how important they were to modern music. Consequently, we were looking forward to our night out. Besides, it was an extra birthday gift for me.

The show was presented as a series of scenes, cleverly backed with original news footage. *Get Back* charts the Beatles' progress from beginning to end. The presentation was so believable and polished, I really felt we were watching the Fab Four perform. However, that night it was a member of the audience that really stole the show.

Everyone had a fantastic time, with lots of clapping and singing, and stamping of feet, but about 20 minutes into the performance Lesley nudged me and pointed towards the right of the stage.

"He's enjoying the show," she shouted into my ear.

In a clear area to the side of the stage, just by the emergency exit, an elderly gent had left his seat and begun to dance on his own. He was a tall, slim man, aged around 90 years old, dressed in a suit, with a shirt and tie, and wearing a knitted cardigan rather than a waistcoat. As the band launched into their rendition of 'I Want to Hold your Hand' he began jumping up and down and waving his arms, as if he were being attacked by a swarm of invisible hornets. The evident passion and joy of his dancing was only exceeded by his enthusiasm and extraordinary stamina. In another country, some official would probably have told him to sit down or leave, but not here. He was encouraged by everyone, even the band. Despite his great age, the elderly gentleman continued to enhance our entertainment for the remainder of the show, only to slip silently into the darkness as the paid performers took their last curtain call.

God bless you, sir, whoever you were, you made our night.

16 – Tumbleweed Chicken

"Did you have a good Christmas?" the nice lady asked.

I groaned internally. Not only had I somehow forgotten her name, she had just asked the dreaded question.

"Ah, it was grand," I replied noncommittally whilst looking over her shoulder and trying to spot my wife across the crowded room.

It was a few days after Christmas and we were at a party hosted by our new friends, Sally and Bruce. In the hour since we had arrived, I'd already deflected the same question five times.

"Tell me about your gifts," she asked, her eyes twinkling with excitement. "Did you get something nice?"

"We didn't exchange gifts," I confessed, grimacing and scratching my ear.

"Oh dear," she gasped, as if I had just announced a death in the family. "Why ever not?"

"We just decided we wouldn't," I explained, not wanting to lie, even for the sake of social acceptance.

"Goodness," she seemed genuinely shocked, "but what do you put under your Christmas tree?"

"We didn't have a tree. Or any decorations. Actually, we haven't *done* Christmas for several years." I gave my best reassuring smile. "It's become rather a tradition."

Wide-eyed, she sipped her drink and sidled away. After a short search, I spotted my wife and gratefully headed for sanctuary. Lesley was in the kitchen chatting with Sally by the breakfast bar.

"Hello, Nick," Sally flashed me a welcoming smile. "Are you having fun?"

"Very much." We clinked glasses. Mine was fruit juice, hers wasn't. I was our designated driver. I munched another vegetarian sausage roll, pausing to wipe some puff pastry flakes from my mouth. "The food is great, and I've met some really interesting people."

"Same here," Lesley added. "But they keep asking about Christmas."

"I guess it's inevitable, as it was only a few days ago," Sally smiled. "I know you're still renovating and didn't feel compelled to participate in the retail festivities. People should be fine with that."

"Or we could tell them we're in some obscure cult," I suggested.

"Good plan," Sally sniggered. "Anyway, Bruce and I had a great time in Dublin. We certainly took up the slack on your behalf."

"And we're very grateful you did," I joked. "That alcohol won't drink itself."

"So we've discovered." Sally drained her glass and reached for another bottle. She topped up Lesley's glass first."

"How did the Christmas market go?"

"It almost didn't," Lesley replied, rolling her eyes. "We were snowed in."

"Nooo!" Sally gasped.

"Yep," I confirmed. "Lesley had dozens of cakes, scones and meat pies all cooked and ready, but we woke on the Saturday morning to several inches of snow. It was all we could do to get out. The ten-mile drive to the market took more than an hour."

"Well at least you made it."

"Unfortunately, it was very quiet," my wife recalled. "We didn't sell very much."

"Oh dear. What a shame."

"She gave most of the pies and cakes to charity," I said.

"Good for you," Sally nodded.

"Santa did quite well though," Lesley said, nodding in my direction.

"You were Santa?" Sally's blue eyes observed me quizzically from under furrowed brows.

"For my sins," I tutted. "But probably for the last time."

Sally's frown deepened. "Do tell."

"Nick was all kitted up in his Santa suit—"

"Over here he's called Santy," I corrected.

"…in his Santy suit and trying to entertain the kids," my wife continued. "But it soon transpired he was no more than a child minder. Quite a few people were quietly leaving their kids with him and heading out shopping."

"Ooh, that's a bit cheeky," Sally laughed.

"It was okay." Lesley waved away the comment. "No harm done."

"So, will you be Santy next year, Nick?"

"I don't think they'll let me, Sally."

"Why ever not?"

"Well…" I grimaced in embarrassment. "Everything was going along swimmingly, with the children telling me what they wanted for Christmas. But after a while I got a bit bored, so I asked them what they got last year."

"That's wicked," Sally's eyes were wide. "I bet they couldn't remember."

"Not one," Lesley said. "The mums were furious with the kids."

"I can imagine," Sally giggled. "The little poppets had probably been hassling their parents for months, begging for some toy or other and now it's stuck at the back of the cupboard and forgotten."

"It got worse," my wife added gleefully nudging her friend. "He ended by telling the children they should all write thank you letters."

"And so they should. You're a very naughty boy, Santy Nicholas," Sally said, raising her glass. "But you're a man after my own heart. Cheers!"

***

A few days later and Christmas was all but forgotten. For many it was no more than a distant happy memory and the stomach-churning prospect of the impending credit card bill – and with good reason. Ireland's financial decline was rapidly becoming a crash. Unemployment reached 326,000, almost ten per cent, and was rising fast. Typically, the job losses were most damaging away from the big cities like Dublin. Rural County Clare was particularly badly hit. Mid-January brought more bad news.

Just three months since the Icelandic banks failed, Anglo Irish Bank was nationalised to prevent a collapse of the entire Irish banking system. It was one of only six banks operating in the state and had previously been my friend, Ticker's, investment top-tip. The Irish government was under increasing pressure to make up the losses incurred by international investors, but the state coffers were all-but empty. Like many people, Lesley and I helplessly watched events unfold with increasing disbelief.

***

At Glenmadrie, with most of the structural work now completed, almost two thirds of the house needed to be decorated. I still had to build and varnish the bannister for the staircase, attach new light fittings, curtain rails, radiators and skirting boards, fit the doors and carpets and do all the other fiddly things that seem to take forever. Lesley is our chief decorator and she was also doing sterling work altering and making up curtains; this helped considerably to protect our meagre savings. All these little extras seemed to cost an incredible amount of money and took a lot of time to source and fit. For a while, we were spending almost every other weekend in Limerick or Ennis, looking for bargains in the DIY and soft furnishing sales. The upside of the ever-deepening recession was that prices were starting to fall and there were some genuine bargains to be had, provided you were patient and prepared to haggle.

Despite a disappointing Christmas, the market was doing well.

"We need more chickens," Lesley said.

"We've already got eight – and two ducks," I pointed out.

"I know, but only three chickens are laying. The duck eggs are fine for us, but too rich for baking. I'm forever having to buy eggs. If we had more chickens, I'd have plenty for cooking and we could sell the surplus at the market."

"Okay," I shrugged in agreement. "But I'm not culling the old chickens, even if they're costing us money. I know we're supposed to kill them once they stop laying, but I just won't do it."

"I agree," Lesley said. "They've done us proud and deserve a long and happy retirement."

"I'll just need to make the pen a bit bigger. How many chickens did you have in mind?"

"About 20."

"20?" I gulped. "I guess I'll have to make the pen *much* bigger."

Alas, my plans for a poultry retirement home came to naught. Nature had other ideas.

***

A couple of days later, on a frosty February morning, I let the chickens out of their hutch and returned indoors for breakfast. Whilst boiling the kettle and cooking some toast, I also made a pint of porridge. This was a special stomach-warming treat for our flock, reserved for chilly mornings. But an hour later, when I went to dispense the porridge, all was not well. The door to the chicken pen was broken and hanging open, dangling from the one remaining hinge. Even from a distance, the carnage inside was obvious.

"Oh no," I gasped.

The pen was awash with chicken feathers and a few splashes of blood. Just two chickens were visible, both very obviously dead. After a futile search for survivors, I returned indoors to share the bad news with Lesley. She was appalled.

"It must have been a fox," she snarled, her features tight with anger.

"I'm not so sure," I replied. "Whatever got into the pen was large enough to break the catch on the gate and snap a hinge."

"Perhaps it was a stray dog?" Lesley suggested.

"It's possible," I shrugged. "Unfortunately, the ground was frozen, so there aren't any tracks. It must have been a large predator to take both ducks."

"The ducks?" Lesley cried, a hand covering her mouth. Her eyes watered as she suddenly remembered our two missing Aylesbury ducks, both as large as swans.

"Sorry." I shook my head sadly. "There's a trail of feathers leading towards the forest and I found a wing in the lane, but that's all. They've both gone."

"Oh, the poor things."

I pulled my wife into a hug, it was all I could do.

Later we decided to press ahead with our plan to expand the flock. I would repair and extend the chicken run and build a new coop, large enough to safely house around 20 chickens, and perhaps a couple of ducks. Once they were established, Lesley planned to source some fertilised eggs from one of the market traders.

"With any luck, one of the new hens will incubate them and, in a few weeks, we'll have some of our own chicks," she explained.

I liked the idea. With a more secure enclosure and a few chicks running around the place, perhaps the pain of that day would soon fade.

***

"I saw a big cat!" I exclaimed, trying to corral the dogs into the house. A tricky task at any time, but doubly so as they were sensing my excitement.

"Like a big tabby?" Lesley asked, holding her hands at shoulder width. "There's supposed to be a giant domestic type on the loose in Ireland."

"It was this big..." I stretched my arms as wide as I could.

"Much larger than Kia – and black, like a panther. It had short fur and a long rope-like tail. It was huge. I swear."

"Where was it?"

"Just up the lane. It was about 50 metres ahead, sunbathing on the road. It spotted us coming and quite casually climbed up the embankment and vanished into the forest. Luckily the dogs were too busy sniffing for hare, so they didn't even see it."

"Did you get a photo?" Lesley asked, somewhat sceptically.

"Ah," I winced. "By the time I'd taken my gloves off, got my phone out, entered the security code and found the camera app…"

"I guess that's why there are no good pictures of UFOs or Bigfoot," Lesley mumbled.

"It was huge," I whined. "Honest."

"Of course it was, dear." My wife patted my slumped shoulder.

***

With our chicken run extended and reinforced sufficiently to deter a wily fox, a panther, or a baby elephant – should one ever visit the hills of Glenmadrie – it was time to replenish our flock. As we had previously discovered, the most reliable source for hens was the Chicken Lady, a delightful woman who visited the local markets and sold live chickens from the back of her van. Equipped with several empty cardboard boxes and my shopping list, along with strict instructions not to deviate from the plan, I parked adjacent to the marketplace in the small town of Gort and waited.

When the Chicken Lady arrived, there was a flurry of activity as a dozen people jostled and elbowed each other in an attempt to buy the best poultry. Feeling rather like an old hand, I shunned such impertinence, preferring to wait until the crowd had thinned. In any event, I knew she had more than enough stock to meet our needs, and those of Ennis market too. Besides, I'd phoned ahead to reserve my order.

Back at Glenmadrie, Lesley was excitedly waiting. She helped me move all six boxes from the car to the safety of the new pen. Once securely inside, we unceremoniously emptied the contents into the coop and closed the door. Lesley tried to peer inside, but I was insistent we kept to the agreed plan.

"We'll lock them in for today. That way they can sort themselves out and roost without undue stress. There's plenty of food and water inside," I said. "I'll let them out in the morning. You'll see them then."

"*Okay*." She pouted like a disgruntled teenager and huffed.

I laughed.

The new chicken coop was a two by three metre walk-in shed, constructed from some old flooring chipboard I had saved during the renovations. Inside there was a heat lamp, plenty of sticks for roosting, a dozen nesting boxes and, at ground level, a duck house. The outside was protected against the elements by a double layer of plastic and roofing felt. For easy access and egg collection, the nesting boxes had a hinged roof.

After a wild night of rain and wind, we were both eager to see how our new flock had faired. In the morning I opened the door to the coop and stood back. One by one, like sleepy dormice emerging from hibernation, the hens shuffled out, blinking at the daylight and pecking inquisitively at their new surroundings. Next came two baby ducks, fluffy white with large yellow beaks and enormous pink clown feet. Both were Aylesburys.

"Oh, they're so cute," Lesley sighed, "and so small."

"They'll soon grow," I replied. "The others doubled in size every week."

"I remember." Lesley craned her neck and peered into the coop. "Did you get them?"

"Don't worry. They're in there."

Right on cue, the final two chickens made their entrance. These were Buff Orpingtons. A hen and a rooster. Much larger than the other chickens, their fluffy feathers were a soft golden colour, puffed out so they looked almost circular.

"They're a heritage breed," my wife said. "Good layers and quite friendly too."

"What shall we call them?"

"I gave it some thought and came up with Bruce and Sheba," Lesley said.

"Sounds fine."

"I officially name you Bruce and Sheba," my wife called out, waving her arm dramatically.

Apparently satisfied with their new designations, the two Orpingtons began exploring the pen. Sheba quickly found the feeder and sampled a few pellets before kicking her heels and scratching the surface in search of a juicy worm. Bruce was more interested in checking out his new harem of attractive hens. Head held high, proudly displaying his magnificent red comb and wattle, our rooster strutted across the cage with all the elegance of the King of Siam.

"He's very handsome," Lesley commented.

Without so much as a by-your-leave, Bruce mounted one of the less observant hens. His unanticipated advance was met with an angry squawk and a flurry of feathers.

"Well that wasn't very romantic," Lesley sniggered.

"Perhaps he needs to pick some flowers," I suggested.

Undeterred, the mighty Bruce headed for the next nearest hen. But forewarned is forearmed and the young girls began to scatter like participants at a bull run. The amorous advance quickly turned into a comical chase. Even the ducks ran for cover, quacking and flapping into the coop. Chickens can run surprisingly fast, particularly when they are not feeling affectionate towards their much larger pursuer. Bruce wasn't helping his case. Being so large and fluffy, he had a lot of bulk to move. Keeping up with the scattering hens was proving to be rather difficult, until he discovered a more efficient method of perambulation. He began to skip.

Lesley burst out laughing.

"Oh, Bruce, you silly bird," she groaned.

"It may be an efficient way of getting around, but he does

look rather effeminate."

Finally admitting defeat, the mighty rooster slowed to a leisurely walk. Making his way to the highest end of the cage, he crowed loudly and ruffled his feathers.

"Never mind, Bruce," Lesley called. "They'll soon come around."

But Bruce's disappointing morning held one more twist. As he puffed out his feathers, there was a mighty gust of wind which blew him over. Like a golden tumbleweed and at the mercy of the wind, he rolled end over end across the muddy cage floor. Stopped only by the netting on the other side, Bruce finished his inelegant undulating journey upside-down and covered in mud.

"Best not to say anything," I whispered.

Hoping to preserve what little pride remained for the hapless Casanova, we crept away, suppressing our laughter until we were safely out of earshot.

***

"This may be my last golf lesson old chap," Ticker warned, as he put his arm around my shoulder.

"Your golf is that good now?" I joked. "I must be a better coach that I thought. Perhaps I should charge more."

"It looks like we'll be moving abroad," he tutted, ignoring my jibe.

"Where too?"

"Probably Jakarta."

"Jakarta!" I exclaimed. "Isn't that in Indonesia?"

"That's right," Ticker nodded. "It's on the island of Java."

"That's great news for you, but I'll be sorry to see you go," I said, as we walked towards the first tee. "I take it this is a promotion?"

Ticker winced and scratched his beard. It was a new feature on his otherwise handsome face.

"It's more of a sideways deployment. At least I've still got a job, unlike some people," he tutted. "What with the recession and everything, my employer is shutting down their operation in Ireland. They've loads of new projects in Indonesia. Plenty of bridges for me to build."

"It's all rather sudden. How's your wife taking the news?" I asked.

"Slightly better than my bank manager," he quipped. "One of my rental properties is empty and the people in the other are three months behind with their rent. The bank was happy enough, right up until they were nationalised."

"Has that caused a change of policy then?"

"It does if you've just lost a bundle betting on their shares." He grimaced and rolled his eyes.

"Oh, I'd forgotten about that," I groaned in sympathy. "I'm so sorry."

"Ack, these things happen. Not to worry." He casually waved my concerns away, then winked devilishly. "Any chance of a discount?"

I laughed and nodded. "This one's on me."

"I hope the rain holds off," he said, glancing at the glowering sky. The cloud base above looked like dark violet cotton wool. "Are you keeping busy here?"

"Not at all," I sighed. "Things have gone very quiet. This is my first lesson this week. For some reason, people seem to think paying the mortgage is more important than golf lessons."

"I know that feeling," Ticker laughed. "Have you finished that golf book you were writing? You promised me an advance copy."

"I'm getting there, but it seems to be taking forever to pull together all the strands. I spent a day with a colleague last week shooting pictures to support the various golf tips. Now I need to edit around three hundred photos, adding lines and arrows and all that stuff."

"With an important project, it's better to do it slowly and right than fast and wrong."

"That's what my wife said," I smiled.

"Clever woman," he winked. He pointed down the fairway. "Shall I go first?"

I was about to agree, but suddenly changed my mind.

"Let's wait until the tornado has passed," I suggested.

"Huh?" Ticker frowned.

I smiled and pointed over his shoulder. A couple of kilometres away, a small tornado had just touched down and begun traversing along the hilltop.

"Oh, my word," Ticker exclaimed, fumbling for his camera. "I must film this."

Tornados are not unheard of in Ireland, but they are rare. For the next five minutes, we watched the twister's eerily silent progress. Although most of the hill was open fields, there were several houses visible along its route.

"I hope it didn't cause any damage," I said, as the whirlwind dissipated.

"It was only a baby. I saw much worse when I was in America," Ticker replied. "I imagine it shook a few tiles at worst."

"It's the first one I've seen." I looked at my watch. "We'd better get on with your lesson."

"One last time," he said.

"One last time," I repeated, as we shook hands.

17 – The Final Roar

Returning from our morning walk, the dogs bounded enthusiastically across the grassy meadow towards Lesley. She was standing by the new chicken run and making a series of complicated hand gestures suggestive that, while she was pleased to see we had all returned safely from our jaunt, it would be appreciated if we could be rather quieter as something magical had happened. Unable to read semaphore, Lady and Kia circled her legs like inelegant cats, whilst Amber yapped and bounced excitedly as she added several muddy pawprints to Lesley's jeans. Romany stoically moved to one side where she balanced precariously on her bum and patiently waited her turn for a fuss.

"Oh for goodness' sake!" Lesley laughed. "I only saw you an hour ago. Be quiet."

"What's the matter?" I asked.

My wife held a finger to her lips and nodded towards the cage. The dogs had settled, but unable to hear anything unusual, I simply frowned and shrugged my shoulders. Lesley rolled her eyes in frustration and gestured more forcefully towards the cage. In one corner of the chicken run I had recently added a small nesting box enclosed within a little cage. For almost three weeks Sheba, our Orpington hen, had been sitting on a batch of eggs. Two were hers, but the other eight had been donated by a kindly friend. I was about to repeat my earlier enquiry when I heard a distinctive sound. It was the gentle cheeping of a new-born chick.

"We have babies," Lesley whispered, her eyes gleaming with glee.

"Have you seen them yet?"

"No. My chicken husbandry book says they'll come out in a day or so."

"I can't wait," I grinned.

"Me neither," she replied.

"I wonder what they'll look like."

"Apparently the flock the donated eggs came from is quite exotic, so the chicks could be an interesting mix of colours and shapes."

"I wish I could see." I leaned forward to peer into the nesting box.

"Leave them alone," Lesley commanded. Taking my elbow, my wife led me reluctantly towards the house. "Come and have a cup of tea."

"It's a good job I made the cage stronger. We saw paw prints along the forest path. A big cat had chased a deer."

"Are you on about that again?" she huffed. My dear wife maintained a policy of polite disbelief when it came to big foot, big cats and big political promises.

"The prints were the size of my fist," I pleaded, pulling out my phone. "I took pictures."

We stopped under the coverway while I shared my snaps.

"You see?" I exclaimed.

"But that's your watch," she grunted.

"It's for scale." I pointed. "This is the foot print."

Without her glasses, my wife squinted, frowned and shrugged.

"I can't see it."

I groaned in frustration, put my phone back in my pocket and led the way towards the house. But before we took three steps, something caught my eye.

"Can you see that?" I asked, pointing upwards.

"Oh wow!" she exclaimed.

Sitting on a stone ledge just below the clearlight roof was a large bird of prey. It had dark brown wings and a speckled beige chest. Above a wickedly sharp looking hooked beak, two yellow eyes watched us with calm curiosity.

"How beautiful," I whispered. "Is it a kestrel?"

"No. It's a sparrowhawk. It probably flew in here after a bird." Lesley gently pulled me towards the house. "Leave it be, it'll fly out on its own."

"Let me take a picture first." I fumbled for my phone. "Just in case you don't believe I saw it."

"Idiot!" My wife laughed and gave me a mighty shove.

***

When we left our busy lives behind and moved to the sleepy hills and sweeping moorlands of rural County Clare, Lesley and I imagined our time would be our own. We pictured long lazy sunlit days where the minutes and hours of our semi-retirement were a bountiful commodity we could squander at our pleasure. It is not so.

For Lesley, the garden and market are like twin furnaces, demanding regular stoking to keep the fire alive, hungrily consuming every minute of her time. My days were similarly devoured.

The bulk of the structural renovations were done, except for the old music studio which I had delayed attacking as it was still in use as a storage area. As Joanne and Mark would be visiting sufficiently close to Christmas to warrant an exchange of gifts, the erection of a tree and various decorations was looking unavoidable. With this in mind, Lesley insisted the improvements to the centre of the house were completed by the beginning of December. Although the required tasks were largely cosmetic, it was fiddly work and therefore even more time-consuming than doing the big stuff. The deadline was months away, but time was tight, particularly as I was writing a book, a regular column for the local newspaper and trying to keep my business afloat.

Despite a pretty substantial drop in the number of golf lessons I was conducting, I hadn't seen a reduction in business costs or a compensatory increase in my free time. In an ideal world, I would conduct all my lessons on a Monday, leaving the rest of the week free to write and work on the renovations to the house. Like a cruel irony, my clients' availability never fitted conveniently into my master plan, leaving my diary untidily dotted with single lessons at odd times. Should a coincidence of golfing enthusiasm deliver two or three clients on the same day, their lessons were inevitably spaced several hours apart. Logistically, with travel time and preparation, one lesson takes almost as much time as three. I have tried using the downtime to catch up on some writing, but to make any real progress I need a clear desk and a quiet room, free from distractions. In the end it's a better use of my time to swap the laptop for my golf clubs and play a few holes while I wait.

I enjoy writing. I find it cathartic and beneficial. Writing instructional material is also an excellent way to test and consolidate your understanding of your own specialist subject. But writing can be a thankless task.

Apart from the challenge of convincing a publisher to take on your work, all your family will see is endless hours at the computer, liberally sprinkled with fear, doubt and self-loathing, while you create, edit and re-edit your writing, without the guarantee of anything positive to show for the time spent. To make any substantial progress, the writing guides tell us an author is supposed to work regular hours, as in any proper job, some even suggest putting on a suit and driving around the block, before beginning work. Once seated, the writer should type diligently for several hours, focusing on volume, rather than substance or quality, as that element will be corrected during the editing stage. I fail miserably on all these points – and many others.

Personally, I can only write when the mood takes me, or as a print deadline looms. Regardless of the pressure, I will frequently become distracted, wasting endless minutes staring out of the window in search of an elusive word or sentence. Sometimes my writing progress is painfully slow, but on other occasions the words seem to flow into my head faster than I can type.

Perhaps the biggest difficulty for an author is there are always other things that I could be doing instead of tapping laboriously at the keyboard, but I know that if I relent the writing will remain unfinished, probably forever. Thankfully Lesley is an incredibly patient and understanding wife. She has generously given me the space and time I need to get the job done. For that I am eternally grateful.

***

As the house was finally taking shape, so too was the garden – only more so. For once the climatic conditions had been perfect for growing; not too hot and just the correct amount of rain. On the west coast of Ireland, spring and autumn can often be the delightfully light and tasty bread to an otherwise dreary sandwich. But this year the summer was a cracker and Lesley's earlier hard work in the garden produced a bumper crop of delicious vegetables along with a dazzling array of colourful shrubs and flowers.

During the years I had worked on the house, Lesley had toiled in the garden. Despite her bad back, she had turned the rocky embankments on either side of our 80-metre driveway into wide flowerbeds, beautiful to behold and attractive to a plethora of butterflies and bees. Around and within the polytunnel she had introduced many plants to act as companions to the food crops. Some of these flowers, like aquilegia and weigela, would attract pollinating insects, whilst the marigold and others would naturally deter pests.

To my eye, the deep flowerbeds were the crowning jewel of the garden. Ireland has a temperate climate, suitable for cultivating many hundreds of plants and Lesley seemed to have grown most of them. To name but a few, there were white flowered choisya, lilac syringa, red potentilla, orange euphorbia, purple phygelius, red white and pink papaver along with broom, deutzia and hibiscus. In the evenings the air was heavy with the scent from roses, dahlia, tulips, philadelphus mock orange, hebe and honeysuckle. Transformed from a bland field of rough meadow grass, this multicoloured palette of scented delight was a fitting companion to our newly renovated house.

Where flowers can grow, weeds will thrive. Throughout that glorious summer Lesley had a challenge to keep the garden tidy and pest free.

"Why don't you get some help?" I suggested one evening.

Exhausted from a day of weeding in the hot sun, Lesley was slumped on the couch, trying hard to keep her eyes open.

"What did you have in mind?" she mumbled. "We can't afford to hire someone."

"Chickens!" I replied.

"What about the chickens?"

"The chickens are constantly scrapping for bugs and worms. They're great at removing weeds, but their enclosure is just dust, except for the wet bit around the duck pond. It hasn't a blade of grass left, so I was thinking we should let them out."

"What about foxes?" she asked.

"It's a bit of a risk, but you're out there all day so an attack is unlikely."

"Well..." Lesley chewed her lip.

"You said ducks are very good at eradicating slugs," I added.

"Okay. We'll give it a go." My wife nodded and smiled. "But the chicks will have to stay in their pen until they are bigger."

"Agreed."

Chickens are quick learners. Soon they were contentedly ranging far and wide around the garden in search of the juiciest bugs. Always watchful for predators, they did a good job of uprooting the smaller weeds whilst leaving the more established plants undisturbed. The ducks were happy to wander about, making quiet 'plock-plock' sounds and filling their bellies with slugs.

There is something very calming about having loose chickens quietly pecking and scratching about the place, it feels so natural. My plan seemed to have worked well, until the day Lesley tried digging the vegetable garden. Within seconds of the spade entering the earth, a dozen chickens sprinted across the lawn to investigate the newly turned soil.

"Gerroff!" I heard her shout, but the chickens persisted.

"Shoo!" she growled, gently pushing them with her boot.

I came over to investigate.

"Having fun?" I asked.

"I can't work like this," she complained.

"I was talking to the chickens," I joked.

My wife delivered a glare that could freeze water at 50 paces and brandished her spade in a distinctly unfriendly fashion. I swiftly stepped out of range and waited until the vein in her forehead stopped pulsing.

"It's not their fault," I explained. "Chickens have two modes, follow or flight. As you are clearly not a fox, they probably see you as a very large chicken, capable of uncovering worms on an industrial scale."

My disarming grin fell on stony ground.

"It was your idea to let them out," she responded through gritted teeth. "So, I suggest you keep them out of my way."

I did my best, but our chooks were rather persistent. Unaware of Lesley's desire to make progress with the gardening, they attempted to outdo each other, making ever more death-defying dives for worms, outwardly oblivious to the angry gardener and her plunging spade. Thankfully no chickens were accidentally decapitated, and I learned to let them out only on non-digging days.

Each evening at around dusk, I walk up towards the chicken pen, rattling a plastic bucket containing some wild bird seed and shouting, "Here chick-chick-chiiickens!" Within seconds they appear, running along with comical enthusiasm, as they follow me back towards their pen. After a quick count I lock them away for the night. Sometimes a chicken is missing, and a frantic search begins. Usually the absent hen is discovered half an hour later, stubbornly digging under some bush to get just one more worm before bedtime.

***

"I believe you," Lesley said, leaning on her spade.

"Makes a change," I quipped, walking towards the vegetable garden. "What do you believe?"

"About the big cat."

"You said there were no big cats in Ireland. What's changed your mind?"

Lesley tutted at my sarcastic comment and pointed towards the pine forest behind our land.

"While you were out, Lady and Kia went exploring up there," she explained. "They were mooching about for a while, then suddenly all hell broke loose. Lady was yelping, Kia was woofing and even Amber and Romany were considering climbing through the hedge and joining the chase."

"And you think they were after a big cat?" I asked.

"Definitely," she rolled her eyes. "Just as it sounded like they had cornered something, there was a mighty roar and a hiss. It sounded exactly like that leopard we saw at the zoo."

"Wow," I exclaimed. "And what did our brave doggies do?"

"More than anything, their response was what convinced me you were right." Lesley grimaced a grin. "Our mighty hunters turned and ran. They were back here in about five seconds and both dogs had their tails between their legs."

The exact nature of the prowling predator would remain a mystery. Two days later the forestry workers arrived with their huge machines to cut a series of firebreaks. For a week, accompanied by the sounds of sawing and stacking, the huge, yellow, diesel-powered vehicles roared and beeped their way through the forest. I guess the noise was enough to discourage even the most determined leopard. I haven't seen it since.

***

On the first frosty morning of autumn I went to light the stove for the first time in many months. It was a shock to realise our wood store was almost empty. During the previous winter we had burned most of the waste wood from the renovations and all the remaining stack of peat that came with the house. Another winter was fast approaching, and we were almost out of fuel. After arranging for our heating oil tank to be filled, I began searching for a supply of kiln-dried firewood. Unfortunately, I was out of luck. Most people had taken their deliveries during the summer and the stock that remained was fearsomely expensive.

"It would be cheaper to burn money," I growled.

"You'll have to keep looking," Lesley said. "I don't want to burn coal and peat is almost as bad for the environment."

Through a friend, I discovered a local sawmill would deliver a lorry load of off-cut timber for just a few hundred euro, all I had to do was cut it into logs. The wood was mostly pine and not of particularly good quality, being largely the slabs of bark and wood created when a round tree trunk is trimmed into a square. Nonetheless, it was cheap fire wood and would burn, although not with the same heat as better quality woods like cedar or oak. Inevitably, just a few minutes after the last bundle was unloaded, it began to rain.

I managed to lash down a large blue gazebo, to keep me and the wood reasonably dry while I set about turning 30-foot long slabs of wood into tidy logs that would fit into the stove. I did my best to keep everything watertight, covering the wood pile with plastic and working under the gazebo, but with the rain and high humidity, our prospective fuel was soon covered in a smelly black slime. The wood was unseasoned, quite damp and, thanks to the nonstop rain, getting wetter by the day. To get any heat efficiency out of firewood, it needs to be cut, stacked and air dried for about a year before it is burned. It quickly became obvious this load was going to do little to heat the house for the foreseeable future and we were going to have to buy a lot of coal or peat if we were going to keep warm.

The rain began falling in October and carried on relentlessly for what seemed like weeks. Soon the lane at the back of the house was running like a small river. Days later the pond overflowed, the meadow was flooded, and the chicken pen looked like a mud bath. We are fortunate to live at the top of a hill where the water can drain away, but down below the effects of the worst rain on record was horrific to behold.

The unrelenting deluge continued day after dreadful day, drenching the soil until the water gradually ran out of places to go. Rivers and lakes overflowed. Inexorably the fields and roads began to flood, so much so that several towns and small villages were completely cut off. Hundreds of farmers were unable to save their stocks of winter feed and many tragically also lost much of their livestock. We heard numerous heart-breaking stories of families and businesses that had lost everything they owned. With tough times already upon us, many of these poor people were uninsured and had to rely on charity or friends for food, clothing and accommodation. Like many others, we couldn't afford much, but we gave whatever we could. In mid-December, the rain finally stopped and the water gradually receded, giving way to recriminations and the inevitable public enquiry.

Because the Shannon basin is low lying with only a gentle gradient to the sea, the rivers are slow to clear excess water. During the boom years there had been an extraordinary increase in the number of houses and industrial estates built on natural flood plains. The flooding was a disaster waiting to happen. Although insignificant when compared to the horrific Indian Ocean earthquake and tsunami, the flooding throughout the west of Ireland was a significant local disaster. Coming on top of an already deep recession and high unemployment, it hit the area hard.

***

Our year finished on a brighter note. Joanne and Mark were to visit during part of the festive period, but only on the strict understanding we would "do a proper Glenmadrie Christmas". With snow laying thick on the ground and feeling enthused with the yuletide spirit, Lesley and I took a trip to Limerick, splashed out on a nice plastic Christmas tree, along with a few boxes of decorations, and in no time our living room resembled Santa's grotto. A few days later, I delicately picked my way along the ice-packed roads to Shannon Airport to collect our guests. Safely back at Glenmadrie, the festivities began.

Keeping to the strict traditions of the festive period, we ate too much, imbibed alcoholic beverages, wore our loosest clothing, watched old movies on television, exchanged silly gifts, played board games, argued passionately about the rules and generally ignored the religious significance of the holiday. Most days we had a late breakfast of French toast with lashings of maple syrup, followed by a long walk through the forest with the dogs. During the afternoon, we sustained ourselves by snacking on satsumas, chocolates, mince pies and crisps. Our evening meal was chicken for the carnivores, with a vegetarian alternative for me, piles of roasted potatoes, parsnips, sweet potato, carrot and delicious boiled vegetables like kale or cabbage, along with cranberry jelly, bread sauce and gravy. For afters I had prepared an American style cheesecake, from my mother's secret recipe. Made with cream cheese, sugar, egg white and sour cream, it weighs in at almost one thousand calories a portion – pure indulgence!

After two days of such slothfulness, we became bored, bloated and restless, so we decided to get active. Mark did sterling work filling a couple of empty barrels with chopped kindling for the fire and helped me clear up the last of the rubbish generated during the renovations. Indoors, Lesley and Joanne sat by a roaring fire doing some mother and daughter crafts.

On the third day the fog and low cloud gave way to a hard frost and crystal-clear skies, which gave Mark and Joanne the opportunity to take some long romantic walks, accompanied by our decidedly unromantic dogs. As they ambled along the wooded hillside, they took some stunning photographs of the misty snow-covered valley below, glinting in the brilliant sunlight. On the last night we had great fun, a few beers and many laughs, playing a family game of darts out in the wing, where I had set up the board. For a while the competition was fierce and the atmosphere lovingly acrimonious, as we battled uncompromisingly to become champions. Despite the fun, our interest slowly began to wane, perhaps distracted by our inability to hit the required double – or even the dartboard. As the newly painted wall became peppered with indentations, proving that alcohol did not compensate for a lack of skill and practice, we called it a draw and gladly returned to the welcoming warmth of the sitting room.

The break was over all too soon. Late on the 31st of December, with Joanne and Mark safely back in England and Lesley fast asleep indoors, I took the dogs out on our meadow. The sky was clear and the quarter moon reflected brightly off the frost-laden snow beneath my feet. Without the need for a torch, we puffed clouds of moisture and crunched our way to the highest point of the land. There, under that magnificent starfield, I silently watched a celestial firework display of meteors flashing across the sky. As the clock ticked past midnight, I welcomed in the new year, missing absent friends but thankful for the privilege of living in Ireland.

18 – That Sinking Feeling

For several reasons, it can be difficult to identify the start of spring in Ireland. Christians and Pagans celebrate the anticipated exit from winter on the first day of February. While Christians call the first day of spring St Brigid's Day, in honour of one of our three patron saints, the pre-Christian name for the same day was Imblog or Imbloc. Perhaps in a nod to the church, the meteorological date for the first day of spring was also on St Brigid's Day, although in what may be a wink towards climate change, this has now been changed to the first day of March. Alternatively, the Old Farmer's Almanac defines the Vernal equinox as the start of spring. In summary, it's complicated.

For me, spring at Glenmadrie begins when nature says so – or the rain gets a little warmer. Soon the moor will discard the dull beige of dormant winter grass, turning green as the new growth pushes through. The heather flowers add swathes of purple, dotted white with cotton heads swaying in the warm breeze. On our meadow the wild flowers attract the first flying insects and the pond rumbles to the amorous growling of frogs. Above us the skylarks play their violin concertos, hanging almost invisible in the azure sky. As we walk through the grass, swallows zip past our legs at impossible speeds, picking off the insects we've disturbed. City dwellers may not realise how quiet nature becomes during the winter months, but living in such a remote rural area, we're particularly aware of when the birds begin singing again. When the still and frosty mornings of late winter are banished by warming sunshine and the air is heavy with the sweet fragrance of flowering gorse, it's time for our feathered friends to lift our flagging spirits once again.

With a melodious harmony of competing yet strangely congruous tunes, every bird will strive to find a mate. In the comparative silence of the forest, far away from the noise pollution of modern life, this avian orchestra is surprisingly loud. But it is worth a few sleepless mornings to experience the privilege of a dawn chorus, unsullied by traffic noise. I have often laid dozing in the half-light and pondered what tales these melodies convey. Do they sing of great deeds of masculine prowess, or of the fantastic nests they will build, or perhaps just a promise of love everlasting? It's fun to imagine the stories they tell. Soon they will fall silent again, for there is danger in being noticed. Once the mating is done the birds become wary of sparrowhawks, kestrels, hen harriers, buzzards, pine martens, polecats and foxes. In a dangerous world, it's best to be a quiet bird – unless you're a chicken.

Chickens are astoundingly noisy birds, particularly when they're announcing to the world the successful laying of another egg. Typically, the layer will begin by squawking her announcement from the steps of the coop. Soon, like sisters in childbirth, a second chicken will add her congratulations, quickly followed by a third. In under a minute the entire flock of hens will join in cackling and screeching and shrieking. To the untrained ear, this commotion is disturbingly like the panicked warning cries accompanying a fox attack. In such a situation, it is acceptable to grab a broomstick and make a futile dash up the garden. Not for the first time have I found myself hanging on to the chicken run netting, breathless, half-naked and wearing only one muddy slipper, whilst the hens peer through the gap in the front of my dressing gown with hungry eyes. Ignoring my shouts for quiet, the cacophony continues to build. The hens circle and shriek like unruly soldiers on parade, only falling silent when Sargent Major Bruce angrily calls them to order.

You may be wondering what became of our baby chickens. Well, they grew up, largely out of sight. Unlike commercially reared chicks born in an incubator, happy to sit on your hand and be photographed for commercials, ours were painfully shy – and with good reason. The natural world is a dangerous place for a tiny hatchling, full of hungry predators and huge scary chickens. Furthermore, Sheba was a magnificent adoptive mother. She kept her little babies inside their coop for most of the day, or hidden away under her wings whenever someone approached. Consequently, apart from fleeting glimpses, neither Lesley or I got a good look at the new arrivals until a month after they'd hatched. By then they had lost most of their fluff and began growing proper feathers. To my mind they looked comically untidy and rather startled. Somewhere along the way, three chicks had gone missing.

"It was probably rats," I suggested.

"Or a kestrel," Lesley replied.

"Possibly." I grimaced. "On the other hand, it's equally likely they were eaten by another chicken. You've seen how quick they are to scoff a mouse, a little chick would stand no chance."

"When you see their enthusiasm for chasing the occasional rodent, there's no doubt they're descended from dinosaurs."

"No doubt at all," I agreed, nodding towards the pen. "Dinosaurs or not, those chicks are cute."

"I agree, although we could have a problem." My wife pointed towards a couple of fledglings apparently involved in some sort of acrimonious territorial dispute. "I think those two are cockerels."

"Is that a problem?" I asked.

"Yep." Lesley pinched her lips and nodded. She'd read our book on chicken husbandry. "They'll fight. Possibly to the death."

"Oh."

Chickens are lovely creatures with a delightfully simple outlook on life. All the hens do is eat, sleep and make little chickens. Cock birds are so focused on the making little chickens bit, they are inclined to forget the other two tasks. However, in the presence of a competitor they will fight with all the aggression appropriate to their dinosaur DNA. All flocks have a very strict hierarchy, the pecking order, with a cock bird at the top of the ladder and the hens below in descending order of size or aggression. It's hardly a management style appropriate to the modern world, but it has served domestic poultry well for almost 10,000 years. Bruce, our mighty Orpington cockerel, sits unashamedly at the top of the ladder – despite his tendency to skip effeminately or blow over in a strong wind. His mate, Sheba, is the largest hen and therefore second in the pecking order. Since becoming a mother she's developed an aggressive streak, particularly if someone is attempting to clean her nesting box. From there on down, the order becomes a little more fluid, depending on how hungry each chicken is and the relative sizes of the fast-growing babies.

Once the chicks had grown sufficiently, they were able to join the other hens on their daily jaunts into the garden. Here they quickly learned to eat bugs, disturb young weeds and keep a watchful eye for predators. Now they were out of the cage, I could conduct an accurate count. Our flock of 29 included two ducks, 24 hens and three cocks.

***

Of all my habits, at least those I'm willing to discuss in public, perhaps the most problematic is my tendency to go off-piste when I'm walking the dogs. Lesley may disappear for hours on unannounced autumnal fruit-picking expeditions but, other than berry-juice stained fingers and a sugar rush, she is unlikely to come to any real harm. My preference is to explore the rugged open moorland, scale high hilltops and roam deep into ancient woodlands, where a slip or fall could prove to be terminal. I'm by no means a risk taker, quite the opposite, but I am an inquisitive explorer with similarly curious dogs. One of the greatest pleasures of living in rural Ireland is the privilege of rambling alone on a carpet of soft moss through a forest of towering trees, in the knowledge I may be the first person ever to have walked here.

When hiking across the uneven surface of the moor with its hidden lumps and concealed grassy hollows, it's easy to stumble and fall. To progress with any appreciable speed across the boggy ground, I have developed a special technique – carry a stick and keep the knees bent. I may look like an old man who has recently suffered an unfortunate bout of incontinence, but the permanently bent knees act as an effective suspension system, efficiently absorbing the unexpected changes in elevation. Thus protected, I can happily stride along with a steely grimace and burning thighs. Despite almost eliminating the risk of a stumble with my bandy-legged silly walk, these peatbogs still hold many dangers for the unsuspecting rambler.

Without its thick layer of peat, the moor would be a desolate but beautiful landscape of bare rock. This is the case in the Burren National Park. In places, the peat on the moor opposite Glenmadrie is several metres deep. Where it has been undermined by subterranean streams, deep fissures can open. These cracks in the peat may be just a few inches wide at the surface, or hidden by moss and grass, but they are dangerous nonetheless. Worse still are bog holes, deep depressions filled with liquid peat and covered with floating moss. They are almost impossible to spot and can easily swallow an unsuspecting cow. A good rule of thumb when walking on the moor is to avoid noticeably boggy areas, unless you are familiar with the route.

As the moors in our area are high in the hills, sudden changes in the weather are an almost daily event. In several places there are steep rocky cliffs, perfect for feral goats and nesting hen harriers, but not so good for hapless walkers. One morning when I was strolling along the exposed clifftops, I was suddenly enveloped by a rolling wave of thick hill fog. Within a few seconds, the temperature dropped by several degrees and the visibility was reduced so severely, I could hardly see my feet. Conscious I was just a few steps from the cliff edge, I hooked the dogs to their leads and let their sense of smell lead me home – or to certain death.

"You should have used your walking stick to tap the ground," Lesley suggested, after I had related my tale.

"I considered that," I replied, "but I imagined standing still for hours, frozen in fear because I couldn't feel the ground, only to discover when the fog had cleared that the end had fallen off my stick!"

"Idiot!" she tutted, shaking her head.

"Anyway, the dogs kept me safe." I reached down and tickled Lady's ear. She pushed against my leg and groaned in pleasure.

"I wouldn't trust them," she laughed. "You're lucky they didn't take you over the edge in pursuit of some goats."

A couple of weeks later my off-piste activities put me in deep trouble.

My wife was off in England, caring for her mother who had just come out of hospital after a bunion operation. The trip was originally planned to last for a few days, but Muriel's age and failing mental capacity were taking a toll, so Lesley's stay was stretched to three weeks. Left unsupervised and perhaps a little bored, the dogs and I decided to explore a new section of forest around a kilometre from Glenmadrie. Deviating from the path that led downhill to the river, we climbed an embankment, scrambled through a ditch and pushed through some bushes, before breaking through into the forest. Beneath the towering pine trees, the ground was relatively clear, but the many low branches made walking difficult. Crouching low I managed to squeeze through. After 20 metres, I found a well-worn deer trail and my progress improved significantly.

It was pleasantly mild and the air smelled like damp earth mixed with pine sap and mushrooms. We walked on for 20 minutes or so, gradually going deeper into the forest. The ground beneath our feet was thick with pine needles and dry, save for a few damp areas caused by underground springs. To avoid sinking in, these muddy patches are best crossed in a couple of quick strides. Without a breath of wind to disturb the trees, I felt a tremendous sense of calm. The sensation of stillness was enhanced by the melodic singing of a lone blackbird sitting in the highest branch. It was a welcome accompaniment and greatly added to my enjoyment of the day.

Just as I was considering back-tracking to head home, we encountered another wet patch. Confidently I took three quick strides forward, but I had been deceived by the thick carpet of pine needles covering what turned out to be a large muddy pool. The surface gave way and I quickly sank into the sticky goo.

"Oops," I laughed, wobbling precariously to keep my balance. I tried to take a retrograde step, but the slightest movement caused me to sink lower.

"Eek," I squealed as the treacle-like gloop spilled into my Wellingtons.

The dogs circled the muddy bog hole with cautious curiosity.

"You lot are supposed to warn me about things like this," I complained.

Lady was eyeing me unsympathetically. I imagined her saying, *"If I played in the mud, you'd tell me off."*

With each movement I was sinking lower. The stinky slime had reached my belt. With a groan, I remembered my new mobile phone was in the pocket of my jeans.

"Aren't you supposed to run for help?" I asked the dogs.

Ignoring my jibe, they settled down to watch the fun.

My downward progress showed no sign of slowing. Feeling nothing beneath my feet, my mind flashed back to tales of cattle drowning in bog holes. Like a mouse in the jaws of a python, I was inexorably being devoured. I began to fear for my safety.

"What are you supposed to do in quicksand?" I asked.

Amber nudged a stick with her nose and woofed, Kia watched with detached interest, Lady gave a wolfish grin and Romany balanced on her bum and farted. So much for my loyal saviours.

"I remember," I exclaimed. "I have to swim to safety!"

The gloop was already up to my bellybutton, but there was just enough of me above the surface to do the job. Hinging from the waist I thrust my chest forward into a muddy swallow-dive. With my neck and chin in the oily peat, I kicked with my feet whilst pulling with my arms. It was like trying to breaststroke through custard. After thirty seconds of grunting and pulling I paused to catch my breath for a few seconds. At first the task seemed hopeless, but realising my body was edging closer to horizontal gave me the encouragement to push on. A full minute later I was swimming on the surface and soon after, my fingers brushed a root. Clinging desperately to my lifeline, I hauled myself to safety. Like a creature emerging from the black lagoon, I flopped face-down on the warm earth and groaned in gratitude. Behind me the pool quivered and bubbled silently, as if it were frustrated by my escape.

Once I'd got my breath back, I staggered upright, and on shaking legs, led the way home. My boots squelched uncomfortably, my underpants felt as if they were filled with treacle, and I smelled so bad the dogs were giving me a wide berth. My clothes were saturated with sticky liquid peat, so there was no way I could wear them indoors. The stink was so foul, even the midges were repelled. Five minutes under the cold spray of the hosepipe made little impression, other than adding gossamer wings of oily water to my crotch and arms. It's a good job Glenmadrie is remote as I had no other option than to strip naked and tiptoe through to the downstairs shower. By the time I was clean, the water was running cold.

"How was your day?" Lesley asked, when I phoned later that night.

"It was quiet," I replied, casually. "But I slipped in some mud and had to wash my clothes."

Over the following two days, I took several more showers and depleted most of our toiletries before the smell of the rotting peat had finally gone. On the up-side, I was alive and my mobile phone seemed undamaged.

***

We named our two new cockerels Bubble and Squeak. From humble beginnings as comically untidy chicks, they grew quickly and soon developed their wattle, comb, hackles, spurs and other cockerel attributes. As the two newcomers were superfluous roosters and therefore likely to be evicted or killed by the mighty Bruce, Lesley tried to rehome them, but without success.

"Nobody wants cockerels," she complained. "Except for food."

"We can't let that happen," I exclaimed. "What about the lady who supplied the eggs."

"I tried her first. She already has a cockerel and she definitely doesn't want a couple more." My wife shrugged and sighed. "The general consensus is we should kill them now or do it in a few weeks when they're ready for the cooking pot."

I grimaced. "I'd rather not."

Like the dinosaurs watching the approaching asteroid, we ignored the problem and hoped it would go away. It didn't.

Awash with the chicken equivalent of testosterone, Bubble grew tall and proud. I suspect he was a cross between an Orpington and a velociraptor. At almost three feet tall, with attractive plumage in gold, brown, and red, he was a magnificent specimen. But behind the handsome exterior hid the DNA of a ruthless killer. His eyes were two sinister, cold, black marbles set above a wickedly sharp steel-grey beak, and his claws – as large as a child's hand – were equipped with deadly razor-sharp talons. All these features combined to produce the most fearsome of cockerels – or they would have done were Bubble not such an abject coward.

Conversely, Squeak was possibly a cross between a bantam parrot and a sparrow. Standing no more than 12 inches tall, he had exotically coloured plumage and long tail feathers in various shades of yellows, reds, browns, and black, which would not have looked out of place on the finest Native American headdress. He was always the first of the three cockerels to announce the coming dawn, which he did loudly and with style, usually whilst sitting atop the chicken coup. Squeak was an enthusiastic competitor for the affection of the hens, and he was as brave as a lion, quite capable of chasing Bubble away. Perhaps because his diminutive size did not make him seem so threatening, the mighty Bruce generally ignored Squeak's presence and regular crowing, and he even turned a blind eye to some of his attempts to romantically engage hens more than twice his size. I suspect Bruce was slightly proud of the little lad. The same cannot be said for his relationship with Bubble.

Although there seemed to be a gentlemen's agreement that fighting inside the chicken coop at roosting time was unseemly, when the chickens were out on the garden or inside their cage, Bruce would attack Bubble at every opportunity. Fortunately, Bubble was careful to keep his distance, and quick to turn tail and run when he saw Bruce approaching. So for much of the day, they maintained a fragile truce. However, the urge to procreate cannot be denied – particularly for a horny young cockerel in the presence of so many attractive hens.

When not hiding from Bruce or eating hurried snacks of worms and corn, Bubble would spend his day sneaking cat-like around the garden, hiding behind bushes and rocks, in an attempt to reach the undefended rear of the flock, and more significantly, the undefended rear of one of Bruce's hens. As soon as the opportunity presented itself, Bubble would dash out from his hiding place and then unceremoniously mount the nearest unsuspecting hen, in a desperate effort to swiftly share his essence. The poor hen – deprived of the usual period of warning provided by the romantic dances and displays of the chicken world – would instantly begin squawking in shock at the unexpected assault. Seconds later, with all the speed and aggression of a sumo wrestler, wearing a chicken suit and riding a pogo stick, Bruce would skip his way through the scattering flock, making a beeline towards Bubble and his squawking victim. This left the cowardly Bubble with somewhat of a dilemma: should he immediately dismount and run for cover, or was there enough time to finish the deed and still reach safety before being caught by the vengeful Bruce? Fortunately for Bubble, whatever he lacked in bravery, he more than made up for with alacrity – and a sportsman's eye for calculating distance and speed.

The endless circle of fighting and fornication was taking a toll, particularly on the hens, who were unable to get any peace with three cockerels competing for their affections.

"I'm sorry, Nick, but we can't let this continue," Lesley said as we watched Bubble stalking another hen from behind the pumphouse.

"You mean...?" I grimaced and slowly drew a questioning finger across my throat.

"It's probably the kindest thing to do. Some of these poor hens are dead on their feet with exhaustion."

As if to emphasise the problem, Bubble burst from his hiding place like a racehorse bolting from a stable. There was a mad scramble to get away, but in the panic he easily caught one very ragged hen.

"You see?" Lesley said. "The slowest hens get caught most frequently. That one's in an awful state."

Bruce came skipping over, but he was rather too late. The deed was done, Bubble was back in hiding and the poor hen was flopping about in dazed confusion.

Acknowledging the inevitable, I nodded, sighed and rubbed my palms across my face.

"Squeak is okay," Lesley added quickly. "He's too small to cause any aggravation."

"I disagree," I joked. "This morning, I was bent over inside the coop cleaning it out when Squeak hopped up behind me and crowed. Scared the pants off me. It was so loud I stood up and hit my head on the ceiling."

My wife laughed unsympathetically. "He is rather loud for such a tiny rooster."

"If I hadn't been seeing stars, I might have wrung his neck right then."

Although she knew I was only joking, Lesley still wagged a warning finger. "Leave little Squeak alone."

"I know," I conceded. "He isn't the trouble."

For a while we watched the chickens in contemplative silence. I knew Bubble was a problem that had to be solved. Keeping him in the flock was cruel to the poor hens, but I just couldn't bring myself to do direct harm. Besides, in a fair fight with such a well-equipped dinosaur, I wasn't confident of winning.

"I'll release him into the wild," I said, breaking the silence.

"Whatever do you mean?" Lesley frowned.

"If I let him go up in the forest, then he's got a fighting chance," I explained. "He might find another flock."

Lesley nodded her consent but whispered 'coward' under her breath as she walked away.

That night, equipped with some stout working gloves for my protection, I grabbed the sleeping cockerel from his perch and slipped him quietly into a box. He was surprisingly heavy. By the light of a torch, I carried Bubble for about two kilometres, before releasing him into the forest. As soon as I opened the box, he sprang forth, squawking angrily, and dived into some undergrowth. I bade him farewell and headed home. In theory the problem was solved, but I was wrong.

It was a warm night and with the bedroom window open I was able to hear Bubble's plaintive calls gradually growing nearer as he trudged his way through the trees towards Glenmadrie. He made so much noise I anticipated every fox, pine marten, and owl in a five-mile radius would soon join the hunt. Yet, when I went to let the chickens out of their coop the following morning, there was Bubble patiently waiting to re-join the flock. Undeterred, on each of the following three nights I delivered the hapless rooster progressively deeper into the forest, only to find by the morning he had again returned to the flock.

"I give up!" I exclaimed. "He's like a bad penny, but with more lives than a cat."

"I guess we'll have to let him stay," Lesley laughed.

We may have conceded defeat, but Bruce had other ideas. Exasperated by the constant abuse of his harem, the mighty cockerel finally cracked. After a huge fight, he chased Bubble away. From then on Bruce refused to tolerate his rival's presence anywhere in the garden, chicken enclosure or coop. Bubble was an outcast.

Unable to catch the hapless chicken, I made a box where he

could sleep in safety, but this was roundly ignored. Bubble soon relocated to the wood, where he could feast on a plentiful supply of bugs, worms and even the occasional mouse. For a week he could be seen patrolling around the periphery of Bruce's territory and eyeing the hens from a safe distance. Then one day he was gone.

I carefully searched the land and the wood, but there was no sign of Bubble, not even a stray feather.

"I so hope he found another farm with a large flock of willing hens," Lesley said.

"Me too," I replied. "But I guess we'll never know."

And we never did.

19 – Crash and Burn

"There it is," I said, pointing towards a magnificent copper beach tree.

Lesley and I were visiting Coole Park, near to the village of Gort, County Galway. It's a 1,000-acre nature reserve, which was once the estate of the Gregory family. The most notable was Lady Augusta Gregory, playwright, folklorist and co-founder of the Abbey Theatre, also known as the National Theatre of Ireland.

"What's it called again?" Lesley asked. "The Writers' Tree?"

"It's the Autograph Tree," I corrected. "According to the guide book, Coole Park was used as a retreat to sooth the fevered brow and inspire the imagination of many famous writers. In 1898 Lady Gregory asked WB Yeats to carve his initials on this tree. Over the following years many more writers were invited to add their own."

"Where?" Lesley leaned forward and squinted. "I don't have my glasses."

I checked the picture in the guide book and pointed.

"Number ten."

"I still can't see it."

"I guess it's faded a bit since then." I consulted the guide book again and pointed to some of the notable names. "George Bernard Shaw, John Masefield, Jack B. Yeats, Sean Ó'Casey and Theodore Spicer Simson."

"When your golf book is published, perhaps they'll invite you to add your name," Lesley said, turning away in an attempt to hide her grin. "Although it's hardly poetry."

"It's a book about golf. That's poetry to some people," I joked.

"When will it be out?"

"In a few months," I replied. "It's off being edited, which will take a good while. After that, I've got to do the layout and add all the pictures. With our slow internet, it took ages to upload the…"

Realising my wife had lost interest in my writing project and wandered off, I jogged after her.

"Let's go this way," she called over her shoulder.

"We just came this way," I said, when I caught up.

Lesley waved the map. "I think we were heading in the wrong direction. Come on."

"This is a bit nicer than when we went to Lahinch for your birthday."

"Hmm," she grimaced. "I'll admit collecting shells on the beach in the middle of winter wasn't one of my better ideas."

"It was funny how we were both hating it, but neither of us wanted to say anything."

We walked past a collection of large grey buildings which was once the stable yard but now housed the visitors' centre. A little further along the path I spied a circular stone structure resembling a toy fort built for a wealthy child. The shape was eerily familiar.

"It looks like one of the pill boxes I used to play in when I was a child," I said. "They were old defensive positions left over from World War Two."

Lesley shrugged and shook her head. "I've never seen one."

"There were a lot on the Air Force bases, particularly in the south east of England."

My wife was squinting myopically at the map.

"It's a lime kiln," I said, helpfully.

"Our lime kiln doesn't look anything like this."

"I think this is the style of kiln you build when you have plenty of staff and lots of money. Ours was a working kiln and so is rather more functional."

"Do you think ours was ever used?"

"Absolutely!" I exclaimed. "It was built at the top of a hill, now it's on the edge of the quarry. All that lime was dug out and burned in the kiln. It probably took 20 or more years."

"But we haven't got one of those little ramps."

"I think we have, but it's under the grass," I replied.

"What makes you say that?"

"Do you remember during the really hot summer, there was a big curve of dry grass up on the meadow?" I asked.

"Uh-huh," Lesley nodded.

"It was about 50 metres long and led right to the lime kiln. I think that was the old path."

"Why didn't you say so before."

I pointed at the kiln before us.

"I only made the connection when I saw that ramp."

Further along the path we saw a horse pump. As we stopped, my wife plucked the guide book from my back pocket.

"It says here, they used to couple a horse to this pump to push it around," Lesley read, her eyes squinting like someone facing a sandstorm. "It uses suction to pull water from the lake below and pump it to the house. Pretty impressive technology for 1850."

"Look at this." I pointed at a sign. "This was all under water during the recent flooding. I bet they didn't think that would happen back in 1850."

We walked on, stopping to pet someone's dog along the way.

"I wish we'd thought to bring our dogs," I said. "They'd have loved it."

Lesley shook her head.

"Lady would have thrown up in the car and Romany is too old to walk this far. Especially after her seizure last week."

"That's the second one she's had."

"Third," Lesley corrected. "The vet says she has a heart murmur, but otherwise she's just old."

"Old, blind and cantankerous," I added. "She seems happy enough for now."

Lhasa Apsos are delightful dogs, but physically frail. Both of our previous Lhasas had passed away long before reaching Romany's 15 years. Outliving several of your loyal and beloved furry friends is a sad fact of dog ownership. Whilst accepting Romany was nearing the end of her life, we were still hoping for the best.

"As long as she isn't in any discomfort."

"I wouldn't let that happen."

"Me neither."

We strolled on, comfortable to silently relish the cool shade under the towering trees and the verdant scenery. Like children at a zoo, we read the noticeboards dotted alongside the path and peered in disappointment at the apparently empty enclosures.

"It says deer pen," my wife read.

"Someone forgot to tell the deer."

"They're probably hiding."

One interesting feature was our first sighting of a ha-ha.

"It's a ditch," I said, somewhat stating the obvious. "Albeit a rather impressive one. What's it for?"

Lesley squinted at the guidebook.

"The ha-ha or ah-ha, is a man-made ditch to confine or exclude grazing stock, but without interrupting the view. Apparently, the concept is French in origin, dating from the late 17th century."

"It's a good idea. Rather like a dry moat."

"Oh look!" Lesley pointed. "It's a red squirrel. I haven't seen one in years."

In England, the small and shy red squirrels have been all but eradicated by competition from their much larger grey cousins. It was the highlight of our day to discover these delightful creatures were still thriving here. Finishing our circuit of the park, we stopped for refreshments and bladder relief at the tea room, before heading home to provide the dogs with something similar.

During the drive we listened to the news on the radio. Greece had recently received a huge financial bailout from the EU and now angry crowds numbering in the hundreds of thousands were protesting the imposed austerity programme. Many financial analysts were predicting Ireland would be the next country to go bust. Despite an emergency budget, further raising taxes and imposing deep cuts to services, the pressure on the Irish exchequer was mounting. With a growl, Lesley leaned over and switched the radio off.

"I can't understand why Ireland needs a bailout."

"It shouldn't," I replied. "Unfortunately, it may be out of our hands. Rather like Iceland, our banks were hugely overextended with billions in foreign debt, but unlike Iceland, we can't let the banks fail and we can't burn the bondholders."

"They mentioned burning the bondholders," she said, pointing at the radio. "Didn't they just take a risky bet and now they've lost their shirts?"

"As such, yes."

"Then why do we, the tax payers, have to bail them out?" My wife folded her arms angrily. "Who are they anyway?"

"Nobody really knows," I sighed. "As I understand it, since the recession started, and tax receipts fell, Ireland needs to borrow money to keep the country afloat."

"Same as most countries just now," Lesley tutted.

"Indeed. But as confidence falls in our ability to repay that money, the cost of borrowing it goes up. Eventually you reach a stage where it isn't financially viable to borrow more."

"A bit like using a payday loan to pay the mortgage?"

I smiled and nodded. "That's a great analogy."

"So why is the government borrowing billions we can ill afford to prop up these bondholders?"

"I believe it's because they are the same people who are lending us the money to keep the country afloat."

"Blech," Lesley frowned. "How ever did that merry-go-round happen?"

I shrugged expressively. "I'm guessing we'll never know."

For a while we drove in contemplative silence.

"If Ireland goes bust," Lesley asked, "how will that affect us?"

"It's hard to say. The austerity programme in Greece is making life pretty grim for the likes of us. This recession has already hit our income hard, there's been a raft of tax rises and I can see more coming down the line. There'll be much worse to follow if the IMF is running things here."

"Will we be okay?" My wife's pale-blue eyes were wide with concern.

I felt my mouth tighten.

"I hope so. We still have a little wiggle room, but not much. For now, all we can do is tighten our belts and pray for a good harvest."

"And hope your book sells well," she added, patting me on the knee.

"That too."

***

All too soon the dam burst.

Like many others resident in this fine land, we looked on with increasing puzzlement, anger and disbelief, while Ireland – until recently one of the world's strongest economies – fell prey to the winds of misfortune.

In September, the Irish Minister for Finance revealed taxpayers were now facing a €50bn bill to bail out the banks. He announced a tough four-year budget austerity programme. In response, Irish Government bond yields rose dramatically higher as international investors fled, fearing the country wouldn't cope with the spiralling repayments. Then, just as it seemed the worst was over, an editorial in the Financial Times predicted a run on Irish banks.

With the country close to bankruptcy, the Finance Minister flew to Brussels to ask for a €67.5bn international bailout for the State. It was an extraordinary debt burden for a country with a population of just 4.5 million people. Negotiating from a desperate position of weakness, Ireland had no option but to accept the terms demanded by the troika of the European Commission, European Central Bank, and International Monetary Fund.

***

Although golf lessons were becoming few and far between, it was important to maintain the standard of my game through regular practice and play. Where once these sessions were fitted around a busy teaching schedule, now they are more likely to be combined with the weekly grocery shopping. Returning from one such trip, I was treated to a rare meteorological phenomenon.

Driving east out of Ennis, with the low autumn sun behind me, I was pleased to have missed the impending rain. Hanging over the Atlantic Ocean, a line of towering thunderclouds was heading towards land. Loaded with rain and with the sun hidden behind, they appeared like a purple bruise on the horizon, bringing an early dusk to our county town. Although sunset was two hours away, it was so dark most drivers had turned their headlights on. Unseen, somewhere in the distance, two storm cells must have parted, allowing the sun to shine through. As if some celestial being had opened a huge refrigerator door, the purple gloom was instantly flooded with a brilliant shaft of golden light. It was so dramatic, several drivers stopped their cars to take a photograph. I was one of them.

The phenomena lasted for barely a minute. As the gap in the clouds widened, the beam of gold diffused from orange through yellow to white. The sky reverted to an ordinary cloudy grey and the distant thunderheads, although still dark, looked considerably less threatening. However, as I set off again towards home, the view ahead was rather more unsettling. High in the hills there was a wide column of smoke of a colour and intensity all too familiar during this dry summer and autumn. Somewhere a large grassfire was raging.

As I drove, I couldn't resist flicking my eyes towards the hill on my left to identify the seat of the fire. Soon my demeanour changed from casual interest to genuine concern. When I turned north and began the long uphill climb towards Glenmadrie, the smoke was directly ahead. Based on its colour and thickness, the fire was intensifying. For a while I feared the very worst, but as

I drove the final stretch, I could see the flames were burning along the moor around a kilometre opposite our land.

Lesley was in the lounge, sipping her coffee and reading a book. I gave her a kiss and fussed the dogs.

"Didn't you see the fire?" I asked.

"What fire?"

"On the moor. There's a huge grass fire." I pointed to the window. "Look."

"Oh, my goodness," she exclaimed. "How did I miss that?"

"The fire's moving away from the house. There isn't even any smoke above us."

"All the same, it's a pretty big fire," she tutted. "I can't believe I didn't notice."

"I'd better call the fire brigade," I said. "Just to be on the safe side."

Once I'd made the call and checked the operator had the correct map coordinates, I told Lesley I was going outside to watch the fun. She declined my invitation to join me on the hill overlooking the moor.

"I've got dinner in the oven," she explained. "You go. I'll stay here and watch the dogs."

I strolled through our meadow and sat at the top of our quarry, where I had a perfect view of the fire. The hot smoke rose quickly, billowing into an angry beige column. I could hear the fire cracking and popping as the tinder-dry grass and gorse bushes were consumed. The yellow-flowered prickly gorse is prevalent on the hills of Ireland, for centuries it was used as a firelighter in rural cottages. The nickname *firebush* is testament to its flammability.

After about 15 minutes, the entertainment took a sinister turn. I felt the wind strengthen and shift, pushing the fire quickly to the north. The change of direction seemed to have put an old cottage directly in the path of the advancing flames. I had previously noticed the house whilst out walking with the dogs. It was about a kilometre down the hill from Glenmadrie, at the end of a long driveway and surrounded by high pine trees. I had always thought it was dilapidated and disused, but in rural Ireland the exterior condition of a property is no guarantee of its occupancy. Afterall, our home was all but derelict when we moved in. With the flames apparently just a few hundred metres away from the cottage, and conscious an elderly person could easily be overwhelmed by such a raging inferno, I decided it would be prudent to drive down and check.

By the time I had sprinted across the lawn and jumped into my car, it looked like the smoke was billowing over the cottage. The drive down took just three minutes. It was a wasted trip. The cottage was indeed empty and, in any event, the fire was nowhere near as close as it had seemed when viewed from up the hill. In fact, it was going to pass safely between the cottage and Glenmadrie. Looking up the hill, I could see the smoke was closing in on the road leading back to the house. Not wishing to be stranded by the flames, I jumped into the car and quickly headed home.

At first the short drive went swimmingly. I could see the fire was closing in from my right, but it appeared to be a safe distance away. However, I was mistaken. Although the direct line back home was well clear of danger, my path would be far from straight. To make the steep climb less severe, the road had been built in a series of tight bends. The last of these turns took me directly into the path of the fire.

Just a few hundred metres from my front gates I was plunged into darkness as the smoke billowed through the hedge. To my right I could see the ominous glow of flames leaping above the trees. Two seconds later, with all the fury and speed of an explosion, the road disappeared in a wall of fire and swirling sparks. My instincts told me attempting to reverse could be disastrous, so I jammed my right foot hard on the accelerator, gripped the wheel tightly and prayed to the blessed angels of acceleration and internal combustion to deliver me from a fiery death. As the car plunged into the cauldron of flame, the heat on the side window was so intense I had to turn my face away. The view ahead looked like the gates of hell, the road was invisible. I only kept my wheels on the tarmac by steering parallel to the embankment. Just as I started to suspect I had made the last bad mistake of my life, the car burst into daylight and roared away from the fire.

Although the drive through that tunnel of flames had taken just five seconds, it felt as if it had lasted an hour. My heart was thumping through my chest and my armpits were dripping with cold sweat. I was coughing and my eyes were stinging as if I hadn't slept for a week. It was only when I pulled into our driveway that I realised the car was full of smoke, sucked in through the heater fan. On wobbly legs and with shaking hands, I walked a slow circle around my car, checking for damage while I blinked away the tears. In the distance, I could hear the crackling of flames and the wail of an approaching fire engine.

As always, the firemen did a grand job. Their strategy was to watch the main fire carefully until it fizzled out for lack of fuel. Any stray bits trying to make a break for freedom, were repeatedly bashed over the head with a spade, until there was nothing left but a sooty mark on the ground. Soon the fire was reduced to little more than some wispy smoke drifting above the scorched earth.

With my heartbeat slowed to a mild gallop, I figured I deserved a nice cup of tea. It was positively surreal to go indoors and discover my dear wife, with her feet up watching television, completely oblivious to my recent brush with death.

"I heard a car. Did you go out?" Lesley asked.

"Yea," I said, "I just went down the road to that old cottage to warn them about the fire."

"I think it's empty, isn't it?" she offered helpfully, glancing back at the television.

"Yes. Bit of a wasted trip, as it turned out. The fire was a bit close on the way back, though," I offered.

"Mmm, sorry? What did you say?" she asked, glancing briefly away from the horticultural delights of Gardeners' World.

"I said..." I stopped and sighed. "I said, the fire's almost out. Would you like a cup of tea?"

"Yes please," she replied, nodding to the television.

20 – Twist and Shout

While I was waiting for my book to complete the editing process, I used the free time to correct an error I had made when reinstalling the central heating. Being a naïve fool, I had assumed the original heating system had been installed by a competent professional and I would be safe to copy the layout when I replaced and extended the plumbing. I was mistaken. Although my design seemed to work, it was only when winter arrived I noticed there was a problem.

The old heating system at Glenmadrie was designed to feed the radiators in sequence, like clothes being hung on a washing line. Although this arrangement will work passably in a small house, with all the additional radiators I'd added, the heat never adequately reached the far end of the system. The correct layout in such a large property would feed hot water to all the radiators at the same time.

It was a silly little mistake to make and demonstrated my inexperience. Fortunately, it would be relatively easy to rectify, provided I could locate the correct pipes and connections, without demolishing the entire house in the process. Of course, by now all the plumbing had been concealed behind the insulation and dry lining. Access was going to be tricky. I spent an hour sitting with my eyes shut, trying to mind-map the various pipes and junctions, before I was confident and ready to proceed. It took much longer to explain the problem and my proposed cure to my dear wife. She was understandably reluctant for me to knock holes in her beautifully decorated walls. My drawings and graphs didn't help.

"You see," I pointed at the diagram I'd drawn. "With just one pipe, the colour goes from red to blue before it reaches the end of the house. That's why it never gets warm up there."

"It's not too bad," she said, trying to back-track from all the times she'd complained of being cold.

"Now look at this," I showed her a second drawing. "See how the red goes to all the radiators at the same time and comes back blue."

"Is red for hot and blue for cold?" she asked, smiling sweetly.

"Ah! Didn't I explain that?"

"No."

"Blast." I grimaced and tapped my pen on a small box in the corner of the drawing. "But there's a key just here."

"I didn't see that."

"Okay. Sorry about that." I grinned and started over. "If you look at this drawing again…"

Lesley covered my diagram with her hand.

"Just get on with it," she sighed reluctantly. "But please try not to make a mess."

Finally armed with the correct work order, I set about carefully removing the skirting boards, cutting some square holes in the plasterboard and stripping away the insulation, until I could access the pipes and reroute the plumbing. Happily, my mind-mapping proved to be accurate, or perhaps I was just extraordinarily lucky. The three small holes I made were spot-on target, exactly where I needed to alter the plumbing. Once the system was drained, it was a straightforward job to make the corrections. When we were confident the heating was working correctly, I cut some new plasterboard and made good the damage. With the heating problem fixed, I could finally get on with some other jobs.

***

Owning an old property, there is always a long list of tasks waiting to be done. From the day we moved in, most parts needed renovating, and those that didn't required some serious maintenance. Aside from writing, teaching and the DIY, I do my best to keep the grass on our lawn and meadow under some sort of control. From late August through to the end of October, most of my spare time is consumed by cutting splitting and stacking firewood ready for the winter.

Lesley was similarly busy baking for the market and looking after the planted parts of the garden. As if the digging and weeding wasn't enough work, each autumn she'd spend hours harvesting free fruit from the hedgerows near to the house and turning it into jam. While I was proud and delighted she was doing so well at the market, with the garden to care for along with baking almost non-stop from Thursday until the early hours of Saturday morning, I was worried my wife was taking on too much. As a long bank holiday weekend was approaching, we agreed it was a good excuse to kick back and have a rest. Arriving home from a rare morning of teaching golf, I was expecting to find Lesley busy gardening, but to my surprised she was on the couch with her feet up.

"Ah," I smiled. "I see you're enjoying the bank holiday already."

"If only," she tutted.

Her face was unusually pale and she winced when she moved.

"Is your back playing up again?" I asked.

"Always, but this time it's my ankle. I was just tidying up where that rubble is under the coverway, when I stepped on a half-brick and twisted my ankle."

"When was this?"

"First thing. Just after you went out," she said. "It's really sore and I can't put my weight on it. I managed to hop indoors, but I've been sat here ever since."

"Let me have a look."

With great care I removed her shoe and sock, then pulled the leg of her jeans up. There was no doubt I was looking at the correct ankle. Even though only a few hours had passed since it was twisted, the joint was swollen and turning an angry purple. The slightest touch caused Lesley to hiss in pain.

"I think it may be broken," I sighed. "There's no point calling at the doctors, he'll only send you for an X-ray. We may as well head directly to A&E."

"Not the hospital again," she groaned. "Last time they almost killed me."

"Bah!"

Although I had dismissed her complaint with a wave of my hand, she made a valid point. After an allergic reaction to some medication, Lesley had become extremely unwell. Close to death with toxic liver failure, she had been admitted to hospital. It was several weeks before she could come home and many more months until she was fit again. Nonetheless, her ankle needed urgent attention.

"Come on," I said, helping her to stand. "It's a twisted ankle. At worst they'll put on a cast and send you home."

At the hospital, the ongoing effects of budget cuts were clear to see. Even allowing for the approaching holiday weekend, the waiting room was overcrowded and the reception understaffed. Every member of staff we saw looked tired and stressed.

"One of my friends works here as a secretary," Lesley whispered. "She said they've had a hiring freeze since last year. None of the medical vacancies are being filled, but all the admin staff seem to have three managers. She isn't very happy."

"I can't say I've seen many smiling faces here," I replied. "Do you think there's people who've been waiting here for days, just because they were in the loo and missed their name being called?"

Lesley rolled her eyes and tutted.

Two hours later, a nurse came into the waiting area, peered at a chart and mispronounced our name.

"Here!" I shouted, raising my hand.

With her arm around my shoulder, I helped my wife through the doors and into the examination area. Once she was laid on a trolley, a frazzled looking nurse briefly examined her ankle, took her pulse and blood pressure and added some notes to the chart.

"We're rather understaffed today," she said. "It may be a while before the doctor can see you."

"Shouldn't she have an X-ray?" I asked.

"Probably," she replied. "But not until the doctor has examined her."

"I was just thinking it would save time."

"It's okay," Lesley said, patting my hand. "Why don't you pop across to the shop and get me a sandwich and a coffee. I haven't eaten all day and I'm parched."

"You'd better not eat or drink until the doctor has seen you," the nurse said, before moving on to the next patient.

"Crikey!" Lesley pointed at the wall clock. "It's after five. The dogs will want their supper and a spin around the garden. It looks like I'm going to be here for a while. Why don't you pop home for a bit?"

"Okay. Do you want me to bring you anything?"

"A book and my reading glasses."

It was two hours later, just as I was getting into the car, that my phone rang. It was Lesley.

"Bring my nightclothes and toiletries." Her voice was tight with tension. "I'm being admitted."

"Don't tell me you need an operation on your ankle," I groaned.

"The doctor didn't even look at my ankle. I had a bit of a funny turn and they got all panicked. They thought I had cardiac problems. I told them I was just light-headed because I hadn't eaten all day, but nobody would listen."

When I got back to the hospital, my wife had already been moved to a ward. Unfortunately, she had missed the evening meal, so I went to the shop anyway. Lesley groaned in delight as she gulped her coffee and munched on her first meal of the day.

"What's the story?" I asked, trying to sound like a true Irishman.

"Your guess is as good as mine." She shook her head then rolled her eyes. "I felt a bit faint and suddenly I was surrounded by medical staff, all in a panic. I think they thought I was having a heart attack or something."

"Oh my goodness." I put my hand to my mouth.

"Tsk." Lesley waved my concern away like a pesky fly. "I was just hungry and a bit stressed about being back in the hospital again."

"But they must be worried about something, otherwise you wouldn't be on a ward."

"Honestly, Nick, there's nothing wrong with me, except for this damn ankle. I feel fine now I've eaten."

"What did the X-ray show?" I asked.

"I haven't had an X-ray. The doctor didn't even look at my ankle."

"No X-ray?"

"Apparently they're closed until after the holidays," Lesley whispered. "The nearest one is over in Limerick, but there isn't an ambulance available for non-critical cases."

"Did they give you anything for the pain?"

Lesley shook her head.

"Why do you think I asked you to bring me some paracetamol?"

Before leaving for the night, I managed to ask one of the nurses why my wife had been admitted. She looked at the chart and shrugged noncommittally.

"Cardiac observation," was all she would say.

As a routine precaution Lesley was given some medication for her suspected heart problem. We never discovered what it was, but by the following afternoon she was noticeably breathless and by the next day she was considerably worse. Unable to find a doctor, I asked a nurse what was going on. She read the notes and gave the same reply as before.

"Cardiac observation."

"What about this breathlessness?" I asked.

"What about it?"

"It only came on since she was given whatever tablets she was given."

"That's highly unlikely," she replied, checking the notes again.

"Is there any chance of seeing her doctor?"

"The doctor won't be here until morning rounds," she

replied, checking her watch. "Look, we're a bit short handed, what with the holidays…"

I nodded my understanding. "Thank you."

Aside from the frustration of being cooped up in hospital when there was so much gardening she could be doing, Lesley was in good spirits. Perhaps it was reckless optimism on our behalf, but we both considered the breathlessness to be no more than a temporary side-effect of the medication – even though the medical staff felt otherwise. On the other hand, the lack of information was infuriating. Lesley felt like an innocent prisoner, forlornly failing to lodge her appeal. On the upside, her ankle was less painful and the swelling had diminished somewhat. Perhaps it wasn't broken after all.

"How long are you going to be in here?" I asked on the third morning.

Lesley shrugged. "I have no idea. The nurses keep saying it's up to the doctor."

"What does the doctor say?"

"No idea. I haven't seen one."

"At all?" I exclaimed.

"Someone in a scruffy suit came by and looked at my chart this morning, but he never spoke to me."

The following morning Lesley's breathlessness was clear for all to see. Even the short limp along the corridor to the coffee machine left her blue-lipped and panting. We were both convinced the link with the medication was unambiguous. Unable to find a doctor, I politely expressed my opinion to a nurse. For once my concerns fell on fertile ground. She made a couple of phone calls, tapped on her computer for a bit and the medication was withdrawn.

"I feel great," Lesley said, the next day. "I'm hardly breathless at all."

"That's wonderful. Now the holidays are over, perhaps they can do some tests or send you home."

My wife shook her head glumly.

"No tests and I'm not going home today."

"Why ever not?"

"Ask the doctor." She pointed towards the nurses' station. "That's him over there."

I jogged across the ward and approached the doctor. Aged around 40, his tall frame seemed hunched, as if weighed down by his workload. He wore scuffed brown shoes, suit trousers and a loose-fitting tie, but no jacket. His shirt was crumpled, sweat stained and hanging loose. There was a stethoscope around his neck and two pens in his shirt pocket. I imagined he had worked a double shift and slept in his clothes, or not at all.

After a moment, I caught his eye.

He smiled stiffly and nodded.

"Oh, excuse me, doctor, I am sorry to trouble you," I said. "Could you please tell me how my wife is doing?"

"Yes, of course," the doctor replied, juggling an arm full of charts. "Who is your wife?"

"It's Lesley, this lady here," I said, pointing.

"Ah yes, Lesley. Now let me see." He found the chart and started to flick through the pages, making "Um" and "Err" and "Ah, yes" noises. Finally, he looked up from the chart and fixed me with a confused stare. "What was wrong with her?"

"What do you mean, what was wrong with her? Don't you know what's wrong with her?" I asked incredulously.

"Ha!" he snorted, "We know what's wrong with her *NOW*, I was asking what was wrong with her when she came in."

Had the poor doctor not looked so obviously tired and overworked, I may have vented my irritation. However, in this case I replied politely and very slowly.

"She-had-twisted-her-ankle."

He flipped through the charts again, chewed his lip and frowned.

"Oh."

After a brief examination, where he found nothing of interest, save for a sprained ankle, Lesley was sent home.

"Well, at least you had a rest," I said, helping my wife into the car.

She speared me with a dagger-like stare.

"Next time I sprain my ankle, I'll just walk it off."

***

Like many small dogs, and particularly those with some hot terrier blood coursing through their veins, Amber thinks her job is to defend her home from attackers – real or imagined. Several times a day, she will stand in the courtyard and woof at the world until Lesley or I angrily call her in. Ignorant to the inconvenience, but content everyone is now safe from ne'er-do-wells, she'll flop onto her bed and sleep until her next shift. Generally, our other dogs are inclined to ignore her yapping, but there is one time when they will take notice. Of all the trespassers Amber barks at, only one produces a response from the little dog that is so extraordinarily apoplectic, we immediately know the cause. The recipient of this volcanic canine eruption is a lonely and permanently horny local dog. He's a cross between a Labrador and something equally harmless and unthreatening. His only ambitions in life seem to be a desire to meet other dogs, make friends, and to sire as many offspring as possible.

His origin and ownership were the sort of mystery which could only be solved with some local knowledge. Old Tom and his son, Tiernan, were sitting in their car counting cows. I was chatting with them when the dog in question came trotting by.

"Do you know whose dog that is?" I asked.

"That's Casey's dog, from down yonder." Tom waved vaguely at the valley below. He could have been referring to any farm from Limerick to Cork, or even the Falkland Islands.

"No, Daa," Tiernan spoke softly, as if wishing to avoid embarrassment. "Casey's dog got killed udder a tractor afore Christmas. That there be Cook's dog. He's called Benny."

"Oo yes." Tom nodded solemnly. "He's a bit of a bugger is Benny. Is he giving you trouble?"

"Not really," I lied. "Most days he'll visit to circumnavigate our land, anointing every bush along the way, before leaving an enormous poop in the centre of the lawn. I don't mind that so much, but at some point he's clearly rubbed our little terrier up the wrong way. She absolutely hates him. I've never seen him showing any sign of aggression, but he's so much bigger than Amber, I do worry."

"Benny's probably just after a bit of skirt," Tiernan smirked. "Terriers can be a bit prudish, like."

"We'd best get on," Tom tutted and shook his head. "I've a lot of work to do and now Tiernan needs to go to confession."

"Daa," Tiernan groaned, as the car pulled away.

To say Amber hated Benny was rather an understatement. As soon as she senses his presence, the little dog will explode out of the door and charge at the hapless mutt, woofing manically. Despite being much larger, Benny will turn tail in shock and surprise, before dancing comically from foot-to-foot as our beige mop growls and nips at his heels. His patience in calmly resisting her attacks is only exceeded by his persistence in repeatedly visiting our home, in the face of such stiff opposition and a total lack of any sex. Although Amber's vehement and noisy dislike for the soppy pooch was irritating, as were the colossal piles of poop he routinely deposited on our lawn, Benny's nocturnal social calls were the real problem.

As soon as he realised Glenmadrie was home to four beautiful bitches, Benny began to visit. Turning up well after bed time, he'd sit on the hill overlooking our house and woof plaintively until well into the early hours. His barks occurred with just enough volume and regularity to send Amber into an apoplectic frenzy, making sleep all-but impossible for the humans. Letting the little terrier out would work as a strategy to chase him off, but I would have to spend the next hour trying to coax her indoors before we could return to bed.

When Benny first began his visits, we tried to ignore him in the hope he would naturally desist. But he is nothing but persistent. With sleep impossible, I was soon spending large parts of the night trudging around my land with a torch, wearing only my dressing gown and Wellingtons, whilst trying to move the pesky dog along. My good manners fell on deaf ears and sterner measures were required. Although I would never do him any harm, I resorted to throwing clots of mud in his direction, illuminating him with torchlight and even waving sticks, but all without success. Typically, he would just meander along to the next convenient spot and resume his mournful woofing. Eventually, and quite by accident, I hit on the answer.

"It's Benny barking again," Lesley growled. "Can't you do something?"

It was 3 am and we had been woken for the umpteenth time that night. Even without the disturbance, it was a foul night. Rain was lashing the windows like a fire hose and the wind was whistling under the eaves.

"I'm not going out there," I exclaimed. "It's too wet."

"Well you've got to do something," my wife cried. "We're exhausted."

"Right!" I snapped. "That's enough."

In a fit of seething anger, I opened the window, pointed my torch and yelled at the top of my voice, "BENNY! F**K OFF!"

Instantly the barking stopped. With a visibly shocked demeanour, Benny did a smart about turn and headed for home. My wife and I shared a look and burst out laughing.

The following morning, I was telling Tom what had happened. He laughed and nodded stoically.

"I guess you just had to find the words he knew."

21 – Mind Your Head

The studio sits at the weather-exposed southern end of the house, directly underneath the master bedroom. We had given it that name because the previous owner, a musician, had used it for band practice. It's about the size of a double garage, with a couple of small windows, twin doors opening to the outside and a low ceiling supported in the centre by a two-foot wide tree trunk running the length of the room. As the doors on the west side gave easy access for deliveries, we had used the studio as our store room ever since we had moved in. Even though it was in the most recently built part of the house, the construction was poor, and we soon discovered water leaking in behind the plasterboard whenever it rained. With nowhere else to store our belongings, it had been a constant battle to plug the leaks and keep everything dry.

Now the studio was empty. It was just wasted space and would remain that way until I had repaired the leaks and the water damage. The room had a lot of potential uses. It could become anything from a gymnasium to a home cinema. Before starting work, I needed a plan. Always the dutiful husband, I first consulted with my wife.

"What would you like to do with the studio?"

"We can't use it for anything. It's too wet," Lesley replied, her face grim. "That sofa bed was so damp and covered in mildew, we had to throw it out."

"I know," I said, gloomily. "I thought the plastic wrapping would keep it safe."

"It was such a waste. We paid a lot of money for that couch. I don't think anyone ever slept on it."

"Sorry," I sighed. "I thought the water had stopped getting in."

"Such a waste," she repeated.

"Anyway," I said, briskly. "I want to begin renovating in there.

I'll have to pull off some of the old plasterboard to find out where the water's getting in, but assuming I can fix the leaks, what would you want to use the room for?"

Lesley frowned and scratched her chin. "I could do with a sewing room."

"Okay," I nodded. "But it's a bit big as a sewing room, unless you're planning to open a factory."

"I could do crafts as well," she suggested.

"How would it be if I divided it into two rooms? I could do with a proper workshop."

"But you've got the shed."

"It's hardly big enough, especially with all your garden tools in there."

Lesley tipped her head to one side. "I could do with a larder," she said, almost to herself. "Then I could bulk buy groceries when they are on offer."

"That's a good idea. It would save a good deal of money and we wouldn't need to make so many shopping trips."

"Could you make three rooms in there?"

"Sure." I grabbed an A4 pad and drew a quick sketch. "If I take that tree trunk out—"

"Isn't it holding up the ceiling?"

"Only just," I laughed. "Unfortunately, it's so rotten, it's got to come out. Don't worry, I'll prop up the ceiling first."

"You'd better." My wife rolled her eyes. "There must be a tonne of books and boxes stored in the room above."

"And your vinyl record collection too. I remember how heavy they were." I pointed at my sketch. "I'll put a wall down the centre, where that tree trunk is now. It will divide the room and act as a support for the floor above. This side will be my workshop and the other side can be split in two, with a larder on the right and your sewing room on the left. As the ceiling is so low, manufactured doors won't fit, I'll need to make some from planking."

With her index finger tapping her pursed lips, Lesley studied my drawing for a moment, before quietly nodding to herself.

"What about those external double doors?" she asked.

"Oh, they're shot – too rotten to be saved. I could replace them, but wouldn't you prefer a window in there?"

Lesley grimaced. "I would, but the cost..."

I grinned. "Not a problem. I saved the windows we removed from the room above. I'm sure I can make them fit."

"Okay." With a flourish, she added her moniker to my plans. "There, you have my permission. When can you start?"

"No time like the present."

***

Despite my initial positivity, things in the studio didn't go well. As soon as I'd pulled up the old carpet and removed the first sections of water damaged plasterboard, I could see the problem.

"I'd hoped to save the floor and most of the walls," I explained to Lesley, "but the water damage is much more extensive than I thought."

My wife stood in the centre of the studio, hands on hips, and glared at the water-stained flooring.

"Some of it's okay," she suggested, tapping the wood with her toe.

"It's not great quality chipboard, so I doubt it'll come up without a fight." I shrugged apologetically. "Although I may save a couple of sheets, it's not worth patching. It'll be better to replace it. If I use the same type of flooring as we did in the house, it won't cost too much."

"Okay," Lesley said, but her despondent expression suggested it wasn't. "What about the walls. They look sound enough."

"You're right. Some of the plasterboard is fine," I replied. "But..."

Lesley closed her eyes for a moment, then heaved a sigh. "Just tell me."

"See where I've pulled the damaged plasterboard away?" I

pointed. "The frame is screwed directly to the concrete wall."

"There's no vapour barrier," Lesley nodded. "It's the same as we found in the house. Nothing to stop the dampness."

"That's right." I smiled.

"You see, I do listen."

I resisted the urge to say 'Sometimes'.

"I'll need to rip out all the walls to install a vapour barrier and insulation," I explained, shrugging. "In any event, it's probably the only way I can be sure to find and fix all of the leaks."

My wife waved away my concerns and headed towards the door.

"Have at it," she sighed. "I'll go and put the kettle on."

"Tea please," I shouted towards her retreating back. "And cake!"

Suitably refreshed, I grabbed the pry bar and sledge hammer and set about removing the wooden floors and plasterboard walls.

Two days later and the ripping out was finished. All that was left in the studio was the bare concrete of the walls and floor, the original ceiling and a couple of light fixings. I was preparing some temporary supports for the floor above, ready for when I removed the old tree trunk, when I spotted another problem.

"What now?" Lesley exclaimed, as I guided her into the studio.

"Look." I pointed high on the wall, where the exposed roof joists met the supporting wall plate.

She peered up, twisting her head for a better view.

"Isn't that wall plate a little small?" she asked uncertainly. "It doesn't look strong enough to support the ceiling."

"You're absolutely right," I replied. "The entire weight of the room above is sitting on just two lengths of four by two timber, attached to the wall with a few carpentry screws."

"I thought as much." My wife nodded to herself. "In the house, you used great big beams fitted with long bolts."

"That's right."

"I'm getting quite good at this building lark," she grinned.

"But there's more." I pointed. "Look again."

Lesley scanned the joists and wall plate like an over-eager building inspector. After a minute she gasped in horror.

"Good grief!" she exclaimed, her eyes wide. "That can't be safe."

"It certainly isn't," I agreed.

On both sides of the room, each of the rafters supporting the entire weight of the floor above were resting on just a quarter inch of wood.

"Whoever built this death-trap probably attached the wall plates before they discovered the rafters were too short. Rather than fitting the correct wall plates, they've just balanced the beams on their tips and hoped nobody would notice."

"How has it not collapsed?" Lesley asked.

I grimaced and shook my head.

"Those beams are 16 feet long, but only the last quarter inch is resting on the wall plate. If there was just the slightest contraction or sagging, they would slip off and the entire floor above would come crashing down. It's a miracle it hasn't happened already."

"Especially with all the wild parties the previous owner apparently had," Lesley said, pointing upwards. "Afterall, it is the master bedroom."

I bit my lip and grunted.

"Yes. I could imagine the floor flexing rather rhythmically."

Lesley rolled her eyes and tutted.

"I meant the dancing."

"So did I," I lied.

Terrified the entire edifice could collapse at any moment under the huge weight of books, vinyl records, craft materials and furniture stored in the bedroom above, I quickly added some additional timbers to act as temporary supports.

The rafter running the length of the exposed south facing wall had suffered most when the water had been leaking into the house. It was so rotten it literally fell apart under my pry bar. The replacement was a 16-foot length of pressure treated, six by three-inch timber which had to be wiggled into place from below. I was grateful Lesley was available to help lift and steady the beam while I attached the new bolts. After a good bit of shoving, pushing and swearing, we managed to get the beam temporarily balanced on the old wall plates. As with the original beams, it was only held aloft by a quarter inch of wood at each end.

"Make sure it doesn't move," I said. "I'll put my ladder at the other end."

"Hurry up," she grunted. Lesley was standing tiptoed on the shorter of our two ladders and stretching up to hold the beam.

"Argh, just a second," I growled. "This is the wrong spanner."

Lesley groaned and shifted position. Correctly equipped, I climbed the ladder and squinted at the beam. Even though I had measured carefully, the pre-drilled holes in the beam and wall were fractionally out of line.

"Hang on," I said. "I've got to move it slightly."

"Will you be much longer?" she asked, her voice squeaking from the strain of standing in such a stressful position.

"Two seconds," I grunted.

With a gentle sideways shove, the bolt holes lined up perfectly.

"There," I whispered.

Incorrectly thinking she was no longer needed to support the beam, Lesley let go and stepped down from her ladder. I was just preparing to attach the first bolt when her end of the beam slipped and fell. From there on, things happened in excruciating slow motion...

The beam headed towards the window. I desperately tried to hold it from my end, but without success. It slipped through my fingers and twisted away.

Looking down and to my left, I saw Lesley bent over massaging her legs.

The beam fell.

"Look out!" I shouted, thinking she might be showered with broken glass.

"What?" she asked, standing to look up at me.

The beam fell faster.

Lesley looked up, standing directly in the way. Her mouth was a perfect O and her eyes were as wide as dinner plates.

"Nooo!" I yelled.

She closed her eyes and scrunched her neck into her shoulders.

"Nooo!" she squealed.

With a sound like a watermelon being hit with a cricket bat, the beam impacted the top of her head.

"Oof!" Lesley grunted.

As her knees buckled, I slid down the ladder and gently lifted the beam from her head.

"Are you okay?"

"I think so," she moaned.

"Sorry. I thought you were still holding it," I pleaded.

"And I thought you had finished," she groaned, holding her head, her face twisted in anguish.

"Let me look." I eased her hands away and checked for damage. Apart from a lump slightly larger than a duck egg and a stiff neck, Lesley was unhurt.

"Look on the bright side," I said later, keeping my face deadpan. "At least your head stopped that beam from breaking the window."

Her reply may not have been particularly ladylike, but it would have kept Benny out of our garden for a month.

***

"I thought I heard the car," I said, as Lesley leaned through the studio doorway.

"How's it going?" she asked.

"Okay, I guess. How did you get on at the vet?"

That morning Romany had experienced two seizures in quick succession.

"Okay I guess," she shrugged and grimaced. "Romany's still

rather confused, but she's bright enough otherwise."

"Is it her heart again?"

"Probably. Katy thinks she may be having a series of little strokes."

"Like vascular dementia?" I suggested.

Lesley nodded, her eyes wet with tears. I pulled her into a hug.

"There's nothing Katy can do," she sobbed. "Other than making sure Romany isn't in any pain."

I stroked my wife's hair.

"We'll keep her happy and warm," I whispered.

"I know," she replied, her face pressed tightly into my chest.

After a couple of minutes, I broke the silence.

"Anyway, the old girl will probably outlive us both."

My wife broke our embrace. She smiled and wiped her eyes.

"She's certainly stubborn enough," she laughed.

"We can only hope."

***

With the old plasterboard and flooring stripped away, I was finally able to discover where and why water was getting into the studio. The leaks had always been a confusing mystery, particularly as this room had only been constructed a couple of years before we had bought the house. However, my experience with the leak in the room above, which was eventually traced to some outrageously shoddy building work, led me to suspect something similar was happening in the studio. Now the concrete walls were exposed and the dog could finally see the rabbit (so to speak), the cause was obvious.

"I suspect this was once a garage or a car port," I said, "Can you see the concrete pillars at each corner of the room?"

"Oh yes," Lesley replied. "But at some point someone's bricked up the holes to turn it into an extra room."

"Unfortunately, they didn't do a very good job." I tutted and pointed to a five-millimetre space along the top of the wall. "Up there they didn't use any mortar. Even with a coat of render on the external walls, there's nothing to stop water getting in."

"It isn't a particularly wide gap," Lesley observed.

"It doesn't need to be, especially in our climate. In fact a narrow crack can draw water almost like a sponge."

"You mean like capillary action?" Lesley asked.

"Good description," I nodded.

"Can you fix it?"

"As it's such a narrow gap, I reckon a good squirt with some expanding foam should sort it out."

"Are you sure?" she asked.

"Pretty much." I held up my crossed fingers. "We'll know when it rains."

For once the weather obliged, delivering three consecutive days and nights of cold lashing rain. Although the water pounded the outside walls like an exuberant firehose, the studio remained mercifully dry. Job done. My fix had worked. Finally, I could begin rebuilding.

Using around 50 of my beloved four by two-inch construction timbers, I built the framework for the new internal walls. Running from floor to ceiling, and set six inches away from the concrete walls, this new layout gave ample space for me to install the vapor barrier, insulation and electrical wiring, as well as providing a solid backing for the new plasterboard. Crucially, it would provide much needed support to the floor above.

With the framework for the walls in place and a few extra props added in the centre for luck, it was finally time to remove the tree trunk. Running the entire length of the room, the trunk was mounted atop two concrete pillars. I suspect it was installed before the floor above was added, with the intention of providing support, but that was no longer the case. A brief inspection suggested the ends of the tree trunk were so rotten, its connection to the ceiling was the only thing stopping it from falling. After some energetic fettling with my prybar, the beam was almost loose. However, at six metres long and 30 centimetres wide, the anticipated weight was going to be a handful. Once the tree trunk was on the ground, my trusty chainsaw would make short work of converting it to firewood, but moving it was definitely a two-person job. I had asked Lesley if she would help me, but for some reason she had developed an aversion to being hit on the head by heavy beams. Fortunately, the solution to my problems was winging its way to Ireland. Mark and Joanne were coming to stay.

22 – The Question

It was lovely to see our darling daughter and her boyfriend again. Joanne looked fit, radiant and delightfully happy. Mark was full of energy and keen to lend a hand with the renovations – I didn't even have to ask, he suggested it.

"Are you sure?" I said. "I wouldn't want to ruin your holiday."

"Tsk." He waved away my concerns. "It'll give Joanne and Lesley a chance to spend some time together. Besides, I'd like to help."

"Okay." I grinned. His offer was timely and I certainly wasn't going to turn it down. "Let's get stuck in."

Just like me, Mark prefers to do some careful planning before beginning a task. So, before any actual work took place, we spent 20 minutes reviewing my drawings and working out the best way to proceed. With an amicable compromise achieved, we had a cup of tea with a slice of Lesley's cake, and cracked on with the job.

No longer supported by the two concrete pillars, the tree trunk was hanging from the rafters in the ceiling, only held in place by dozens of six-inch nails. These final fixings had been hammered in from above, but now they were only accessible from below. Mark and I hoped to pry the trunk away from the nails and rafters without dropping it, or unduly damaging the plasterboard of the ceiling.

Using crowbars, hacksaws, hammers and wedges, we teased the tree trunk away from its fixings and gently lowered it to the ground. From then on it was a simple enough task to cut it into short sections, which we could split and stack along with the other firewood.

"Great team work," I said. "Thanks very much."

"That's fine," Mark replied. "It was fun."

"Well, I'm very grateful."

"You're welcome." Mark tapped his finger on my plans. "Shall we start building this dividing wall?"

"Sure thing."

Not only was I delighted to be making such good progress with the studio, I was enjoying Mark's company. He seemed to be a fine young man, with a good work ethic. We got on well, had a similar sense of humour and shared a liking for dreadful puns. Furthermore, we both loved my daughter. However, despite his outwardly cheerful demeanour, I could see something was troubling him. Conscious Mark may have felt compelled to help me when he would much rather have spent time with Joanne, I asked why he was so preoccupied.

"Honestly, it's fine," he replied, holding up a reassuring hand.

"As long as you're sure," I said. "You look tense. Like someone waiting to see the dentist."

Mark sighed.

"I guess I am a little on edge," he admitted. "I didn't realise it was so obvious."

"It must be," I replied. "Afterall, I'm hardly a sensitive soul."

He laughed and shook his head. Perhaps he'd heard about my unreliable appropriateness filter. Wondering if perhaps I had inadvertently offended him, I scoured my memory of our conversations, but nothing stood out.

We worked on in silence for 10 minutes or so. Once the floor and ceiling beams were in place, we added the first four uprights to the wall and checked with a spirit level to ensure it was perfectly positioned. Finally, Mark broke the silence.

"I wanted to ask you something..." He grimaced and scratched his chin. "But perhaps later..."

"No time like the present," I suggested.

Mark heaved a sigh.

"Well–"

"Do you want tea?" Lesley called from the doorway.

Mark and I both jumped at the unexpected interruption.

"Yes please," I croaked. "We'll come in."

Like a man leaving a burning building, Mark was out of the door and around the corner before I had taken a single step.

Whatever it was he had wanted to ask would remain a mystery – at least for now.

***

Ireland was enduring another bitterly cold winter. At Glenmadrie, high on the hill, we had a thick blanket of snow and a succession of deep overnight frosts. Although Mark and I were keen to progress the renovations, in the unheated studio it was too cold to work for more than an hour without taking a break to thaw our hands and feet. On the third day, I called time.

"We've done enough," I told Mark. "I'll finish up when the weather improves."

He scanned the fruits of our labour and nodded approvingly.

"It's coming on," he said. "You've both done wonders with this house. Joanne showed me some of the photos you took at the beginning, it's hard to believe it's the same building."

"Thank you. We're very pleased with the way it's shaping up."

"I know these things are never truly finished, what with the continuous cycle of decorating and suchlike," Mark said. "But you should consider celebrating the end of the renovations."

"What do you mean?"

"When a large commercial building project is finished, they usually recognise the significance of the event with some sort of a festivity," Mark explained. "It's sometimes called a topping off party."

"Oh, as if you've just finished putting the roof on a house?"

"Or adding the last beam to a building," he added.

"So you think we should have a party?" I asked.

"I'm not sure Lesley would appreciate wrecking the house with some wild party," Mark laughed, "but a celebration might be appropriate."

I rubbed my chin and nodded.

"You know, it's not a half-bad idea," I whispered. "Lesley has put up with a lot in the last seven years. Finishing the renovations is an achievement worthy of a celebration. What's more, our 30th wedding anniversary is coming up soon. Perhaps I'll arrange a surprise holiday – kill two birds with one stone."

"Or you could have two celebrations…" he suggested, tactfully.

"Let's not get ahead of ourselves," I laughed, pointing towards the door. "Go spend some quality time with Joanne."

"Okay," he said, rubbing his hands together and stamping his feet. "I won't argue."

I began putting my tools away.

"Unless you want to talk about something else…" I suggested, conscious of his still unasked question. Mark didn't answer and when I looked round, he had already gone.

I'm a sensitive soul, but not very good at picking up social cues. Mark's continuing edginess left me feeling ill at ease. I would be mortified if I'd inadvertently offended Joanne's boyfriend. Difficult as it was, for now I would have to remain patient.

***

While Mark and I had bashed, levered and sawed in the studio, Lesley and Joanne cooked dinners, chatted, did jigsaws and generally bonded together as mother and daughter. With the renovation paused, we all took advantage of the sunshine to take long walks in the forest and across the moor. Despite the bone-chilling cold, the blue skies and thick snow made for pleasant walking whilst enhancing the already beautiful scenery for those of us wishing to take pictures.

At about seven o'clock on the fourth evening, we were watching a movie when there was a sudden hullabaloo outside. The dogs were all in the garden performing their evening ablutions and had begun barking excitedly.

"What's all that about?" Lesley asked, her expression grave.

The frantic racket was unlike our dogs usual 'barking at the moon' noise, clearly they were disturbed by something.

"There's probably a fox about, or perhaps some deer," I suggested, with a sigh. "I'll go and check."

The moonless sky was an infinite black dome, but the starlight was so bright as to make the frost-laden snow glow a ghostly white, emphasising the slight mist hanging in the air. I hadn't brought the torch, but I hardly needed it to see what was going on. At the bottom of the garden, the dogs were facing the road in a wide defensive semicircle and woofing relentlessly. On hearing my footsteps crunching through the snow, their barking redoubled in volume and intensity.

"Shush," I hissed. "Come here."

Remarkably they obeyed, albeit grudgingly. Whatever was out there, it wasn't a fox or deer. I peered unsuccessfully into the darkness for any sign of movement. At some previously agreed signal, all four dogs began barking again.

"Quiet!" I demanded.

Mark and Joanne came out to join in the fun. They had brought the torch.

"Something's upsetting them, but I can't see what," I said.

Mark swept the powerful beam of light slowly back and forth. It sliced through the mist like a searchlight. On the third sweep of the torch, just as I was about to call time, we spotted something at the end of the driveway. For a brief instant, two brilliant dots glowed like fire as the torchlight reflected from an animal's eyes.

"There!" I pointed.

Mark swung the beam back.

"It's a dog," Joanne said.

"Probably a stray," Mark added. "Perhaps it's been dumped."

"It's a possibility," I replied. "Since the economic crash here, the number of homeless pets has gone up alarmingly. Many of the shelters are full."

Our mutts began barking again. The stray dog cowered in fear but showed no sign of leaving.

"What are we going to do?" Joanne asked. "It can't stay out here, it'll freeze to death."

She was right.

"So will I if I don't put my coat on," I said, my voice involuntarily shaking as I shivered. "It must be minus 10 out here."

With the offer of biscuits and threats of censure, we managed to get our loopy dogs back indoors. Wrapped up warmly in gloves, coat and hat, I went back outside. Mark and Joanne were still watching the stray. It was clearly very scared and unsure of itself, refusing to leave, but unwilling to come closer. For 20 minutes we tried to get nearer, using kind, calm and gentle voices, and offering biscuits, but without any success. We were all getting so cold and frustrated, we decided to go back indoors.

"There's only so much we can do," Joanne said.

It was sad, but she was correct. As they turned away, I had one last desperate idea. Summoning as much confidence as I could and attempting to quell my shivering lips, I gave the two-tone whistle I use to summon our pooches. Amazingly the dog immediately limped over and sat obediently at my feet, looking up as if to say, "Okay, you are my owner now."

"How remarkable," Joanne gasped.

I reached down and gave the dog a gentle stroke. He leaned against my thigh, groaning in delight.

"What breed is it?" Mark asked.

"It's a Rough Collie," I replied. "The same breed as the dog in the Lassie films."

I gave the dog another stroke, then leaned down to give him a quick check over. This was a fine-looking animal, with a light beige coat of long soft fur and a thick white rough, like a lion's mane but streaked with a little black. He had a long snout, gentle brown eyes and large pointed ears, one of which flopped over at the end, like a humorous afterthought. Although I could find no obvious injuries, his limp was pronounced.

"He seems to have some hip pain," I reported. "There's no collar and he's clearly very thin and underfed, but someone must have cared for him once. He's been neutered and that's unusual in these parts."

Mark pulled a face. "He stinks."

"I suspect he's been living in a barn or shed. Most dogs in rural Ireland are never allowed indoors."

"What are you going to do with him?" Joanne asked.

"Same as you're doing with Mark," I replied, giving him a wink. "Keep him warm and fed until we can find his rightful owner."

Even though it was dark and beginning to snow, I took all of the dogs for a short walk to ensure they bonded and understood the new arrival was now part of our pack. Although he was clearly an outdoors dog, it was so cold he needed little encouragement to come in and take pride of place by the fire. As he had nominated me to be the boss and I was heady with my new-found power, I decided we would call him Jack. When I tried out the name on our new friend, his ears pricked up and he looked at me quizzically for a moment before giving an almost imperceptible nod of agreement, as if to say, "That will do nicely". And so Jack came into our lives.

***

On the morning Joanne and Mark were due to return to England, we had a cooked breakfast and prepared for one last walk together. As the girls were putting on their boots, Mark attracted my attention.

"Why don't we stay behind and wash the breakfast dishes?" he whispered. "That way Joanne and Lesley can have some time together before we go."

"Good idea."

When I suggested the idea to Lesley, she frowned then nodded.

"I'll leave Romany with you. She's been really shaky on her legs this morning."

"Perhaps she should see the vet again," I suggested.

Lesley shook her head, her face showed her sadness.

"Katy said the next time she'll see Romany, will probably be the last time. She's an old dog with a heart murmur and her kidneys are failing. There's nothing more we can do for her, except make sure she doesn't suffer."

I chewed my lip and watched the little dog squiggling on her bed to find a more comfortable position. She looked like an overweight lamb. I knew her time was near, and that she'd had a happy life, but it didn't make the prospect of losing another dog any easier to stomach.

"Come on, Mum!" Joanne called from the door.

"I'd better go," Lesley said, with a tight smile.

"Try Jack on the lead again," I suggested.

"I'll give it a go, but it's new to him," she replied. "Anyway, he's happy just following along behind."

When the four dogs and the girls were gone, Mark and I got on with washing the breakfast dishes. Once the last plates were put away, he hung the tea towel over the Rayburn to dry and leaned against the kitchen unit. His casual stance did little to hide an undercurrent of tension.

"Nick?" Mark's voice was an octave too high and trembling slightly.

"Yes?"

"Can I ask you something?"

"Of course," I replied. "You can ask me whatever you like."

Clearly whatever had been troubling the young man all week, was about to burst forth.

He coughed and licked his lips.

"To be honest, washing the dishes was rather a subterfuge," he explained. "I wanted to ask you something – something really important, before we went back."

I nodded and waited.

Mark drew a deep breath.

"As you know, Joanne and I have been seeing each other for a while now. We get along very well, like peas in a pod." He paused and licked his lips again. "I've got a good job, with excellent prospects. Err…and I'll always put her needs first."

I nodded and waited.

Mark took another deep breath.

"May I have your permission to ask Joanne if she'll marry me?"

Although Lesley and I had often speculated Mark may turn out to be The One, somehow I hadn't seen this coming. Nevertheless, I knew in my heart what to say. For once I managed to avoid any attempt at inappropriate humour.

"Of course." I smiled and shook his hand. "You're obviously both very much in love. I would be honoured to have you as a son."

"Thank you." His grin was as wide as the Cheshire Cat. "I would appreciate it if you could keep the secret until I've had a chance to ask Joanne."

"No problem. When will that be?"

"Sunday," he replied, his eyes shining with excitement. "I've booked a romantic weekend at a hotel in Ipswich. It's one of our favourite places. If she says yes, we may have the wedding there."

"I'm sure she will. Do you have the ring yet?"

He shook his head.

"I'm picking it up from a jeweller in London on Wednesday."

"You have it all planned then," I quipped. "Down on one knee and all that?"

"Hopefully," he grimaced a grin.

A thought occurred. I held up a finger.

"One thing first" I said. "As a part of your prospective husband training…"

Mark nodded and leaned forward expectantly.

"Although you have my permission," I explained. "It means nothing unless my wife agrees."

"Oh…"

I patted his shoulder and smiled.

"Don't worry, Mark, I'm sure it'll be fine. Welcome to the family."

23 – 300 Eggs

Despite our best efforts, distributing flyers in the local village, asking at the post office and checking with the dog pound, we had been unable to find where Jack had come from. Nobody recognised him or knew of anyone missing a dog. It seemed he was here to stay. Indeed, he had quickly settled into the daily routine of life at Glenmadrie, intent on becoming a permanent and worthy part of our family.

The poor dog was in a dreadful state. He was malnourished, very unsure of himself and his coat was filthy and matted. Over the next ten days, we gave him several baths to remove the muck and smell. Every day for a week, Lesley brushed him for at least an hour, gradually working her way through the tufts and knots in his long hair. While he revelled in such undivided attention, the other dogs paced impatiently, glaring at Lesley through the conservatory windows with ill-concealed irritation.

With most of the loose hair removed from his coat, it was painfully obvious just how underweight Jack was. There were also signs of joint problems in his hips and knees, which the vet put down to the canine equivalent of rickets, probably caused by a bad diet when he was a puppy. She gave him a multivitamin injection and a course of tablets, along with recommendations for an improved diet, rich in protein and minerals. To improve his overall conditioning and build up his muscles a bit, we encouraged him to eat a little more food than perhaps he had been used to. The turnaround was remarkable. Soon Jack was showing promising signs, he could walk a bit further and sometimes he even ran a little along with the other dogs.

He is a delightfully good-natured dog, although dreadfully unsure of himself, which makes him appear to be rather shy. For such a large dog, he is pathetically scared of any loud noises, especially running water, heavy rain and, his greatest fear, thunderstorms – particularly when combined with hail drumming on the conservatory roof. The first such event was painfully disturbing to watch.

As soon as the hail began to fall, Jack jumped to his feet and began circling and whining, as if he was desperate to escape from the noise, but unsure of where to go. He salivated uncontrollably, dribbling on the carpet in agitation and orbiting the room in pathetic anxiety as the storm built. With a mighty crash of thunder the squall reached its peak, mercilessly pounding the house with hail and vivid flashes of lightning, prompting poor Jack to bury his head in Lesley's lap and repeatedly howl in terror, oblivious to her attempts to provide any comfort. Even after the storm had passed, he continued to pace and dribble for an hour, unresponsive to our kind words and comforting strokes. Unfortunately, with warm south-westerly winds trying to push our winter away, Jack's arrival at Glenmadrie coincided with a succession of such storms. Naturally, his hyper-anxiety triggered a similar response from our otherwise laid-back pooches. With two or three storms a day, soon the house was in uproar. We did everything we could think of to lower Jack's stress, Lesley even tried spraying him with a calming pheromone liquid, but it had no effect.

"Forget the dogs," I said in desperation, "perhaps you should spray it on me."

Lesley laughed at the irony.

"This can't go on much longer," she said. "He's going to have a heart attack."

"According to the weather forecast, there's a cold front moving in," I said. "This unsettled air should push away sometime tomorrow."

"Thank goodness for small mercies," Lesley sighed. "I've never seen a dog so scared of storms. Whatever could have caused it?"

"I have a theory he was locked in a shed as a puppy, perhaps newly separated from his mother," I replied. "Frightened and alone, the sound of a thunderstorm overhead and the beating of torrential rain on a tin roof would have been terrifying."

"You could be right," Lesley nodded and stroked Jack's ear. "Such an experience would have left him mentally scarred for life. Poor thing."

Whatever the cause of his aversion to thunder, Jack is a neurotic dog. If he were human, I suspect he would test high on the autism spectrum. For example: He won't eat if his food bowl is in the wrong place. Jack refuses to use a dog bed. There is a favoured spot where he will sleep at night and no other will do. He refuses to climb stairs and is unable to walk across a tiled floor. This has caused us quite a bit of inconvenience. Although all of the other dogs will walk through the kitchen to get from the conservatory to the lounge, Jack has to go outside and back indoors through the French doors. To add to the entertainment, he is so polite he refuses to go through any door before a human, consequently I have to go out in the lashing rain and lead him from the conservatory around to the other door. We've tried all of the conventional strategies to encourage Jack to walk through the kitchen and climb the stairs, but without success. At bath times, he has to be carried upstairs and back down again – but I guess that's the same for most dogs.

"Perhaps he isn't neurotic after all," I said.

"What makes you say that?" Lesley asked. It was a couple of weeks since Jack's arrival.

"I was throwing a ball for the dogs a little earlier, but Jack wasn't doing very well."

"That's not unusual. I told you, he's never learned how to play. It just confuses him. That's why he just barks and runs around."

"I thought so too," I explained. "So I tried a little training. While the other dogs were running after one ball, I threw another to Jack."

"Did it work?"

"Sort of." I gave an embarrassed grimace. "It bounced off his head."

"Oh dear," Lesley sniggered.

"Three times," I added.

"Oh." Lesley hid a smile with her hand. "So he's not very coordinated then?"

"Actually, he's almost blind," I replied. "His reaction got me thinking, so I did that test the vet showed us with Romany, covering one eye and waving a hand in front of the other. I don't think he can see out of his left eye at all."

"That's the same side as his floppy ear," Lesley pointed out. "With only one eye, he wouldn't have any depth perception. That would explain his difficulty with tiled floors and stairs too."

"And catching a ball," I added.

Armed with this new information, I finally managed to get Jack across the river at the bottom of the hill. Although the water isn't particularly wide or deep, thus far it had been an impenetrable barrier, truncating one of my favourite walking routes. Imagining how someone with poor depth perception would feel when confronted with a glassy expanse of water, I came up with a plan. To prove the water was only ankle deep, I twice carried Jack to the centre of the stream, gently lowered him down and led him out again. Whilst not delighted with the experience, he remained reasonably calm. On the third time, I left him in the stream and crossed to the far side with the other dogs. With some gentle reassurance from me and some louder encouragement from Lady, Kia and Amber, Jack cautiously tiptoed to our side of the stream.

"You should have seen him," I said, recounting the event to Lesley. "Jack was so proud of himself, he positively danced along for the next half-mile with a huge grin on his face."

"Oh, how sweet," she sighed. "Did he cross the water on his own on the way back?"

I frowned and scratched my ear.

"No. I had to carry him."

"Give it time." Lesley leaned down and patted his head. "He'll get there."

Jack is so shy, he won't even take an offered biscuit from my hand. Unlike Lady, who will happily take most of my hand as well, Jack's biscuit must be laid on the ground where it can be sniffed and examined, before being eaten and savoured ever so slowly. Although he has become rather partial to having his head patted and his ears rubbed, he is slow to ask for such a favour. Shyly edging forward, he will place his chin on my knee and wait patiently. Should I honour him with a tickle behind the ear, Jack will roll his eyes and hum with pleasure. If the gentle stroking stops before he is satisfied, he will give my knee little bumps with his chin and continue staring at me pleadingly, until he is forcefully pushed away. When he is certain that no more attention is forthcoming, Jack will wander off to the corner of the sitting room, where he will slump down on the carpet, giving out a long, contented rumble of satisfaction, like distant thunder echoing from deep within his chest.

If excited by the other dogs, Jack has a curious habit of woofing into his own ears, by turning his head alternately left and right with each bark. His only vice is ripping up plastic, which he may have learned through being around farms where silage bales and the associated plastic were common. We have discouraged him from simply destroying any and every bit of plastic he finds whenever the mood takes him, but not before he had stripped all the plastic from the chicken coop and uncovered several rolls of loft insulation. Luckily he hasn't set about dismantling the polytunnel, and he now has his own large sheet of plastic, which he likes to play with on windy days. Outside of the occasional game of chase with Lady, the only time I have seen Jack play was when he found a chicken feather on the lawn. He carefully picked it up in his mouth and then ran wildly around the lawn with such enthusiasm that I honestly believe he thought he might fly.

***

"Congratulations!" Lesley and I shouted together.

"Thank you," Joanne replied, her beaming smile pixelating momentarily as our slow internet struggled with the video stream. "And thank you for calling."

"We'd have called earlier," I said, "but we only found out about the engagement this morning, when we saw your posts on Facebook."

"Oh. I thought I'd sent you a message," she replied. "It's been hectic."

"I love the ring," Lesley said. "It looks stunning."

"How did the proposal go?" I asked. "Mark said he was taking you to a posh hotel in Ipswich."

"It nearly didn't happen."

"Oh no. It was so well planned. What went wrong?"

"The day before we were going to the hotel, Mark suddenly announced he was driving to London for a meeting. Of course that was just a ruse, he was really going to Hatton Garden to collect the engagement ring," Joanne recalled. "Unfortunately, it was the day of the big snow storm here. I thought it was an unnecessary risk to make a 120-mile round trip in such dreadful conditions for a meeting that would probably be cancelled anyway – and I told him so in no uncertain terms. He couldn't put it off or tell me the truth, so he insisted on pressing ahead. I'm afraid we had rather a row before he left."

"Oh no!" Lesley exclaimed, laughing. "At least he made the journey safely."

"Hardly," Joanne snorted. "London was gridlocked. It took him six hours. He got stuck in the snow twice and nearly had to abandon the car. I was furious. The following morning, during the drive to the hotel, we hardly spoke a word to each other."

"I'm guessing you kissed and made up when he proposed?" I suggested.

"Yes," she smiled, waving the ring-bejewelled finger. "It was all very romantic."

"And chivalrous," I added. "Like a knight winning the hand of a fair maiden."

"That too," she conceded, laughing.

"We're delighted you said yes," I said.

"Likewise," Joanne replied. "I hear he asked for your permission when we were in Ireland."

"That's right," Lesley said. "We thought it was a nice gesture."

"I said he was a handsome lad and he didn't need to compromise," I joked.

"Thanks, Dad!" Joanne snorted, rolling her eyes.

"Actually, I said I'd have to ask your mum first."

"Very wise," my daughter nodded. "Teaching him who's boss."

"Have you set a date yet?" Lesley asked.

"Yes, the 11th of September. We booked the hotel while we were there."

"Ten months," my wife said. "Plenty of time for planning."

"We've already started," Joanne replied.

I inadvertently groaned.

"Don't worry, Dad," Joanne laughed. "Mark and I aren't planning anything too extravagant. We don't want to start married life in debt, or by making you guys destitute."

"Very wise," we replied.

***

Although London's snowstorm had mercifully missed Ireland, a week later we received a double dose – and it couldn't have happened at a worse time. It was the final market before Christmas and Lesley had been baking flat out to capitalise on the anticipated surge of shoppers looking for tasty treats and homemade Christmas cakes. Allowing enough time to bake six trays of scones and load the car, we rose at 5 am only to discover it was snowing heavily.

"It's already ankle deep," I reported. "The chickens weren't too keen to come out."

"I'm not surprised. It's a good job you installed that heat lamp." Lesley swore and banged her fist on the cooker. "This won't light."

"Don't worry. The regulator on the gas bottle is probably frozen again. I'll go outside and pour some hot water on it."

My solution worked. With the gas flowing again, Lesley began preparing the scones.

"It must have been really cold last night," I said. "With this snow falling onto icy roads, the drive down the hill is going to be tricky."

"Do you want to drive?" she asked. "I know how you fuss."

I smiled and nodded. "How well you know me."

As it turned out, the roads were beyond treacherous. The first three miles weren't too bad, as the thick snow provided some reasonable traction, but lower down the hill, the surface was thick with ice. I crept along at walking pace, carefully negotiating the steep slopes and tight bends. We arrived safely, but several others didn't. Along the way we saw a jeep suddenly lose control and spin around three times. Luckily the boxy vehicle somehow stayed upright and on the road, so the only casualty was the driver's pride and perhaps his underpants. Another driver was less fortunate and collided with the embankment, but despite one front wheel flopping about like a broken leg, he pressed on with his journey.

Unfortunately, the bad weather hit the market hard. More than half of Lesley's cakes and pies went unsold.

"I can freeze some of the pies and flans," she explained, as we drove home, "but what we can't eat will go to waste."

"The chickens will eat some of the cakes," I suggested.

"And so will you," she added. "I've already given away a dozen cakes and pies. They went to help some of the families that are struggling with this recession. There's a lot of people out of work."

"Well at least someone benefited." I patted her knee. "I'm sorry it didn't work out."

"Not to worry," she sighed. "At last I can have a rest. The market's closed for a month."

"That's nice. You should go over and see Joanne."

"Good idea," she replied. "You should too."

"Obviously we can't go together. Someone has to be here to care for the dogs and chickens and the ducks."

"I know," she tutted.

"Hang on... How are we going to get away for the wedding?"

"Already sorted," my wife replied with a casual wave of her hand. "My friend, Christine, knows a girl who will be happy to house sit for us. She's very reliable, loves animals and is happy to walk the dogs."

"That's great."

We drove in silence for the remainder of the journey. The availability of a house sitter had got me thinking about Mark's earlier suggestion. With the renovations all-but finished and our 30th wedding anniversary approaching, perhaps I could arrange a surprise celebratory holiday.

It wasn't until we were unloading the car that I spotted the flaw in Lesley's plan to take a long break from the market.

"What are we going to do with all the eggs?" I asked.

"I know I didn't sell any today, but there's only three dozen left. We'll soon get through them."

"That's true, but I wasn't talking about these eggs," I replied, tapping the boxes with my finger. "The chickens are still laying around a dozen a day. If there's no market for a month, that means no baking, so you won't be using many eggs. We're going to have loads left over."

"Oh..." Lesley bit her top lip and did the calculation. "That's potentially–"

"300 eggs!" I exclaimed. "Whatever are we going to do with them all?"

"Err..." My wife grimaced.

***

At the height of food rationing during World War Two, a lot of money and effort went into researching methods to effectively preserve and ship American produced eggs to their British allies. Although it was not particularly palatable, dried egg powder was the least worst outcome. Since then, there have been no new developments. I found the internet was full of suggestions of how we could unburden ourselves from our growing pile of spare eggs. Most of them were well-meaning but unhelpful, as they revolved around variations of joining a local market and selling the eggs whole or made into cakes. Other discarded suggestions were to protect the eggs by immersing them in salt, clay, wood ash, vinegar, vegetable oil or sodium silicate. We experimented with various methods of freezing raw eggs, but the outcome was always disappointing. Although the yoke will freeze well, the egg white does not. It becomes watery and will henceforth refuse to participate in the makings of an omelette or French toast.

Unable to give away or sell our eggs, our only other option was to consume them. Despite the risk to our cholesterol, Lesley and I doubled our intake, but our best efforts couldn't keep up with the enthusiastic laying of the hens and ducks. Fortunately, the dogs love eggs – and so do chickens. It may seem counterintuitive, but eggs are an excellent source of protein and perfectly suitable for chickens. Throughout that month, it became a daily ritual to cook up a large pot of rice and eggs for the dogs and fresh scrambled eggs for the chickens. The animals were delighted and so were we. When the time came for the market to restart, we had the healthiest chickens in Ireland and just enough fresh eggs left to make the first consignment of cakes and scones.

***

A week later, I was sitting at my computer, clicking through a succession of pictures, each seemingly more beautiful than the last. There were herds of red deer casually feeding on sweet meadow grass, rocky snow-capped mountains, glassy lakes, oak forests and magnificent waterfalls.

"Killarney National Park," I whispered. "It looks perfect."

My secret search for a suitable holiday destination where my wife and I could celebrate our 30th anniversary was over. All I needed to do now was contact the house sitter and book a hotel. As Lady barged her way into my office, I swiftly swapped browser tabs.

"What are you looking at?" Lesley asked suspiciously, as she followed our foxhound through the door.

"Just checking my book sales," I replied casually. "We're doing rather well."

"That's nice," she replied, squinting at the screen.

My golf book had been on sale for three months. Already it was receiving excellent reviews and topping the charts.

"Look. It's the number one golf instructional book in Canada," I said, tapping the screen with my pen.

She leaned over my shoulder.

"How many copies has it sold there?"

"Probably about three," I tutted. "I don't think they sell a lot of golf books in Canada."

"So we can't buy that private jet then?" she joked.

"Leave it a couple of months," I grinned. "Sales are good in America and Europe. That's where the money is."

"What about the local bookshops?"

"They've all sold out again," I reported, smiling proudly. "I've ordered some more books to be delivered next week."

"That's great." She squeezed my shoulder. "Did *they* pay you yet?"

"Ah..." I stammered, well aware of which bookshop she was referring to. For many years my wife had worked as a bookkeeper. She had an accountant's eye for numbers and a reputation for debt collection worthy of the mafia. In an effort to avoid an international incident, thus far I had avoided asking for her help.

"Honestly, Nick!" Lesley growled. "You said you wouldn't send them any more stock until they'd paid you what they owe. They've already had two invoices–"

"Three," I corrected, mentally wincing at admitting my lack of courage in chasing down the unpaid debt.

My wife crossed her arms and glared at me.

"I think they're having a bit of a cashflow crisis," I offered, weakly. "What with the economy…"

"Well they can jolly well have a crisis with someone else's money," she snapped.

"I'm thinking of writing another book," I said, quickly redirecting the conversation.

"Another golf book?"

"I was considering a memoir about how we moved to Ireland and renovated the house," I explained. "There are lots of funny stories to tell. People are always suggesting I write a book."

"Isn't that what they say when they're bored with the anecdote you're telling?" she joked.

"As if their glazed expression and futile attempts to sidestep the conversation weren't enough?"

"Probably," Lesley laughed.

For a moment, she scratched her chin as if lost in thought.

"Perhaps you *should* write a book," she said. "It's up to you."

"Right, that's settled then." I gave a thumbs-up. It was rather more hopeful than I felt. "I'll get started on it."

***

Spring is usually the season of hope and joy, but that year began with dark news from several fronts. The recession was hitting County Clare particularly hard. Businesses were going bust at an alarming rate, unemployment was soaring and in Ennis there seemed to be more vacant shops and closing down sales than there were viable businesses. At the conclusion of a rare trip to the golf club, I was chatting to Eugene, a former client, also unemployed, when he asked if I knew Graham Morgan-Tucker.

"Oh, you mean Ticker?" I laughed, remembering happier days. "Lovely fellow. He moved to Indonesia."

"Did you know he died?" Eugene asked.

A cold chill ran through me.

"Oh my goodness," I stammered. "W…when?"

"I think it was around October last year, but I only heard yesterday."

"I didn't know," I said, fighting the lump in my throat. "I sent him an email at Christmas, but didn't get a reply. Do you know what happened?"

"Helicopter crash," Eugene said, looking down and kicking at the gravel with his shoe. "He was flying to survey a new project, but the weather was bad. I think it crashed into a mountain."

It seemed almost surreal to discover someone I knew and liked so much had died, especially as it had happened several months earlier. I still had dozens of videos of his ungainly golf swing on my laptop, many included quick flashes of his goofy but endearing smile. I felt a great sorrow for the sad passing of such an engaging man.

When I arrived back home, all thoughts of Ticker were momentarily forgotten. Lesley was red-eyed and crying.

"Jack's gone," she sobbed, throwing herself into my arms. "They came and took him away."

24 – Highs and Lows

"Who came?" I demanded. "Who took Jack away. Tell me what happened."

My wife sniffed and wiped her nose.

"A...A man and a woman c...came this morning," she said between sobs. "It was just after you went out. They said Jack was their dog, only his name is Duke. They came to take him back."

"Just like that?" I exclaimed. "He's been here for ages. How did they track him down?"

Lesley wiped her eyes with a tissue. Her sad expression was now tinged with anger.

"Farmer Jim told them Jack was living here just after Christmas."

"Christmas? That was weeks ago!" I was open-mouthed in shock. "Why did they wait until now to come and get him?"

"You tell me," she snapped. "They gave me some story about thinking he was dead in a ditch somewhere. Jim mentioned we had a new dog, but they didn't know if it was their dog Duke. Today they only popped in on the off-chance."

"Where do they live?" I asked.

"I'm not sure." She pointed north. "It's somewhere near Jim, about five miles away."

"And since Christmas, they couldn't make the time to pop around and check if it was their dog?"

Lesley shrugged.

"Apparently they've been too busy."

Feeling my jaw clenching involuntarily, I took a deep calming breath.

"I guess their story holds water," I sighed. "Given the distance, it would be unlikely for their dog to pass a dozen houses and end up here. What's more, I never thought to head north when I was putting up the posters, so they probably didn't see a picture."

Lesley looked unconvinced.

"Are you sure he was their dog?" I asked.

"No doubt about it," she conceded. "Jack— I mean Duke, went nuts as soon as he saw them. He hopped into the boot of their car at the first invitation."

"They put him in the boot?"

"Apparently that's how he likes to travel."

"He was quite happy on the back seat when we took him to the vet," I said. "Did you tell them that?"

Lesley nodded. "I also said about his hips and that he has rickets."

"And?" I raised my eyebrows.

"They seemed rather irritated by the innuendo. Obviously, my concern was for Jack's health, but they didn't seem to read it that way."

"How do you mean?"

"When I mentioned the vet, it was as if I was asking for a refund of the money we'd spent."

I waved away her concerns. "I'm sure that wasn't how they felt. Perhaps they were just a little embarrassed."

Regardless of the circumstances, Jack was gone and the house seemed strangely empty without him. It was as if his presence added a dimension far greater than that of a single dog. Perhaps his neurotic demeanour was responsible. I tried to look on the positive side. Whereas our Jack was going to be missed at Glenmadrie, their Duke was back with his rightful family, hopefully happy and loved. The dogs quickly returned to their old routine, going in and out of the correct doors and taking long walks without diversions or interruptions.

***

Despite the warm and sunny weather, Lesley's spirit remained stubbornly melancholy. Bunches of flowers, hugs and even day trips to her favourite garden centre did little to brighten her mood. Not only was she upset by Jack's sudden departure, but Romany's health was failing. The little dog's soft white coat now looked grey and wiry, her eyes were dull and listless, and the once bouncing trot of a young Lhasa Apso was no more than an exhausted shuffle. It seemed Romany's final days were approaching with unavoidable inevitability.

Fortunately, one elusive source of potential joy had finally succumbed to my clutching fingers. Lesley's dance club was going to start.

An inordinate amount of time had passed since the night Lesley and I had first discussed the idea of her teaching American Round Dancing in Ireland. I remained supportive of the idea and she was sporadically enthusiastic, particularly just after she had attended dances in England and Germany, where this style of dancing is still popular. Four things had held us back: time, viability, facilities and insurance.

At first we were just too busy to commit to another venture, but nearing the end of our renovations, combined with the impact of the recession on my business, solved that problem. The popularity of televised pro/celebrity ballroom dancing competitions in the UK had spawned a renewed interest for formal dance instruction in Ireland, suggesting Lesley's dance club could do well. Locating an appropriate dance hall had taken time, but here the economic downturn was in our favour. Several suitable venues had become available, and all at reasonable prices, provided we had our own insurance. The best by far was a posh town centre hotel with a magnificent ballroom. Easily large enough to facilitate 300 wedding guests, it was rather large for our needs, but at less than the price of a pub lunch, it was too good to miss. Our final hurdle was finding insurance.

You may be wondering why on earth a dance club with potentially a dozen elderly ladies cautiously twirling bust-to-bust, would need public liability insurance. After all, it's hardly a high-risk activity. Unfortunately, aside from being one of the friendliest and beautiful locations on the planet, Ireland is also among the most litigious. Personal injury claims are almost routine, and the pay outs are typically many times higher than those awarded elsewhere in Europe. Consequently, public liability insurance in Ireland is eye-wateringly expensive and difficult to find – more so if your wife is seeking to teach an obscure type of dancing nobody seems to have heard of. Undaunted, I persevered and eventually secured the required cover for slightly more than the cost of a decent lawnmower.

With everything in place, we put adverts in the local paper and parish magazines and waited for the enquiries to flood in. After a tentative start, they did. With 20 curious students signed up, Lesley enthusiastically began her preparations. All the old music equipment was unpacked, dusted off and tested. Several hundred 45 rpm vinyl records were unboxed, carefully cleaned and stacked in categories on the dining room table. With all the furniture pushed to one side, our living room took on the resemblance of a dance studio.

I'm proud of my wife's dancing talents, so I was happy to support her in organising the club. Naturally, I had expected her to be grateful, and she was, but not in the fun way I had imagined. My reward left something to be desired…

"You want me to what?" I squealed.

"Be my dance partner," she repeated, smiling enthusiastically. "I'll need you to demonstrate the correct steps."

"You're kidding!" I exclaimed.

Although I round danced with Lesley for around a year when we first met, that was many years ago. I am a clumsy and uncoordinated dancer, not the nimble-footed model she would need.

"Don't be such a baby," she huffed, dispatching my objections with a casual flick of her hand. "You'll be fine. Anyway, you've a couple of weeks to do some practise."

"But…but…" I stammered, but my objection fell on deaf ears. Sometimes it's just easier to give in.

American Round Dancing uses similar moves to ballroom

dancing, but because it is cued the students do not need to memorise the choreography. The dancers move in a circular pattern, counter-clockwise around the dancefloor, hence the name. The two major categories of ballroom rhythm found in round dancing are the smooth or international rhythms, such as foxtrot and waltz, and the Latin rhythms, such as cha-cha and rhumba. Unfortunately, they all sound the same to me.

"Ow!" Lesley squealed, as I trod on her foot for the third time.

"Sorry." I grimaced.

"I swear you're doing it on purpose," she growled.

"I am not! Anyway, I'm the man, so I'm supposed to lead and you should follow," I said, rather more firmly than perhaps was necessary. "You told me to dance a *box* and that's what I was doing, dancing a waltz box."

My wife gave a sigh of exaggerated patience.

"But we're dancing a rhumba," she said, "not a waltz."

"Oh. Then that would explain it," I conceded.

Despite my clumsy clodhopping moves and lack of rhythm, Lesley again proved to be a patient and skilled instructor. After a week of regular practise, she declared I was ready for my role as her dance partner.

"Even if it's only to show them how not to do it," she added, somewhat unkindly.

It was heart-warming to once again see my wife so bright-eyed and brimming with excitement. Unfortunately, that emotional high was short-lived.

***

The following day Romany died. Her passing was swift and mercifully painless. It was her time.

That little white Lhasa Apso was the last connection to our former life. Romany had been our constant companion for so many years. She was the tiny puppy who fell in a stream on her first walk, the hilarious young dog that changed colour by mud surfing on a beach in Devon, the mature dog that gladly came with us to Ireland and enthusiastically embraced our new lifestyle, the old dog that had been so central to our lives for so long and the real owner of Glenmadrie.

We left her body in the conservatory for a while, so the other dogs could say goodbye. Lesley and I hugged and cried, sad for our loss but relieved Romany's passing was without discomfort or pain. Later that day I buried our little dog beneath her favourite spot on the front lawn.

My wife was beside herself with grief and our dogs remained strangely subdued for several days. Lady seemed to miss little Romany the most. Although deeply saddened by her passing, whenever I am mowing the lawn near the hazelnut tree that marks the spot where she lies, it pleases me to remember her sitting there and barking at her own voice echoing from the cliffs across the moor. I like to imagine that she is still watching over our new life in Ireland.

***

"Oh look!" Lesley exclaimed, pointing at the French door. "It's Jack."

She was right. Jack was sitting patiently outside and staring through the glass, his one floppy ear complimenting the goofy smile on his face. My wife threw the door open and enveloped Jack in a huge hug. He groaned in pleasure.

"Yuck. You stink," she groaned, her eyes wet with tears of joy.

"Hello, Jack." I reached over and patted his head.

Once released from Lesley's bearhug, Jack said hello to the other dogs, circled the room twice and flopped down in his favourite spot. If he noticed Romany was missing, it wasn't obvious in his demeanour.

"It's like he's never been away," Lesley said.

"He smells like he's been sleeping in a cowshed." I waved my hand in front of my face.

"He probably was," she replied. "*They* said he was an

outdoors dog."

"All evidence to the contrary." I nodded towards Jack. He was already fast asleep.

"I'm so pleased he's come back." My wife was smiling wider than I'd seen for some time.

"*They'll* come for him again," I said gently. "You do realise that, don't you?"

"I know," she nodded, wiping her eyes. "I'm just so pleased to see him again, what with Romany…"

As she sobbed, I pulled my wife into a hug. There was nothing left to say.

They came for Duke/Jack the following morning. This time I was there to complete the handover. Lesley stayed indoors, too upset to participate. Although I had anticipated this meeting to have all the tension and acrimony of an exchange of spies, to my surprise I found Brenden and Mary to be a lovely couple. We chatted amicably for about 20 minutes and they told me the backstory to Duke's recent roving.

Brenden had been in the army, but a back injury the previous year had forced him to take early retirement. He now worked with his brother in a factory manufacturing kitchen units. His wife was a district nurse, a very busy district nurse. While they were at work, Mary's mother would come to the house to take care of their two children and Duke. He had always been an outdoors dog, happy to lounge around the house and watch the world go by. The arrangement worked splendidly, until the children began their schooling. With Mary's mother no longer visiting the house, Duke was alone. He happily tolerated this arrangement for a few months, then one day he began to roam, wending his way along the road and across fields, quietly exploring. Sometimes his trips would last a few hours and occasionally a day or two. It is unclear why he suddenly began wandering off. Perhaps he was disturbed by an unexpected noise, possibly a thunderstorm, or maybe he was just lonely. In any event, when Duke/Jack came to Glenmadrie, he was missing for so long Brenden and Mary assumed he had been hit by a car and died in a ditch somewhere far from home. They were as delighted to have him back as we were sad to see him go. This time our handover was friendly, with a hint of humour.

"He'll probably come back again," Brenden said, as I helped him heave Duke into his car. I suspect he felt a little like a father, yet again asking for the return of his son's soccer ball.

"Almost certainly," I laughed. "At least you know where he is."

"Or…" Brenden handed me a slip of paper with directions to his house. "You can always drop him down."

"You're well prepared," I smiled, tucking the note in my pocket.

"Just pop him in the front garden," Mary said. "If it's not too much trouble."

"It'll be fine." I waved them on their way.

Jack was back the following morning, just in time for his breakfast. I took him back in the afternoon.

"They won't even know you've been away," I told him.

At 3 am he returned to Glenmadrie, sitting in the courtyard and woofing plaintively until I climbed out of bed and let him in. Oblivious to my dagger-like stares, he flopped down on his favourite spot and went to sleep. After breakfast I took him back again. He seemed happy to be home, but in the early hours he returned again. And so it went on. Every day for a week I took Duke/Jack back to his home and each time he returned, seemingly determined to stay at Glenmadrie.

"This is getting embarrassing," I said to Lesley, as Jack appeared at our French doors once again. "Something will have to be done."

***

Brimming with excitement, we set off early for the first night of Lesley's dance club. Our estate car was loaded down with equipment. There were several boxes of records, a turntable, two tall speakers, a mixing deck, hand and head microphones and seemingly miles of wires.

"Are you sure you're going to need all this stuff?" I asked.

"I'd rather have it and not need it, than need it and not have it," she replied.

"But you're only going to teach one or two dances. Surely you don't need 400 records. Afterall, you must have a plan."

"I do – sort of," she mumbled. "But I might change my mind."

Therein lay the difference. Whereas I would have a plan and stick to it, my wife was flying more seat-of-the-pants.

"Oh well..." I muttered.

"What if nobody turns up?" Lesley asked, her face tight with tension.

"It'll be fine."

"But what if it isn't?"

"It'll be fine," I repeated, patting her knee.

"What's the matter with this fan?" she snapped. "The windscreen's all misted up."

"The demister is on full." I pointed. "It's rather humid this evening. Just give it a minute."

We waited, but it only got worse. The windows were opaque with condensation.

"Give me a cloth," I said. "I can hardly see."

Lesley hunted under the dashboard. "There isn't one."

I wiped the windscreen with my handkerchief. It was too small to be effective for more than a couple of wipes.

"It's no wonder the windows are misted up, there's steam coming out of this vent," I reported. "We must have a leaky pipe somewhere."

"We're not going to breakdown, are we?" Lesley exclaimed, her voice tight with anguish. "I can't be late for the first night. It'll be a disaster."

"The engine temperature looks okay, it's probably just a small leak in the heater. I'll turn it off and open the windows, that should fix it."

My solution worked. The humid air whistling through the car, had dried the windscreen enough so I could see out.

"I think we're okay now," I said reassuringly.

Glancing at my wife caused me to gulp involuntarily. Her expression was grim. With the wind blowing through the car, Lesley's long and carefully coiffed hair was whipping around her head as if she were sitting at the centre of a tornado. Conscious she had wanted to present herself to her new students as smart and professional, I grimaced and drove on in silence.

Fortunately, we arrived at the venue with time to spare. While I unloaded the car and set up the equipment, Lesley found her hairbrush and went to the ladies. Although she managed to brush out the tangles and knots to the point where most of her hair was pointing in the same direction, the new style had acquired a somewhat flouncy quality.

"It looks fine," I lied. "Very 1980s."

One look at her eyes encouraged me to stay out of kicking range for a few minutes.

The new students soon began to arrive, cautiously drifting into the hall, their faces displaying a mixture of excitement, curiosity and a little anxiety. We had laid on some light refreshments to help them feel relaxed and welcome. Whilst Lesley did the registrations, I circulated and chatted. Our advertising had delivered 15 people, all keen to learn this new dance style. There were 12 individual women, in an age range from their early thirties to somewhere north of 70. Four were acquainted, but the other eight had arrived alone. The other three people were a young engaged couple, keen to learn and prepare a wedding dance for their upcoming nuptials, and a man called Martin.

"What's the story with the women?" he whispered. We were standing by the refreshments table as Lesley finished registering the last arrival. Martin was a tall gangly man, aged about 65 with untidy white hair and a scraggly beard. He wore dusty leather shoes and a threadbare brown suit over a grey check knitted cardigan.

"What do you mean?" I asked.

"Haven't you picked one out yet?" He grinned and winked

licentiously.

"Err...not really. I'm just here for the dancing."

"I'm not really interested in dancing," he admitted. "I thought it would be a good place to meet women."

"I'm not sure that's the intention of this club," I suggested, realising he had mistaken me for a fellow student.

"Oh..." Martin squinted at me as he wrongly assessed my sexual ambivalence. He smiled and nodded knowingly. "That's okay. I'm not one to judge. I expect the pretty teacher's off limits, but at least you won't mind if I split up the herd and pick off a couple of weak ones?"

I was momentarily lost for words. Fortunately, I spotted Lesley waving to attract my attention. It was time to get underway.

"Excuse me," I mumbled, pointing towards my wife. "I'm needed."

"Good luck," Martin said.

"You too," I replied.

With more than 30 years in Round Dancing, Lesley has run hundreds of beginners' sessions. Even though it had been a while since she'd been front and centre as the teacher, she quickly got into her stride. With the students paired up, and me as her partner, Lesley demonstrated a few basic steps. Somehow, I managed to avoid looking out of place or treading on my wife's toes. Slowly and without accompanying music, for the first half hour she walked the students through the new steps one cue call at a time. Being the second most experienced dancer in the room, I was tasked to partner with each lady in turn. Almost wilting under Martin's envious glare, I did my best to help where I could. Once everyone was showing a reasonable level of competence in their ability and responding correctly to the changing cues, Lesley put on the first record.

Although simple in principle, like a game of Simon Says to music, Round Dancing is harder than you might imagine. Not only must you move your body correctly in time to the beat, you also have to listen to and process the cue for the next series of steps. One moment of inattention will leave you very obviously heading in the wrong direction. It was testament to Lesley's excellent teaching and the determination of the dancers, that they were all moving identically around the dancefloor – with one exception.

Although Martin had mastered the steps rather well during the dry run, apart from a tendency to put his hands in entirely the wrong place, as soon as the music started he discarded everything he had learned and began to trot swiftly around the outside of the circle of dancers, with his somewhat startled partner staggering alongside. I was dancing with Julia, a recent widow, keen to socialise and learn a new skill. By the time we had circled the dancefloor once, Martin had overtaken us three times, jogging along with all the musicality of a frightened emu.

Ever the professional, Lesley paused the music and gave Martin some one-to-one instruction. This break also gave his unfortunate dance partner an opportunity to regain her breath and swap places with another lady. Once Lesley had removed Martin's hand from her bottom for the second time and ensured he knew the steps, we got back to business. But no sooner had the music begun, then he broke into a canter and raced around the outside once again. His new dance partner was clinging on tightly, but not with the affection he had hoped for. They were cornering so violently the poor lady dare not let go, terrified centrifugal force would throw her to the wall.

A second break was called and more instruction followed. Martin's partner quietly hobbled away, feigning stitch and a sprained ankle. Undeterred, he cut another unsuspecting dance partner from the herd. Despite Lesley's patient instruction, once the music began Martin launched into another floor shaking gallop. As he passed me for the fourth time, I looked towards my wife.

"What am I to do?" she mouthed.

Ironically, my shrugged reply was in perfect time with the music.

In desperation, Lesley swapped to the head mic and danced

with Martin herself. Somehow, she brought him under control.

"I thought it went rather well," I said as we were driving home.

"Do you?" she asked. "I hope everyone had a good time."

"I'm sure they did. They were all smiling and dancing rather well."

"Except for Martin," she groaned.

"You sorted him out in the end," I said. "How ever did you do it?"

"It's a trade secret," she replied.

"Come on." I beckoned with my fingers. "Out with it."

My wife smiled wickedly.

"Whenever he put his hand on my bottom, or tried to gallop off around the dancefloor, I trod on his foot!"

***

The following morning, we had a surprise. Jack was back – and this time he was here to stay.

25 – Adare

Jack stayed overnight again. In the morning I took him back to his home. When I pulled up in their driveway, Brenden was in the front garden. Smiling, he came over to say hello.

"I'm returning the prodigal son again," I joked.

"Oh dear," he tutted. "This is happening a lot."

"By my reckoning, this is the 23rd time I've brought him back."

"Feck!" he exclaimed. "I didn't realise he had been up to you that many times."

"I wouldn't expect you to." I lifted a calming hand. "Particularly if he left when you were at work and we returned him before you got back."

Brenden ran his fingers through his hair and exhaled heavily.

"This won't do at all," he sighed. "I'm so sorry for the fuss."

"It's okay. No trouble at all really," I little-white-lied.

"I'm sure it must be."

I grimaced a pained shrug. "In truth this back-and-forth is upsetting my wife," I explained. "One of our dogs recently passed away. Since then Lesley's become very attached to Ja– I mean Duke. She's in tears each time I take him away."

"Oh." He chewed on his lip thoughtfully. "That won't do at all."

"I have a suggestion," I offered.

Brenden looked at me quizzically.

"Go on."

"I appreciate he's your dog, and I wouldn't want to force the issue, but he's a free agent… I mean he can come and go as he pleases, both here and up at my house. Isn't that right?"

Brenden nodded. I suspected he was thinking along the same lines as me.

"I was going to suggest we let him stay wherever he wants," I said. "Afterall, there's nothing to stop him coming back here on his own."

Brenden slowly nodded. "I guess it wouldn't be entirely inconvenient if he stayed up at your place," he said. "Especially with Mary and me being out so much. What's more, we're away on our holidays this weekend."

"So, you're okay with this?" I asked, just for clarification. "If he comes to mine, he's welcome to stay as long as he wants."

"Sure." Brenden nodded. "That's grand with me."

"Can I pay you for him?" I asked.

"There's no need for that." He politely waved away my offer.

We shook hands to seal the deal. I knew Lesley would be delighted. I couldn't wait to tell her the good news. Even though there was no guarantee Jack would stay with us permanently, at least he had the choice and I could retire my canine taxi service.

"Shall I take him back with me today?" I asked.

"No need." Brenden smiled and pointed over my shoulder.

Jack was but a small dot in the distance. While we had been talking, he had quietly crossed the road and set off on the cross-country route leading towards his new home. By the time I returned to Glenmadrie, he was already waiting at the door.

***

While the wedding planning was going on in England, back in Ireland it was still business as usual. Lesley was working almost flat-out tending to our garden and vegetable plot, cooking, baking and producing jams for the market, while I was trying to add as much money as I could to help with the wedding costs. Inevitably, and with viciously exquisite timing, the recession in the west had worsened considerably. Book sales were healthy, but my teaching business was now no more than an interesting hobby. On the up-side, I'd had the extra time I needed to put the finishing touches to the rebuilt studio.

It was quite a moment when I applied the last lick of paint and declared the renovations finally finished. It had taken almost eight years of hard grafting, with numerous mistakes, hundreds of cuts and bruises, and tens of thousands of euros worth of materials. Considering I am not a builder, plumber or electrician, or even particularly skilled mechanically, by patiently and carefully following the instructions in a DIY manual, applying a little common sense and a lot of money, we had transformed a run-down old farmhouse into a delightful family home. It was indeed time for a celebration.

"Well, that's it all done," I said.

Lesley was in the polytunnel. She groaned as she straightened her back. "What's all done?" she asked, leaning on her spade for support.

"The renovations." I smiled and waved my arm, expansively encompassing our domain and striking a tomato plant in the process. "Oops. Anyway, we've finished the house. I know there will always be decorating and maintenance to do, but we've done a magnificent job turning the old place into a beautiful home. I think we should celebrate."

"Pub meal?" Lesley suggested.

"As you've been so patient and supportive, I was thinking of something a little more luxurious. How about a long weekend away in a nice hotel?"

"I'm sure it would be lovely," she laughed ironically. "But we can't leave the animals unattended. Anyway, it would be too expensive, especially with the wedding coming up."

"Not at all. You deserve a little treat," I said. "Think of it as a dry run for the house sitter before Joanne's wedding."

Lesley pursed her lips, deep in thought. "Okay," she nodded. "When did you have in mind?"

"Friday!" I said, excitedly. "It's our 30th wedding anniversary this weekend."

"That's just a week away. Isn't it rather short notice?"

"Not at all." I wiggled my eyebrows and grinned. "The hotel is already booked and I've arranged for Danni to care for the house. We're going to Killarney National Park."

***

"I didn't think this was going to happen," my wife said as we drove away from Glenmadrie. "My mum couldn't have taken ill at a worse time."

"It could have happened the week of the wedding," I countered.

"Don't!" Lesley rolled her eyes. "That would be a disaster."

"I was just thinking the same thing," I replied. "I'm glad Muriel is feeling better."

"The doctor said it was just a urinary tract infection," Lesley said. "Mum should be fine now she's on antibiotics."

"It's strange how it caused her to become so mentally altered. I suppose the infection somehow magnified the symptoms of her dementia." I pursed my lips and sighed. "With such a sudden onset of confusion, slurred speech and a loss of balance, it wasn't surprising her neighbour thought Muriel was having a stroke."

"It was good of her to call Joanne and the doctor."

"Absolutely," I agreed. "I hope Joanne wasn't put out too much. I know she had plans."

"She was just worried for Mum. It was fine."

I sighed and rubbed my face. It had been a stressful couple of days, trying to manage the care of an elderly relative over the phone. To my mind, the situation was at best unsatisfactory, and likely to get worse.

"We can't keep relying on Joanne or Muriel's neighbours to help out," I said. "Sooner or later something will have to be done."

"I know." My wife's mouth was a tight line of supressed anger. "That care assistant should have noticed something was wrong."

"Minimum wage workers," I tutted. "The company gives her 45 minutes to do an hour's work. You told me that. With the best will in the world, the poor girl was probably too busy to even notice Muriel was altered. Her neighbour only spotted something was up when they were chatting over tea and cake."

We drove in silence for a while. I tried to relax and look forward to our holiday. My wife seemed calm, but her fingers were tapping an angry staccato on her knee.

"Well, I don't know what the answer is," she mumbled, disturbing my tranquil thoughts. "We can't put her in a care home, especially after seeing that dreadful documentary the other day."

"It was pretty shocking," I agreed.

"Perhaps we should increase the hours for Muriel's carers?" Lesley suggested. "A little more time every day would help a lot. We agreed we could do that, didn't we?"

"Of course. Every little will help." I patted her knee reassuringly.

We both knew it was only a stop-gap solution. Muriel's condition was inevitably going to worsen, and eventually she would need around the clock care. The only practical solution would be for her to come to Ireland and live in our wing – the self-contained Granny-annex I'd built.

"We have the space," I said, reflecting the conversations we'd had over the previous week.

"She won't like it," Lesley reminded me.

"I know," I sighed. "But it's our responsibility to look after her. It's that or a care home and she definitely won't like being in a facility."

"Mum just had a bladder infection," Lesley said, trying to reassure herself, "that's why she was so confused. She's feeling much better now, and mentally she's doing okay."

I didn't say anything.

"I'm over there in a couple of weeks," she continued, "cooking cakes for the wedding. I'll see how she is then."

"Okay. That seems like a reasonable plan." I pointed ahead. "Let's stop worrying and enjoy our holiday."

For a while we listened to music and appreciated the scenery. With the sun shining and the trees in full leaf, the countryside seemed to overflow with greenery. The traffic was light as we passed through Limerick city and we were soon heading south west towards Killarney.

"Do you think you gave Danni enough instructions?" Lesley joked.

"Whatever do you mean?" I replied, my voice heavy with mock innocence.

"She's only looking after the house and a few animals. Don't you think four pages of advice, suggestions and emergency telephone numbers is rather over the top?"

"I was just covering all the bases," I explained. "If one of the dogs is taken ill or something, you'll be pleased she can contact us or know which vet to call."

"Agreed," Lesley tutted, "but it does make us seem like doting parents leaving our firstborn child with a new babysitter."

I laughed. "It does rather feel that way. Afterall, this is the first time we've been away for a long time."

"Yes, but *four* pages?" My wife rolled her eyes dramatically and giggled.

"I guess I got a little carried away," I admitted reluctantly.

It was nice to see Lesley so relaxed and happy. From the day we had decided to discard our old life and move to Ireland, the constant river of renovations to the house and gardens, along with my hectic work schedule, had been unrelenting. Under such circumstances, it had been all too easy to forget why we had moved to Glenmadrie in the first place. Sometimes you need to stop and smell the roses. With the facelift of our new home complete, we finally had the time to enjoy the new life we had sought. Today really was the first day of the rest of our lives.

"This looks like a pretty village," Lesley said.

"It certainly is," I replied. "Do you want to stop and look around?"

"Very much." She nodded enthusiastically. "Where are we?"

"This is Adare. I didn't realise it was so quaint. Andy and I came here when the Irish Open was on, but we went directly to the golf club, so I've never seen this part of the village before. It really is quite striking."

We parked on the main street, directly opposite a long row of thatched cottages. It was a terrace of around ten tiny houses, all connected under one continuous roof.

"I bet it took a while to thatch that lot," I said.

"It's very impressive. I've never seen such a long thatched roof."

"There's another block further along the road."

Although a few of the cottages appeared residential, the majority had been given over for commercial use. There was a tea shop, an art gallery and a couple of gift shops, selling Irish and Adare-themed souvenirs and craft to the tourists. The right-hand end of the block was in use as a pub.

"Do you want to grab some lunch?" I asked, pointing my nose towards the pub and the distinctive aroma of chips.

"It's a little early." My wife patted her bag. "Anyway, I've brought some sandwiches and cake. Let's walk up to that park we passed. We can eat there."

"Do you want to look at the craft shops?" I asked, immediately kicking myself for such a foolish suggestion. I needn't have worried. Lesley had other ideas.

"I'm sure we could spend a happy afternoon browsing through these little shops, but I'd much rather see that castle we passed on the way in."

"Very wise," I said, trying to hide my relief. For me, shopping is a necessary evil, best approached with a list and some military discipline. "Anyway, we've still got the thin end of a two-hour drive to Killarney."

Lesley took my wrist and squinted at my watch.

"We'll stay here until four." She flashed a smile, her blue eyes twinkling. "Okay?"

"Okay," I nodded.

Compared to our sleepy and economically depressed county town, Adare was teaming with tourists, shoppers, buskers and street performers dressed as unidentifiable historic figures or silver painted statues. After lunch, we crossed the road and headed towards a smart modern building which appeared to have a tea shop and, hopefully, toilets.

"This is the Adare Heritage Centre," Lesley said, pointing at the sign.

Suitably refreshed and relieved, we decided to have a look around. Inside there were several shops selling Irish wool, souvenirs, crafts, and one specialising in heraldic research and production.

"This must be very popular with tourists searching for their Irish roots," Lesley said. "It looks very professional."

We browsed the tourist information displays, picking out anything interesting for this trip or for the next. Inevitably, Lesley's selection was predominately garden themed.

"Ooh look," she pointed. "There's a guided tour of Desmond Castle. Shall we go?"

"Sure. We have time."

It was only after we had bought our tickets that the lady mentioned there would be a wait of almost an hour.

"The coach leaves from the carpark at the rear. Perhaps while you wait, you'd enjoy looking around the historical exhibition." She pointed to a dark doorway across the hall. "It's free and really rather good."

And she was right. Far away from the noisy and bustling crowds of happy tourists, Lesley and I strolled alone through the dimly-lit serpentine corridors which connected the main display areas. Along the way spotlights drew our attention to items of interest. There was much to see. In a series of historically themed sections using paintings, beautifully created plaster tableaus and three-dimensional maps we learned the history of Adare.

Known to be one of the prettiest and most photographed villages in Ireland, the site dates back to 1200 AD. It has been the subject of many rebellions, wars and conquests, leaving behind a legacy of historical monuments, along with an understandable distrust of anything British. In the early 19th century, the Earl of Desmond drew up plans for the layout of the streets and houses in the village. Much of this map is unchanged today. The farms and cottages on the estate were rented to local tenants under various agreements, some of which are still in force.

"The name Adare means the ford of the oak," Lesley said, reading from one of the information boards. "The River Maigue is tidal as far as Adare, so the ford was a strategically important crossing point. There was a settlement on the eastern bank of the river, overlooking the ford. Desmond castle was built to provide protection."

"It's certainly imposing enough."

"Adare was a market town," she continued. "By the Middle Ages it had three monasteries."

"Three?" I exclaimed. "Good grief, that's a lot of monks for such a small village."

Ignoring my clumsy attempt at humour, my wife carried on reading.

"The Trinitarian Order established their only monastery in Ireland in Adare in 1230. Apparently, the Trinitarian monks may have come from Scotland."

"I'm genuinely impressed with their dedication and seamanship," I said. "The journey from Scotland to here would be a significant challenge in a small craft today. I can't imagine what it would have been like back then."

"The Augustinian Priory was founded in 1316," she read, "and the Franciscan Friary in 1464."

"Isn't the Franciscan friary the ruin inside the golf club grounds?" I asked, pointing at a picture on the wall.

"That's right," Lesley said. "Apparently they still celebrate mass there, at dawn on Easter Sunday."

"I saw the ruins when I was here at the Irish Open. It's quite a feature," I said. "Of course, it's not as impressive as the manor house. I wonder when that was built?"

It took a minute to locate the correct information.

"Here it is," I said, pointing at the text printed below a photograph of Adare Manor. "The present building was reconstructed in the early 19th century," I recited. "It was built in a Tudor-revival style, whilst retaining parts of an earlier structure. Located on the banks of the River Maigue, Adare Manor is the former seat of the Earl of Dunraven."

"Can we visit?" Lesley asked.

"Only if we're rich and famous," I joked, sadly shaking my head. "It's a luxury resort hotel. Much too posh for the likes of us."

"But you're an international bestselling-author," Lesley quipped.

"Six copies sold in Canada won't open many doors," I pulled a mock-sad face. "Especially in these clothes."

"Jeans and a t-shirt. Comfortable and functional." My wife smiled and gave a little twirl. "Perhaps they'll let us in after your next book."

"Perhaps..." I checked my watch and nodded towards the exit. "We should go. It's time for the guided tour."

We strolled casually through the reception area to the rear carpark where around a dozen people were standing alongside the tour coach.

"You know, that historical exhibition was really rather good," Lesley said. "Yet, even with so many tourists here, we were the only people who saw it."

"It's a shame," I agreed. "A lot of effort went into those displays. Perhaps they need a bigger sign."

Desmond Castle stands on the banks of the River Maigue to the north of Adare village. After a short coach journey, we followed the other passengers to the castle gates where the tour began. With typical Irish efficiency, the coach driver doubled as the guide. Fortunately, he was a safe driver and an excellent guide. Polite and knowledgeable, he pointed out the key features and related some of the interesting history.

"The castle was erected on the site of an ancient ring-fort around the early part of the 13th century. It became a strategic fortress during the following turbulent years. It was the property of the Earls of Kildare for nearly 300 years until the rebellion in 1536, when it was forfeited and granted to the Earls of Desmond, who gave the castle its present name," he said. "Much of the castle has been renovated. This work began in 1996 and continues today."

"We've finished our renovations," I whispered. Lesley shushed me with a nudge to the ribs.

"This is a fine example of an Irish medieval fortified castle," the guide continued. "It is one of a number of outstanding castles situated in County Limerick. As you can see, the castle is sited on the bank of the River Maigue in a strategic position, able to oversee and control traffic on the river. It was an important stronghold for the Earls of Desmond."

After leading us to a higher position, he pointed out some of the features.

"Many so-called castles in Ireland are no more than over-large, tall and square houses. Built for show, they are not practical as a defensive position. Desmond Castle is the real deal." He nodded with pride. "The strong square central building is called the keep, it forms the defensive core of the castle which stands within a walled ward surrounded by a moat. This is encircled by a robust battlemented rampart with semi-circular bastions. The only entrance is the gate to the south, which has a drawbridge to allow people to cross the moat. As you can imagine, a structure such as this could resist a determined attack for a considerable time. You may have noticed the steps we just climbed are uneven and of differing sizes. This is not poor workmanship. They are called stumble-steps and are deliberately difficult to negotiate without looking at your feet. Of course, such an action would be fatal to an attacker during a swordfight."

The tour ended in the large courtyard at the centre of the castle grounds.

"Here you can see the remains of the great hall, with its early 13th century windows looking out on to the river. The smaller building to the side was a kitchen and bakery. Besides being a defensive position, this castle and its surrounds were also home to many people. It was quite an industry just keeping them all fed. Speaking of which, if you are hungry, there is a wonderful restaurant back at the Heritage Centre."

Although it was close to 4pm by the time we got off the coach, we couldn't resist the temptation of stopping for tea and some scrumptious cake. As we were leaving, Lesley diverted towards the heraldic research and production stall.

"Look what I found while you were in the toilet." She waved a key fob under my nose. "Read the name."

It was strangely familiar. I frowned momentarily.

"It's Mark's surname!" she prompted.

"Oh!" I exclaimed, as the penny dropped. Although our future son-in-law was decidedly English, apparently his name had very Irish roots.

"You know what this means?" I asked, smiling mischievously.

"What?"

"Our daughter could become Irish before we do!"

26 – Happy Anniversary

"Turn right, now." The electronic female voice had a disturbingly sexual warmth.

"I can't turn right here," I growled, lurching the car back onto our side of the road. "What's the matter with this satnav?"

"Perhaps you haven't set it up correctly," Lesley said, covering a smirk with her hand.

"Recalculating. Recalculating."

"I've set it up perfectly. It's been fine all the way to here," I said.

"Recalculating. Recalculating."

"Well it's lost now," my wife sniggered. "A bit like us."

"Continue for five kilometres, then turn right."

"There! You see?" I pointed at the infernal machine. "It's not lost after all."

"I don't know why you bought it," she said. "It seems like a waste of money. Can't you just use a map?"

"I bought it for you, to help when you're driving over to England. You know how complicated Dublin is, particularly if you aren't familiar with the streets. Anyway, it was second-hand, so it didn't cost much."

"That's probably why it isn't working," Lesley whispered to herself.

"Should we call Danni?" I asked, smoothly changing the subject.

"Whatever for?"

"Just to make sure she's coping, and the dogs are alright."

Lesley groaned and rolled her eyes. "Don't be such a fusspot. She'll phone if there's a problem."

"I don't think my phone has had a signal since we left Adare."

"Stop fussing. Danni's perfectly capable." My wife pointed ahead. "Wow! Look at that windmill."

We were passing a commercial windfarm. It was the first

317

we'd seen in Ireland. The base of one windmill was just a few yards from the road, the slowly turning blades gleamed brilliant white and towered high above us.

"I've never seen one up close before," I said, squinting low to see through the top of the windscreen. "I can't get over how tall it is."

"The upper blade is hitting the cloud base." Lesley tapped the side window and pointed. "It's leaving little swirls, like cream in coffee. How pretty."

"With all the wind we get in Ireland, it's surprising there aren't windfarms on every hill."

"They certainly seem a long way behind the curve on the sustainable energy front," Lesley said. "Although, it wasn't always like that."

"What do you mean?"

"You know the canal we crossed near the garden centre on the other side of Limerick?"

"You mean Ardnacrusha?" I asked, smiling at my wife's preference for navigating by garden centres or any other garden-related landmarks.

"Is that what it's called? Anyway, I saw an environmental programme the other night. That isn't a canal, it's actually the bypass river channel for the Shannon hydroelectric power plant."

"That's right," I said, clicking my fingers in recognition. "There's a big dam there somewhere. I've seen pictures of it."

"Apparently it was built just after Irish independence. It cost about a fifth of the country's annual budget to build."

"Wow," I exclaimed. "That's some commitment to the future of Ireland."

"Well it certainly paid off," Lesley continued. "For a while that power plant was producing almost all of Ireland's electricity."

"But not now?" I asked.

"Unfortunately, the production of renewable energy here hasn't kept up with the expansion in demand." Lesley frowned and scratched her chin. "I think they said it only accounts for around two percent now."

It was my turn to frown. "That can't be right."

"It is," she nodded. "Think about it. Back in 1922 hardly anyone in Ireland would have had electricity, now they all have washing machines, fridges, televisions, computers and outdoor lighting."

"Except for that cottage down the hill. The one with the two elderly brothers," I said.

"Oh yes." She smiled at the memory. "They must both be in their 80s, but they're still living quite happily without any electricity."

"That's County Clare for you," I grinned. "We like to keep it quirky."

For a few minutes, we were content to take in the scenery. Three kilometres later, the satnav broke the silence.

"In one hundred metres, turn right."

"But there isn't a junction," I exclaimed.

"Perhaps we're a little off-piste," my wife said, her face deadpan.

"Turn right, now."

"But I can't!"

"Recalculating. Recalculating."

"Just turn it off," Lesley sniggered.

I growled and jabbed at the satnav with my finger. Perhaps fearing for its life, it jumped from its cradle, fell to the floor and hid under my seat.

"Recalculating. Recalculating."

"Oh shut up, you infernal machine!"

Lesley laughed, her face radiant and relaxed.

A short while after entering County Kerry, near to Coolick, we passed through a high valley between two cloud-topped hills and began the long downhill run to Killarney. As the land fell away and the cloud dissipated, we had the first glimpse of our destination.

"Oh wow," Lesley exclaimed. "What a view."

"It feels like were in an aircraft coming in to land," I added.

We were looking to the south, down the hill towards Killarney and the surrounding 20,000 acres of National Park. Even from five kilometres away, it was easy to see why this was such a popular tourist destination. The terrain below had the green flatness of quality farmland, dotted with cottages and small agricultural buildings. At this distance, Killarney town was no more than a thumb-smudge on a painting, where the colour changed to shades of grey and beige. Beyond the town, I could see the vast sky-blue waters of Lough Leane, glistening in the afternoon sunshine and surrounded by the verdant green of the National Park. Like the sides of a bowl rising from the valley floor, the backdrop to this beauty was a stark and intimidating curve of mountains.

My wife took a map out of her bag and unfolded it.

"You brought a map?" I tutted. "It's no wonder the satnav isn't working. It's probably sulking."

"The highest mountain is called Carrauntoohil," Lesley pointed to an imposing granite monolith on the right. "It's over a thousand metres tall."

"What's the purple one called?" I asked.

She squinted at the map and laughed. "That's Purple Mountain."

"Very apt. I wonder why it's purple."

"Perhaps it's covered in Rhododendron bushes," she said. "They're an invasive species in Ireland and rather a problem in Kerry."

"Where's Torc Mountain?" I asked. "It's on the same road as our hotel."

Lesley consulted the map. "It's the greenish one, directly behind the town. That must be where the Torc waterfall is. Perhaps we can have a look this evening?"

"Sure," I said. "We can do whatever we want. Afterall, we are on holiday."

The remainder of our drive was uneventful. I knew our hotel was situated on the main road leading to the National Park and the famous Ring of Kerry, so navigating our way through the town was a simple matter of following the signposts.

"There's the hotel," Lesley pointed.

I indicated to turn and waited for a break in the seemingly endless stream of oncoming traffic.

"Plenty of tourists here," I said.

Fortunately, a slow-moving pony and trap created a natural gap. I nipped through and pulled into the first available parking place.

"Here we are." I stretched and smiled.

As I opened the door, a muffled voice spoke brightly from below my seat.

"*Arriving at destination, on the right.*"

We burst out laughing.

***

Once we had checked into our hotel room and had a refreshing beverage, we jumped back into the car and drove a mile further to the base of Torc Mountain, where the Torc upper carpark gave us easy access to the walking trail. It was a five-minute walk through the thick woodland to the base of the waterfall. Although the path was good, the climb was steep. It was okay for a veteran mountain goat like me, but with her bad back and aching hip, Lesley found the going a little harder. Nevertheless, once the blood was pumping, she lengthened her stride an began to enjoy the exercise.

The waterfall is a rocky cascade falling steeply for around 70 feet. At times of drought it has been known to slow to an unimpressive trickle, but we were lucky to have arrived at the back-end of some typically inclement Irish weather. I could hear the waterfall from the carpark. Up close, the noise was almost a physical assault. Spray wet our faces, adding to the sheen of sweat we had acquired during the climb, and the roar of the thrashing water smashing against the rocks pounded into our chests.

"Let's go this way," I shouted, pointing to a stepped pathway.

The ascent was a good workout for the legs and buttocks, but otherwise quite easy going. We stopped at each waypoint to take some pictures and even engaged in a camera-swap with a Japanese couple so we could both have a husband-and-wife-standing-by-the-waterfall photograph. Near the top, there was a large signpost with a pictorial representation of the various walking routes we could take, along with notes on the distance, difficulty and time needed. With an hour to spare, we chose a path which would take us in a wide clockwise loop through the thick forest and across the river to a high viewpoint, before curving back down to the carpark again. Hand-in-hand, we set off.

"Let's eat somewhere nice tonight," I suggested, "to celebrate our anniversary."

"You've got the wrong date," Lesley laughed. "Our anniversary isn't until the day after tomorrow."

"I know." I rolled my eyes. "But that's the day we're heading home, so I thought I'd treat you tonight – and tomorrow too if you like."

"One posh meal will be lovely," she replied.

"Or if you prefer, I could pop down to the garage forecourt and buy you a bunch of flowers," I joked.

"How romantic. Let's stick with the meal," Lesley laughed. "I hope they have a nice vegetarian option for you."

"Don't worry about me, we'll go wherever you want. It's your treat."

"I'd prefer if we both had a nice time." She squeezed my hand.

I sighed. "You know, sometimes I wish I wasn't vegetarian. It can be so inconvenient."

"Don't worry about it," she tutted. "Anyway, as soon as you quit eating meat, your stomach problems disappeared."

"That's true," I grinned sheepishly. "Now we only have to open the windows when Lady has eaten a hare."

"Oh yes," Lesley laughed at the memory. "That was a really,

really bad day."

At the highest point, the path turned south following a ridgeline through the forest. It was a pleasantly warm afternoon, with a gentle breeze nudging the occasional fluffy cloud across the otherwise clear blue sky. Although we were walking on well-maintained gravel, to the sides there were thick grass and bushes. I had great fun spotting the frequent signs left by the passage of foxes, badgers, deer, hares and smaller wild animals. Through gaps in the treeline we could see the glowering grey peak of Magerton mountain, leaning over us like a mini Matterhorn. High above we spotted two raptors turning lazy circles as they rode a thermal. We squinted and peered, but they were too distant and we were too myopic to identify the species.

"Perhaps they're white-tailed sea eagles," Lesley suggested. "I read they have been breeding them here."

"We'll have to look out for them."

A little further along the path, we reached the viewpoint. Through a small clearing in the forest we had a clear view of Muckross lake and gardens and beyond that Lough Leane with Ross castle just visible on a spit of land.

"Phew!" I gasped, clicking away with my camera. "That's some sight."

"It was certainly worth the climb."

"It's all surprisingly flat down there," I noted.

"Good job too," Lesley replied, massaging her calf muscles. "It'll make for easier walking tomorrow."

Although the view was spectacular, the gap in the treeline was quite small, limiting our field of vision.

"I feel like I'm looking through a castle window," she said. "It's a shame we can't see a little more."

"Perhaps if you were taller…" I joked.

My wife gave me a friendly shove.

Without a care in the world, standing on top of a hill, next to my wife, on such a beautiful and sunny day, I was unexpectedly stuck with a great sensation of sadness. Hearing my deep sigh,

Lesley looked concerned.

"What's wrong?"

I sighed again, searching for the words.

"Looking at all this," I waved my hand at the view and forest, "and thinking of how things have worked out so well for us, I suddenly thought of Ticker dying so unexpectedly…and Romany…I guess…"

"What do you mean?" Lesley asked, her face dark with concern.

I paused and tried again.

"When we got married 30 years ago, Ticker would have been just a kid, with his whole life ahead. Now he's gone and we're here celebrating our anniversary, a new lifestyle and finishing the renovations. I suppose I was just struck by the cruel impermanence of life."

"I think I know what you're getting at," she said, squeezing my hand. "Our lives would be very different if we hadn't moved here."

"True." I nodded. "I'd have probably burned out or had a heart attack by now."

"But you didn't. And we're here now."

"I suppose I was warning myself not to take all this for granted. Not just the scenery, but our lifestyle too."

"Live for the minute?" Lesley asked. "Is that what you mean?"

"Sort of. We still have to plan for the future, but perhaps we need to take a little more time out to enjoy the now." I said. "You know what I mean? Don't forget to stop and smell the roses."

"At last, we're talking about gardening!" Lesley laughed.

We continued along the path, glad to begin the downhill section towards the carpark.

"I meant to tell you Joanne phoned while you were out yesterday," my wife said. "She called to wish us a happy anniversary."

"That was nice. Did she say how the wedding preparations

are going?"

Lesley nodded. "The dress has arrived. Apparently it looks beautiful. It's exactly as she wanted. She said thank you to us both."

"Oh, that's wonderful. Are they still sticking with this Rock 'n' Roll theme?"

"More or less. She said it's loosely aimed at that late 50s and early 60s period. Mark and her have had great fun buying loads of cheap memorabilia from car boot sales and second-hand stalls. They've even managed to find some squiggly illuminated signs."

"You mean neon signs?" I asked.

"That's it." Lesley grinned.

"Have you sorted out what cakes you're baking?"

"Yes. She wants a couple of hundred cupcakes and muffins for the after party. I'll do the bulk of the baking at home, then take it over in the car. The rest I'll do at Joanne's house."

"What about the wedding cake?"

"She's asked me to do a small cake, but the centrepiece is going to be a wedding cheese."

"A cheese?" I frowned.

"It'll be made from several different exotic cheeses. It's all the rage."

"Well, Joanne would know," I replied. "She must have been to a dozen weddings this year alone."

After another 20 minutes, winding our way down the hill, we finally reached the carpark – or so we thought.

"Where's the car?" Lesley asked.

"Where's the waterfall?" I replied, cupping a hand to my ear. "It should have been just above us."

Somehow, we had taken a wrong turning and become completely lost. Luckily, there were plenty of enterprising jaunting car drivers who, for a small fee, offered to take us back to the correct carpark.

These horse-drawn open carriages are either two-wheeled types, which seat two passengers facing forwards, or larger four-wheeled carts that carry around a dozen people – precariously balanced on bench seats, facing sideways. There are literally hundreds of jaunting cars around Killarney. Wherever we went, we could hear the steady clop, clop, clop of horses and the lilting commentary of the official drivers, enthusiastically relating stories of witches, fairies and the like to their appreciative audience.

Just before our trip, we read there had been considerable complaints from the drivers and even threats of strikes and blockades, because of a new rule requiring all the horses to wear a sort of equine nappy to collect their poo. After much negotiation, both in the press and behind closed doors, they reached a consensus with the authorities – which may have resulted in some local councillors having particularly well fertilised rose bushes. In any event, given the sheer number of horses parading around the area, it was not surprising something had to be done before Killarney disappeared under a mountain of horse manure.

After our walk and a quick dip in the hotel pool, we were both ravenous, so we strolled the short distance up the Muckross road to the town centre, in search of an eatery that met with our approval. Compared to our sleepy county town, Killarney was positively heaving with people.

"At this time of night, every shop in Ennis would be closed," I said.

"Half the shops in Ennis are empty and boarded up anyway."

Lesley was right. The economic downturn had hit many rural towns particularly hard, but Killarney's quaint side streets with their multi-coloured shop fronts, were bustling with tourists from all corners of the planet. The contrast in fortunes was quite surprising.

"There's no sign of a recession here," I said, shaking my head in disbelief. "It's hard to understand how 90 miles can make such a difference."

For an hour we window-shopped and hunted for a suitable restaurant or pub where we could celebrate our anniversary.

"Do you see anything you fancy?" I asked, as we studied the menu outside of yet another pub.

"Not really," Lesley frowned. "There doesn't seem to be much variety."

"It's not too bad," I offered.

"I quite fancied a roast dinner," she said, "but it's not on the menu. Anyway, the only vegetarian option they've got is sweet and sour vegetables."

"It was the same at the three other places we tried."

"What? Sweet and sour vegetables?" she frowned. "I didn't notice."

I nodded.

"Goodness." Lesley shook her head. "How odd."

"It can't be a coincidence," I grinned and wiggled my eyebrows. "Perhaps it's a union rule."

"What if you don't like sweet and sour vegetables?"

"We could always go back to the hotel," I suggested.

My wife of (almost) 30 years shook her head firmly.

"No. We'll find somewhere here."

Our search continued.

"With so many tourists here, particularly Americans, I'd have expected a wider selection of foods on offer," I said, as we randomly turned into a side street.

"Perhaps I'm biased," Lesley whispered, "but whenever we've eaten out around in County Clare, there's always been a brilliant spread on offer."

"That's not a bad compliment from a blow-in. Oh look!" I pointed to a tatty blackboard leaning against the wall alongside a faded green door. The hand-written menu seemed to fit the bill.

"They'll do a roast dinner," Lesley said, "but what about a vegetarian option?"

"Don't worry about me." I guided Lesley through the door. "I can always eat cake."

The pub's restaurant area had around a dozen functional tables on a bare wood floor. The interior was a little dark and unwelcoming, but the food smelled delicious. Only two tables were occupied. Before we could change our minds, the barmaid spotted us and waved.

"Grab a table," she called. "I'll be right over."

We relented, selecting a table next to a window.

The barmaid appeared at my shoulder with two menus and a basket of bread. She was a neat and pleasant-looking girl, probably aged around 20.

"I'm Siobhan," she said, smiling warmly. "Are you on your holidays?"

"Yes," Lesley replied.

"It's our anniversary," I added, immediately receiving a glare and a kick on the shin from my dear wife.

"You're English?"

"That's right," I replied, "but we live in Ireland."

"Where're you at?" she asked.

"County Clare." I pointed upwards, indicating north.

"How long are you here for?"

"Eight years," Lesley replied.

"You have family here?"

"No," I admitted. "Moving here was a snap decision."

"Before we came to look at houses, we'd never even visited," Lesley added.

"G'way outta that!" she exclaimed. "You're joking me."

"It's true."

"Come here to me," Siobhan whispered, leaning closer. "I'm a Galway girl me-self. How're ye finding Killarney?"

"It's a bit like Torquay in England," Lesley whispered. "Very nice to look at, but rather too touristy for a long visit."

"Spot-on," Siobhan exclaimed and clicked her fingers. "Look it. I'll leave you to read the menu."

"No need," Lesley said. "I'll have the roast beef with vegetables please."

"Chips and mash?" she asked.

"Just the mash please," Lesley smiled. Serving mashed potatoes and French fries on the same plate was common practice in Ireland.

"I'm vegetarian," I replied, when Siobhan asked for my order.

"Fair play to ya," she smiled genuinely. "So am I. The menu special is fecking sweet and sour again, but chef sometimes does something else."

"Could you ask him?" I asked, adding my sweetest smile. "*Afterall*, it is our anniversary."

Lesley kicked me again.

Siobhan returned with our drinks order.

"Chef's in a good mood tonight. He'll be happy to prepare something special." She smiled warmly. "What would you like?"

I was delighted. After scanning my mental database of vegetarian dishes, I chose something both exotic and challenging.

"Two fried eggs, chips and peas – please, I said with a big smile. Siobhan rolled her eyes dramatically and Lesley gave me another swift kick.

Despite my bruised shins, I thoroughly enjoyed my expertly prepared meal and I was relieved to see Lesley was happy with her roast dinner. At the end of our meal, my wife of thirty years even smiled coyly when I saluted her coffee cup with my Guinness glass and wished her a Happy Anniversary.

27 – Tout and About

The planned highlight of our short trip to Killarney, was a visit to see Muckross House and its gardens, which sits below Mangerton Mountain on the banks of beautiful Muckross Lake.

Built in 1843 and designed by William Burn, Muckross is a spectacular Victorian country house, similar to many I had seen in Scotland during my childhood. The house is so large it has 62 chimneys. Originally owned by Henry Herbert and his wife Mary, who was an excellent amateur artist, Muckross House was used for entertaining the rich and famous – including Queen Victoria.

Unfortunately Mr Herbert's entertaining skills far outshone his earning potential, particularly with regard to the Queen's visit. To cover his enormous debts, in 1899 he sold the house and the 13,000-acre surrounding estate to Lord Ardilaun of the Guinness brewing family. For the next 12 years the house was used as a holiday let, giving wealthy visitors a suitably lavish place to stay when they were shooting deer and game. In 1911, the wealthy American, William Bourn, bought Muckross as a wedding gift for his daughter, Maud. When she died in 1932, her husband, Arthur Vincent, and her parents donated the house and estate to the Irish nation, a gift which allowed the creation of Ireland's first national park.

Although the morning began dull and overcast, with bouts of light rain, it failed to dampen our enjoyment. The gardens of Muckross are huge, far too large to cover in a day, but we decided against riding the minibus for the guided tour, preferring to explore on foot. After several years of following our dogs up steep rocky forest paths and along muddy tracks across the moor at Glenmadrie, we thoroughly enjoyed strolling along these well-maintained tarmac lanes. They were set on gentle slopes and we were happy to take our time, pausing to chat with the staff and reading the information posters along the way.

The first attraction was at the top of a hill, where a long winding lane meandered its way through a series of traditional Irish farms. Some were just small cottages with a bit of land and a few chickens, rather like our home, while others were grander affairs with antique farm machinery, heavy horses and dozens of exotically coloured chickens. One barn held our attention for several minutes. In the corner, hidden behind a low wall of straw bales, we discovered a litter of delightfully friendly and energetic sheepdog puppies. I finally dragged Lesley away by tapping my watch and threatening to withdraw her garden viewing privileges.

The tour of Muckross House visited most of the beautifully maintained rooms and lasted around an hour. Starting with the huge entrance hall, our journey took us across the dining room with its exotic red velvet wall covering, through the library, along the awesome main hall, leading up the hand-carved oak staircase to the billiard room, which is hung with exquisitely hand-painted Chinese silk wall coverings. Every room seemed to be filled with beautiful furniture, carpets and fittings, and our guide was enthusiastic, knowledgeable and interesting as she enthralled us with the history and story behind each piece.

We were particularly impressed with the beautiful examples of locally made Killarney furniture, which is of the highest quality, intricately inlaid with arbutus, yew and holly. I have since discovered this exquisitely attractive work is greatly prized by collectors, commanding high prices. Strangely, we had never seen or heard mention of this spectacular work on any of those antiques television programmes. Little wonder Killarney furniture is sometimes called the forgotten industry.

After a delicious lunch of thick vegetable soup with fresh wholemeal bread, we perused the gift shop before walking around the walled garden.

"Isn't this fantastic?" I asked.

Strangely, my wife seemed rather underwhelmed. "It's very pretty," she grudgingly admitted, "but it was never meant to be a flower garden."

"What do you mean?"

"At one time this walled garden would have produced fruit and vegetables in sufficient quantities to feed the household, guests and the Queen," she said. "Those greenhouses were heated all year round. They even grew grapes and peaches. It's rather a shame it hasn't been returned to working order."

"Trust a horticulturist to find fault with a garden like this," I tutted, with an ironic smile.

In dappled sunshine, the remainder of the day was taken up with a somewhat less than gentle stroll around the 35 hectares of well laid-out and beautifully maintained gardens. It was much too extensive to explore in detail in the time available. To see everything on Lesley's list, we needed to get a bit of a move on. Perhaps inspired by my attention to detail, Lesley used the guide book map to navigate the well-trodden paths, ensuring we saw most of the attractions, without either getting hopelessly lost or walking in circles.

The garden is famous for its display of rhododendrons. Even in August, they were still showing hints of their earlier splendour. At Lesley's direction, we criss-crossed the lawns and switched from path to path, in search of the most notable plants. Moving along at what felt like a gentle canter, we passed through the arboretum to seek out alder trees, yew, hazel and oaks, before visiting the mighty Monterey pine. Along the way we also saw the sunken garden, the stream garden and finished our tour by climbing through the beautiful fern and heather-encrusted rock garden. Before leaving, we visited an exhibition about the oak woods of Killarney National Park.

"At the end of the 16th century, much of Ireland was still heavily wooded, mostly with oak and alder," Lesley read from the guide book. "The south west was particularly rich in woodland, which provided natural concealment and protection for the Irish armies in their on-going battle with the English forces of Queen Elizabeth."

"I remember watching a documentary about how many great British warships, like the Victory and the Mary Rose couldn't have been built without Irish oak," I said.

"That's right." Lesley tapped the guide book. "It says here, shipbuilding and deforestation for industrial use, along with land clearance by the new settlers, destroyed most of the forests. Today, Killarney is one of the few places in Ireland where the majesty and splendour of these ancient native woodlands can still be seen."

"I'm so glad we came," I said. "Perhaps we'll get to see a little more of the forest before we go home."

***

The following morning, as I was contemplating my choices at the breakfast bar, I happened into a conversation with an affable American tourist. I had chatted with this distinguished-looking gentleman the previous morning, so I took a moment to ask if he and his wife had enjoyed their tour around the Ring of Kerry. This spectacularly scenic drive loops along the mountains, cliffs and beaches for 179 kilometres of the Iveragh Peninsula, and is popular with tourists. He reported that the weather had been kind and the views were spectacular, but the journey had taken a long time because of the amount of traffic.

"These Irish roads are so narrow, you have to pull over each time you meet any oncoming vehicles," he said, in a refined Boston accent. "We seemed to meet so many cars and coaches. I had to pull over almost every hundred yards or so." He gave me a tooth-perfect smile. "But everyone was very friendly, they all seemed to be waving at us."

Somewhere in my head, a bell was ringing.

"Which way around the loop did you go?" I asked. "Clockwise or anti-clockwise?"

"Well, we just followed the satnav. I guess we were going clockwise," he answered, sensing my suspicion.

"Well then, there's your problem!" I laughed. "Because the road is so narrow and busy, you are only supposed to drive the Ring in an anti-clockwise direction." I gently patted his shoulder in sympathy. "I expect that the people were waving to warn you that you were heading in the wrong direction."

"But it can't be one-way," he complained. "We would have seen the road signs."

"Ah... Yes. Well, this is Ireland – it's a sort of unofficial one-way system. It's mentioned somewhere in the brochures and on some web pages. Other than that, you're just expected to know."

He thanked me for the information and added another sausage to his breakfast plate. As he walked away, he smiled, shook his head and mumbled, "Nutty country!"

***

With a few hours spare before we had to head home, we donned our jackets and sensible shoes and ambled aimlessly towards the town. Quite soon we saw a sign for Killarney house and garden.

"Garden." Lesley pointed, like a child hoping for ice cream.

"I guess so," I nodded stoically. "Afterall, it is our official anniversary today."

We turned left and began to explore.

Sadly, the magnificent French chateau style house had fallen into a wretched state of disrepair. The garden was a twisted mass of bracken and weeds and the house but a crumbling shadow of its former glory. A new billboard style sign announced the pending commencement of an ambitious three-year renovation project.

"It's probably too long for us to wait," I joked, tapping my watch.

Lesley scowled and tutted as if I were an unruly child, which I am.

Deciding to explore a little further, we strolled along the cherry tree-lined buggy track which leads away from Killarney. To our right, trees and bushes blocked our view of the town, but the land to the left was a huge expanse of flat meadow edged with trees. In the distance, the leaden darkness of Cnoc na Péiste mountain rose steeply from the water's edge and thrust its summit into the cloud base. It appeared dark and unwelcoming until the sun broke through the cloud, turning its slopes into a gleaming beacon of lavender and gold. From the obvious tracks and scat deposits, I knew there were hundreds of red deer around, but they remained stubbornly hidden.

After half an hour strolling along the well-maintained path, we reached a junction. The tourist finger posts indicated one path would take us to the town, whereas the other went to Ross Castle and the lake, around three kilometres away.

"These aren't really walking shoes," Lesley said, nodding left, "but I guess we can always turn back when our feet begin to hurt."

It was a pleasantly warm day, the walking was easy and enjoyable across level land, but I was glad to be wearing my latest trilby hat for protection from the sun. There were plenty of other walkers, as well as whole families of cyclists on rented mountain bikes, who gave a friendly wave as they rode past. Every few minutes we had to stand aside as another horse drawn jaunting car trundled by.

For a while the path was enclosed by magnificent oak trees and we were unable to see much scenery, but nearer to the shoreline where the low-lying land was prone to flooding, the trees thinned out teasing us with tantalising glimpses of Lough Leane. Encouraged and hoping for a better view, we pressed on, but our hopes were dashed. A hundred metres ahead, the native waterside rushes gave way to a forest of three-metre tall bamboo plants. They lined the path sides like a solid impenetrable wall which continued for a kilometre. Where a small stream bisected the path, we could see the bamboo forest was a hundred metres deep, extending all the way to the water's edge. It was like stepping out of rural Ireland and finding we had been instantly transported into deepest China. I almost expected to see a giant panda leap out at any moment. The mud flats and marshes, once a haven for all types of wading birds and a dazzling variety of plants, were now just an impenetrable wall of monotonous bamboo.

During our tour of Muckross House, much was made of the on-going battle that Coillte (the State Forestry Service) was waging against the rhododendron and bamboo gradually taking over the park and mountains. These invasive species grow so vigorously, if left unchecked, they will starve most other plants of food and sunlight. On our walks around Killarney, the sheer scale of the problem was depressingly obvious. Many of the mountains are now completely covered in a solid mass of rhododendron. In the native woodlands, thousands of bushes cover the ground between the trees. Beautiful as these plants can be when they are in bloom, rhododendron sour the land and gradually exclude all other vegetation.

I have no idea how these invasive plants will ever be cleared, or even if they can. Rather like the Irish sovereign debt, the growth far exceeds that which we can cut down. Perhaps there is an opportunity to solve two problems at once. Surely there is money to be made here – if only someone could find a market for Irish bamboo.

After 20 minutes, the bamboo thinned out and we could finally see our intended destination. Ross Castle is an impressive 15th century tower house and castle keep. It sits on the boat-lined lake front, surrounded by grassy embankments. The picnic area was alive with gaggles of tourists and children excitedly running to and fro, intent on consuming all the crisps, sandwiches and ice creams in the garden-shed style tuck shop.

"Tea?" I suggested.

Lesley frowned at the queue.

"Let's go on a little further," she suggested, pointing at the mixed woodland ahead. "It's so nice just spending time together."

Walking on past the castle towards the Bronze Age copper mines, our progress was stalled when an excitable dog came bounding across the grass and threw itself at our feet as if desperately begging for rescue. It was a scruffy looking collie/springer cross. The owner, a tall and slightly eccentric looking Englishman, came trotting along behind.

"Sorry, sorry!" he called. This is the standard apology, used by every dog owner since the Stone Age, to excuse the impolite actions of their pooches. "He's a bit unruly."

"It's okay," I replied, casually using my hand to rearrange the dog-slob on my trousers. "We have dogs too."

"You're English," he said. "Are you on your holidays?"

"Just visiting," Lesley replied. "We live in County Clare."

"I'm Derek," he said, pointing a thumb over his shoulder. "I live hereabouts."

"We're Lesley and Nick," I announced, as we shook hands.

"I'm a tour guide here," Derek announce, "but it's my day off."

"That must keep you busy," I replied. "Do you have to sit exams for that?"

"Bah! Exams is overrated." He tapped the side of his nose with his index finger and winked. "You just have to know the right people."

"Oh. Is that all?"

"For some," he countered quickly. "Fortunately, I know a lot about the local geography and history. It's made me a busy tour guide." He winked meaningfully. "Even on my days off."

For a hundred metres or so, we chatted politely with this amiable fellow. I'd hoped he'd leave us to our romantic stroll, but he continued walking alongside, apparently oblivious to our desire to be left alone. Lesley caught my eye and frowned.

"Your dog's run off." I stopped and pointed, hoping our uninvited guest would take the hint.

"Ah. He'll be grand." Derek waved dismissively. "He knows his way home."

"Perhaps you should check," I suggested. "Goodbye."

Hand-in-hand, Lesley and I walked on. Derek followed, half a step behind.

"It's lucky we met," he said. "I know some parts of Ross Island most people miss."

"We're just having a little walk together, before we go home," Lesley replied.

"It's our anniversary," I added, praying I wouldn't get another kick from my wife.

Unfortunately the subtle undertone of our comments completely missed their target. As Lesley and I strolled along chatting quietly and admiring the scenery, Derek followed behind like a lost puppy.

A few hundred metres later, we stopped at the entrance to the copper mine. Our ad hoc guide stepped forwards and, after taking an almost comically theatrical stance, launched into his spiel.

"Many artefacts have been discovered during archaeological excavations of the copper mines at Ross Island, proving strong links with the Bronze Age. Copper mined from this island provided the very first metal to be used in Ireland over 4000 years ago, and again during the early Christian period in Ireland."

As he stumbled through his presentation like an inexperienced air hostess reciting the pre-fight safety instructions, I nodded politely. Then I noticed he was actually reading surreptitiously from a tourist information panel conveniently close to where he was standing.

"Substantial shipments of copper ore were also delivered to British smelters during the 18th and 19th centuries to meet the demands of the Industrial Revolution," Derek continued, oblivious to the fact we were reading from the same board, but somewhat faster.

Further up the trail we reached Governor's Rock, which provides a spectacular view across Loch Leane. Again, Derek stood directly in front of the information panel, openly reciting the words, but pretending that they were from his own encyclopaedic memory. Despite the humour of the situation, we were becoming a little fed up with the charade, particularly as it was interfering with our romantic walk together.

Lesley nudged me and mouthed, *"Say something."*

I shook my head and mouthed back, *"You say something."*

In typically British fashion we were unable to bring ourselves to confront the problem for fear of being thought rude.

A little farther down the path, we paused to look at some of the huge oak trees.

"This one is magnificent," Lesley whispered, pointing to a particularly large example.

"Do you know trees?" Derek asked.

"She's a great horticulturist," I replied proudly. "Very knowledgeable."

My wife smiled demurely.

Our ad hoc tour guide pointed to a large tree on the other side of the path. "What species is that?"

"It's a pine tree," she replied, trying to cover her smile.

Derek nodded slowly and repeated, "P-i-n-e T-r-e-e," as if to commit this nugget of information to memory, for later use.

"Say something!" Lesley hissed in my ear.

I cleared my throat.

"I say, old chap—"

I was saved by the bell. A perfectly timed mobile phone call from our daughter gave us a good excuse to move away for some privacy.

"Happy anniversary!" Joanne said.

"Thank you," I replied, switching my phone to speaker mode. "We're in Killarney National Park, sat on a rock overlooking the lake and bathed in glorious sunshine."

"It's raining here in London."

We both laughed, feeling no guilt whatsoever.

Our daughter was delighted to hear Lesley so happy and enthusiastic.

"You should get out and about more often," Joanne said.

"We plan too," Lesley replied.

"Even if it's only to visit more garden centres," I added.

After the call ended, I gave my wife a hug, happy we could enjoy our time together in such a beautiful location.

"All clear," I said, peering over her shoulder. "I think our limpet tour guide has gone."

"I reckon he latches on to unsuspecting passing tourists, gives them a little spiel and hopes to get paid," she said.

"I think you're right. Did you notice he was just reading from the signs?"

Lesley laughed and nodded.

"It was rather obvious."

We started to walk back towards the castle.

"Next week, he'll probably be pointing out all the pine trees," I said.

By the time we arrived back at Ross Castle, we were hot, hungry and desperate for a nice cup of tea. The queue at the small tuck shop had thinned a little, probably because the shelves were almost empty. I was fortunate to snag the last two cheese and pickle sandwiches. We sat at a bench overlooking the lake while we sipped our tea and ate. Life was good and so were the sandwiches.

Refreshed and energised, we began walking back towards town. Lesley pointed at a sign at the head of a small pier. It was for a boat tour of the lake.

"Do you want to go?" I asked.

"I would love to," she sighed, "but it's too late."

The engine was running, churning the water as the boat began to move. Grinning widely, I grabbed my wife's hand.

"Run!" I shouted.

Giggling like teenagers, we raced down the pier and jumped onto the boat, just as it was pulling out. The cruiser was like a floating bus, with a dozen rows of seats and a domed Perspex roof. The journey lasted for around an hour giving us ample time to relax while we were shown the attractions. We saw Library Point, Governor's Rock (again), the Devil's Punchbowl, Lover's Rock and several spectacular hotels which were very obviously beyond our budget. Without a doubt, the highlight of the trip was seeing the recently reintroduced white-tailed sea eagles, as they nested and fed along the shoreline. For a few minutes the boat held station about 60 meters offshore while the guide explained how these beautiful and magnificent birds are regularly fed on the beach to discourage them from flying away in search of food.

"In time we hope they will consider Lough Leane to be their home," he said.

As the boat pulled up to its mooring at the end of the tour, Lesley pointed out one further attraction. Derek, our erstwhile guide had attached himself to a group of tourists and was pointing out the interesting features of Ross Castle. She noted he was standing conveniently close to the information panel.

28 – New Beginnings

The morning after we arrived back home, my wife began baking for Joanne's wedding. A week ahead of the ceremony, Lesley left for England, taking her car on the ferry so she could transport the wedding cake (yet to be decorated), and the boxed ingredients for the hundreds of cupcakes she would make. As my presence was not required in the preparation process, I would fly over just two days before the wedding.

Left alone at Glenmadrie, I had anticipated a few days of quiet relaxation, dog walking and the chance to do some planning for the book I wanted to write, but an inexplicable flurry of golf lessons kept me rather busy. Although Killarney has some excellent golf courses, they weren't on the agenda during our visit, so it was rather nice to see some friendly clients and play a little golf. The writing could wait for a bit.

The flight to England was uneventful. My future son-in-law kindly gave me a lift to the hotel where the festivities were to take place. I thought Mark seemed a little distracted.

"How are you feeling?" I asked.

He chewed his lip.

"To be honest, Nick, I think I'm getting cold feet."

My heart raced, pounding blood in my ears.

"Oh…err… These feelings of doubt are perfectly normal–"

Deadpan, Mark cut me off with a raised hand.

"Hang on…" he said, leaning forward to adjust the car's air conditioning. "That's much better. It was blowing cold air onto my shoes."

Trying hard not to laugh, I looked out of the window and waited for my blood pressure to fall.

Whereas Mark looked tall, young and handsome, my daughter seemed hot and flustered. Joanne was delighted to see me, but far too busy to stop and chat. After delivering a quick welcome hug and kiss, she hustled off to deal with some last-minute preparations.

"How's everything going?" I asked Mark.

"It's fine," he smiled. "Joanne's fussing because she wants things to be just perfect."

"That's understandable," I said. "Is there anything I can do to help?"

"Not just now, everything's taken care of. We'll probably need a few extra hands in the morning." Mark checked his watch and grimaced. "I've got to pop out and collect my brother. I think you'll find most of the relatives are in the garden. We're all meeting for a meal this evening. It's nothing formal. Just a chance for everyone to get reacquainted."

I found Mark's parents, Dave and Linda, chatting with Lesley. They are a lovely couple, full of life and laughter. My wife was chuckling at some comment Dave had just made. She looked surprisingly sprightly, considering the amount of baking I knew she'd recently done.

"Are you going grey, or is that just flour in your hair?" I joked. It didn't get a big laugh.

***

The hotel was a magnificent converted country manor house. It was an understandably popular wedding venue, as it had a large function hall, a ceremonial room and well-maintained gardens. As the bride's parents, we'd snagged one of the best rooms.

"Whatever was that racket last night?" I asked, peering out of the window.

"I think it was a motorbike," Lesley mumbled. She was putting the final touches to her makeup.

"It sounded more like a chainsaw. Perhaps someone was cutting wood over in those trees."

"At 3 am?"

"Who knows?" I shrugged.

"Mum was very confused at dinner last night. She got lost twice, just going to the toilet."

"That's understandable. The layout of these old country houses can be quite baffling," I said. "She seemed alright at breakfast."

"It's much worse when she's tired, or in unfamiliar circumstances," Lesley explained. "I took her shopping to her local supermarket the other day. Unfortunately, they'd changed the layout."

"Oh dear. Did she get lost?"

"I was with her, so she didn't get lost, but she got so upset and confused, I had to take her home." My wife's face was grim at the memory.

"I'm so sorry," I sighed. "We'll have to keep a close eye on her tonight."

Lesley shrugged, trying to make light of the situation. "Perhaps these new tablets will help. The doctor said they take about a month to show results."

"Fingers crossed." I gave a thin smile.

"Joanne has her own life now. If these tablets don't work…"

"Muriel can always come to live with us." I patted my wife's hand. "Don't worry."

Lesley nodded and pointed at the bathroom.

"You'd better get ready."

"It's so warm today, I didn't want to get dressed too soon. I've only got to shave, trim my hair and have a shower," I said. "It won't take long."

"Why didn't you go to the hairdresser like a normal person?" she sighed.

"I've been cutting my own hair since I was 20 and I'm not about to change now," I insisted. "Anyway, I just need to tidy the back and sides. It's hardly rocket surgery."

"You've only *got* hair on the back and sides," Lesley sniggered.

I plugged my hair trimmer into the shaver socket and began. Something didn't feel right.

"Oops!" I groaned.

"What's wrong?"

"I usually have this trimmer set to 7mm, but it must have been knocked while it was in my suitcase."

"What's it set to now?"

"3mm," I sighed.

With my first exuberant sweep of the trimmer, I'd ploughed a furrow up the back of my head. Lesley winced.

"You'll have to do the rest. It's going to be very short though."

"Luckily, everyone will be looking at Joanne," I said.

"But you're giving her away," she growled, "and you've a speech to make."

"Perhaps I can wear my hat…"

***

With the help of friends, family and the hotel staff, Mark and Joanne had done a magnificent job preparing the hall and ceremonial room. The tables were arranged and beautifully decorated with flowers, old fashioned sweets and other retro touches. The walls were hung with bunting, disco lights and vintage posters of advertisements and music stars, while the garden was charmingly bordered with ribbons and outdoor candles. In pride of place, the wedding cake was resplendent in white icing with a navy-blue ribbon to match the flowers. The side tables were laden with cupcakes, wedding cheeses and every conceivable sweet treat from the last three decades. Overall the effect was one of a very personal, but totally professional wedding.

Mark had put his prodigious organisational skills to good use, creating a well-planned and widely distributed running order, ensuring everyone knew where they were expected to be and when. Our bride and groom had decided to forgo the usual speeches, choosing instead to have a reading by Mark's father before the ceremony, with an entertaining table quiz prior to the serving of the meal, followed by a short toast from me to congratulate the newlyweds.

Perhaps dreading I would say something inappropriate, accompanied by a PowerPoint presentation and slide show, Mark and Joanne had been adamant they did not want me to attempt the usual father of the bride speech. To help keep me on track, they kindly provided some detailed instructions on what to say and how to prepare. After several hours and much head scratching, I was able to put together some sweet words and a few light witticisms I felt would acceptably fill my allocated timeslot.

My primary task for the day was entirely in keeping with tradition. It would be my honour to give the bride away. When the time arrived for the wedding to begin, dressed like James Bond at a casino, but with much shorter hair, I made my way to the bridal suite to collect Joanne. Looking at my daughter, resplendent in her white silk wedding dress, with her hair in a side bun and her makeup exquisitely applied, my heart sang.

"You've never looked more beautiful," I said, fighting the lump in my throat.

"Thanks, Dad," she squeezed my hand then frowned. "What the hell happened to your hair?"

Outside, it was sunny and warm. Perfect weather for a wedding. With a little time in hand, Lesley and I posed with our daughter in the side garden while every guest with a camera took their pre-wedding photos. Lesley hates having her picture taken, but for once she was happy to be photographed and rightly so. My lovely wife looked stunningly elegant in her new dress. Mother and daughter, like peas in a pod.

"We're fashionably late," I said, checking my watch. "It's time to begin."

In a moment of calmness, as Joanne and I stood outside the ceremonial room waiting for our cue to enter, I was struck with a sudden choking fear. What if Mark said no and ran screaming from the hotel? How could I possibly comfort my daughter? Perhaps sensing my concerns, or more likely projecting those of her own, Joanne squeezed my hand and smiled. My racing heart slowed to a gentle gallop. Moments later we walked arm-in-arm to the head of the room and the wedding got under way.

The civil ceremony was a touching and romantic affair, with the usual exchanging of oaths and rings to the soundtrack of tears and the honk of repeated nose-blowing from delighted friends and relatives. As the exchange of vows began, Joanne took Mark's hand and squeezed it gently, as if to say, "We can get through this together". After the legal formalities were completed, David, Mark's father, was invited to say a few words. After hesitantly making his way to the front of the room, he shyly cleared his throat and in a powerful and confident voice, recited a beautiful poem. As I listened to his soaring oratory about love and commitment, I imagined Laurence Olivier or Anthony Hopkins could not have done a better job. Fingering the scrap of paper in my pocket carrying my notes for the upcoming toast and, realising my reading glasses were still on my desk in Ireland, I fought back the tears.

While the newlyweds went off for some scenic photographs, the guests moved to the reception garden where we could chat and quench our thirst. Acclimatised to the cooler Irish climate, I was rather warm in my black tuxedo.

"Phew! James Bond never had this problem," I whispered, draining my sixth glass of juice.

"What are you drinking?" Lesley asked.

"It's only mixed fruit juice. I'm really thirsty."

"That's fruit punch and it's packed with booze!" she exclaimed.

"Oh," I slurred, swaying slightly. "Thash would eshplain it."

Conscious I was many years past being a regular drinker, I cautiously sidled away from the punch bowl and went in search of some water. As I circumnavigated the room, chatting with the guests, thanking them for coming and agreeing how lovely Joanne looked, I somehow acquired a glass of beer. Keen to avoid insulting anyone, I drank it. When a second beer was thrust into my hand, I repeated the process.

Once the happy couple returned and everyone was seated, the wine was served and the table quiz began. The best man compered an excellent and keenly fought competition. As the shouting and laughter continued, cross-eyed with alcohol and without my reading glasses, I surreptitiously tried to read my notes for the impending toast. In the end I need not have worried. Most people were too kind, or too drunk, to recollect what was said – including me. I can only remember starting nervously, by calling David "Alan" by mistake, and finishing by advising Mark to remember, "No wife ever shot her husband while he was washing the dishes!"

After the meal, the dancing began. With so many young, energetic and enthusiastic sales people on the guest list, the reception was always going to be an exhilarating affair. The dancing was happy and unrestrained, continuing well into the early hours of the morning.

"When did we get so old?" I asked, as Lesley and I sat panting on the side-lines.

"About 20 years ago," she laughed.

Most people only left the floor to refill their glasses, or replenish their blood glucose with stacks of Lesley's delicious cupcakes. As the dancing got ever more frenzied, the room became as hot and humid as a tropical rainforest. The men had removed their jackets and most of the ladies had sensibly opted to wear something slinky and lightweight, but Joanne was still adorned in her wedding dress.

"She must be sweating like a racehorse under that lot," I laughed.

"I told her to change her clothes, but she didn't want to," Lesley replied.

We needn't have worried. Our daughter came up with a uniquely practical solution. She removed her multiple layers of petticoats, giving one to each of her bridesmaids, then used a pair of scissors to deftly turn her wedding dress into a mini skirt.

"A slice of cake and a piece of wedding dress. It's rather a nice keepsake," I said.

"Perhaps it'll catch on," Lesley replied.

The following morning, bleary-eyed and tousle-haired, we

waved the newlyweds off to Italy for their honeymoon, before setting off home ourselves.

***

Back in Ireland our lives have fallen into an easy routine of early rising, long walks with the dogs and relaxing days out whenever we fell the desire. We are living the dream again.

Jack has shown no yearning to leave. He is still every bit as neurotic, but somehow he fits well with the other dogs. Lady continues to be the undisputed pack leader, always out in front during our walks and quick to track a scent into the woods. Kia will shadow Lady wherever she goes, 10 metres behind, covered in mud and brambles but smiling with joy. Little Amber continues to believe she is the biggest dog, despite all the contrary evidence. She's a little old and stiff for the rough and tumble of chasing a ball, but in a quiet moment, she's happy to play long games of tug with whoever will oblige. We still miss Romany. Perhaps one day we'll get another dog. I've always wanted a golden retriever.

Joanne and Mark are happily married, busy in their new life. They're planning to move to a new house, one with more bedrooms and a nice enclosed garden. It sounds like the sort of place where they could start a family. We look forward to long summer holidays with our grandchildren enjoying the space and fresh air here in Ireland.

With the aid of the new medication, Muriel's health has improved a little, but we know this is only a temporary reprieve. Dementia is a progressive disease. At some point she will become unable to care for herself. Her bed here in Ireland is ready and waiting.

Finishing the renovations brought a sense of completion. For seven years Glenmadrie had been a hungry mouth to feed, ravenously consuming our time and money. Finally, we were free to pursue other projects. Lesley was happy to fill her time with the garden, the market and her dance club. My golf teaching business wasn't dead, I'd just stopped worrying about it so much. Besides, I had the writing bug and was determined to make a go of it as an author. I was keen to write a memoir about our move to Ireland.

"It's up to you," Lesley shrugged, as supportive as ever. "What will you call it?"

"An English couple and their unruly dogs, searching for a better life in rural Ireland?" I suggested.

"That seems a bit unwieldy," she replied.

"I'll try and think of something shorter."

My wife patted my shoulder.

"Do the writing first," she said. "You can worry about the title later."

THE END

You can read more about Nick and Lesley Albert and their Irish adventures, in book four of the Fresh Eggs and Dog Beds series.

Acknowledgments

Writing a book is very much a team effort and there are many people who I would like to thank:

First of all, to Victoria Twead and the staff at Ant Press, thank you for your vision and belief.

Many, many thanks to Zoë Marr, for your keen eye, honest opinion and exceptional editing.

Stefan Nikolic for his excellent cover illustration.

Lesley, my beautiful intelligent and supportive wife, who gave me the time and space to finish my books, thank you for accompanying me on this search for a better life – and for all the cakes.

Joanne, our daughter, who gave her unflinching support to each of our nutty ideas; she politely pointed out my mistakes and gave me the motivation to continue writing.

Richard Clarke, you are a great friend and an inspiration.

Thanks to our dogs, cats, chickens and ducks, past and present, you make our lives richer and more interesting.

Finally, thanks to the good people of Ireland, who have made us feel welcome and at home in a foreign land.

About the author

Nick Albert was born in England and raised in a Royal Air Force family. After leaving college in 1979, he worked in retail management for several years, before moving into financial services as a training manager. In the mid-1980's he qualified as a martial arts instructor and began a parallel career coaching sport. In search of a simpler life, and the opportunity to write full-time, he and his wife, relocated to the rural west of Ireland in 2003.

Nick signed with Ant Press In 2016 to write the comedy memoir series, Fresh Eggs and Dog Beds. He has also written and published Better Golf Tips and Wrecking Crew, the first in a series of twisty thrillers featuring reluctant hero Eric Stone.

Ant Press Books

If you enjoyed this book, you may also enjoy these Ant Press titles:

MEMOIRS
Chickens, Mules and Two Old Fools by Victoria Twead (Wall Street Journal Top 10 bestseller)
Two Old Fools ~ Olé! by Victoria Twead
Two Old Fools on a Camel by Victoria Twead (thrice New York Times bestseller)
Two Old Fools in Spain Again by Victoria Twead
Two Old Fools in Turmoil by Victoria Twead
Two Old Fools Down Under by Victoria Twead (coming 2019)
One Young Fool in Dorset (The Prequel) by Victoria Twead
One Young Fool in South Africa (The Prequel) by Joe and Victoria Twead
Fat Dogs and French Estates ~ Part I by Beth Haslam
Fat Dogs and French Estates ~ Part II by Beth Haslam
Fat Dogs and French Estates ~Part III by Beth Haslam
Fat Dogs and French Estates ~ Part IV by Beth Haslam
From Moulin Rouge to Gaudi's City by EJ Bauer
South to Barcelona: A new life in Spain by Vernon Lacey
Simon Ships Out: How One Brave, Stray Cat Became a Worldwide Hero by Jacky Donovan
Smoky: How a Tiny Yorkshire Terrier Became a World War II American Army Hero, Therapy Dog and Hollywood Star by Jacky Donovan
Smart as a Whip: A Madcap Journey of Laughter, Love, Disasters and Triumphs by Jacky Donovan
Heartprints of Africa: A Family's Story of Faith, Love, Adventure, and Turmoil by Cinda Adams Brooks
How not to be a Soldier: My Antics in the British Army by Lorna McCann
Moment of Surrender: My Journey Through Prescription Drug Addiction to Hope and Renewal by Pj Laube
One of its Legs are Both the Same by Mike Cavanagh
A Pocket Full of Days, Part 1 by Mike Cavanagh
Horizon Fever by A E Filby
Horizon Fever 2 by A E Filby

Cane Confessions: The Lighter Side to Mobility by Amy L. Bovaird
Completely Cats - Stories with Cattitude by Beth Haslam and Zoe Marr
Fresh Eggs and Dog Beds: Living the Dream in Rural Ireland by Nick Albert
Fresh Eggs and Dog Beds 2: Still Living the Dream in Rural Ireland by Nick Albert
Fresh Eggs and Dog Beds 3: More Living the Dream in Rural Ireland by Nick Albert
Don't Do It Like This: How NOT to move to Spain by Joe Cawley, Victoria Twead and Alan Parks
Longing for Africa: Journeys Inspired by the Life of Jane Goodall. Part One: Ethiopia by Annie Schrank
Longing for Africa: Journeys Inspired by the Life of Jane Goodall. Part Two: Kenya by Annie Schrank
A Kiss Behind the Castanets by Jean Roberts

* * *

FICTION
Parched by Andrew C Branham
A is for Abigail by Victoria Twead (Sixpenny Cross 1)
B is for Bella by Victoria Twead (Sixpenny Cross 2)
C is for the Captain by Victoria Twead (Sixpenny Cross 3)
D is for Dexter by Victoria Twead (coming 2019)

* * *

NON FICTION
How to Write a Bestselling Memoir by Victoria Twead

* * *

CHILDREN'S BOOKS
Seacat Simon: The Little Cat Who Became a Big Hero by Jacky Donovan
Morgan and the Martians by Victoria Twead

* * *

Chat with the author, other memoir authors, and readers at We Love Memoirs:
https://www.facebook.com/groups/welovememoirs/

Printed in Great Britain
by Amazon